Children Behaving Badly?

THE NSPCC/WILEY SERIES

in

PROTECTING CHILDREN

The multi-professional approach

Series Editors: Christopher Cloke,
NSPCC, 42 Curtain Road,
London EC2A 3NX

Jan Horwath,
Department of Sociological Studies,
University of Sheffield,
Sheffield S10 2TU

Peter Sidebotham,
Warwick Medical School,
University of Warwick,
Coventry CV4 7AL

This NSPCC/Wiley series explores current issues relating to the prevention of child abuse and the protection of children. The series aims to publish titles that focus on professional practice and policy, and the practical application of research. The books are leading edge and innovative and reflect a multidisciplinary and inter-agency approach to the prevention of child abuse and the protection of children.

All books have a policy or practice orientation with referenced information from theory and research. The series is essential reading for all professionals and researchers concerned with the prevention of child abuse and the protection of children.

Children Behaving Badly?

Peer Violence Between Children and Young People

EDITED BY

CHRISTINE BARTER AND DAVID BERRIDGE

⊛**WILEY-BLACKWELL**

A John Wiley & Sons, Ltd., Publication

This edition first published 2011
© 2011 John Wiley & Sons Ltd.

Wiley-Blackwell is an imprint of John Wiley & Sons, formed by the merger of Wiley's global Scientific, Technical, and Medical business with Blackwell Publishing.

Registered Office
John Wiley & Sons Ltd, The Atrium, Southern Gate, Chichester, West Sussex, PO19 8SQ, UK

Editorial Offices
The Atrium, Southern Gate, Chichester, West Sussex, PO19 8SQ, UK
9600 Garsington Road, Oxford, OX4 2DQ, UK
350 Main Street, Malden, MA 02148-5020, USA

For details of our global editorial offices, for customer services, and for information about how to apply for permission to reuse the copyright material in this book please see our website at www.wiley.com/wiley-blackwell.

The right of Christine Barter and David Berridge to be identified as the authors of the editorial material in this work has been asserted in accordance with the UK Copyright, Designs and Patents Act 1988.

Wiley also publishes its books in a variety of electronic formats. Some content that appears in print may not be available in electronic books.

Designations used by companies to distinguish their products are often claimed as trademarks. All brand names and product names used in this book are trade names, service marks, trademarks or registered trademarks of their respective owners. The publisher is not associated with any product or vendor mentioned in this book. This publication is designed to provide accurate and authoritative information in regard to the subject matter covered. It is sold on the understanding that the publisher is not engaged in rendering professional services. If professional advice or other expert assistance is required, the services of a competent professional should be sought.

Library of Congress Cataloging-in-Publication Data

Children behaving badly? : peer violence between children and young people / edited by Christine Barter and David Berridge.
    p. cm.
  Includes index.
  ISBN 978-0-470-69440-4 (cloth) – ISBN 978-0-470-72705-8 (pbk.)
    1. Children–Institutional care. 2. Children–Violence against.   3. Peer pressure in children.   4. Children and violence.   5. Violence in children.   6. Bullying.   I. Barter, Christine.   II. Berridge, David.
  HQ778.5C535 2011
  303.6083'0941–dc22

                                                    2010036012

A catalogue record for this book is available from the British Library.

Set in 10 on 12 pt Times Ten by Toppan Best-set Premedia Limited
Printed in Singapore by Ho Printing Singapore Pte Ltd

1   2011

Contents

List of Contributors

Les Back teaches sociology at Goldsmiths, University of London. His recent books include *The Art of Listening* (Berg, 2007) and *Out of Whiteness: Color, Politics and Culture* (University of Chicago Press, 2002). He writes regularly for non-academic audiences and is a contributor to *Eurozine, openDemocracy, The Times Higher Educational Supplement* and *The Guardian*.

Christine Barter is an NSPCC Senior Research Fellow at the School for Policy Studies, University of Bristol. Previously she was a Senior NSPCC Research Fellow with the University of Bedfordshire. She has published widely on a range of children's welfare issues including children who run away, protecting young people from racism and racial abuse, boys' use of advice and counselling services, institutional child abuse, and involving children and young people in social research. Currently her work focuses on the neglected area of young people's experiences of partner exploitation and violence in their intimate relationships.

Jo Bell is a Lecturer in the Department of Social Sciences at the University of Hull. Her research interests are broadly around health, development and education in young people. She has extensive experience of research on sensitive issues with young people and families, and has researched and published work in the areas of adolescent development, domestic violence, young suicide, young parenthood and sexual health and behaviour in young people.

David Berridge is Professor of Child and Family Welfare and Head of the Centre for Family Policy and Child Welfare at the School for Policy Studies, University of Bristol. He has been a researcher for 25 years and is author/co-author of 12 books and numerous other chapters and articles. With Christine Barter, he has collaborated with the NSPCC for 15 years on projects concerning mainly adolescents and child protection issues. His latest co-authored book is *Educating Difficult Adolescents: Effective Education for Children in Care or with Emotional and Behavioural Difficulties* (Jessica Kingsley, 2008). David was awarded the OBE in January 2005 for services to children.

Jane Brown originally trained as an art therapist, specialising in child protection. She started life as a researcher in 1992, observing children giving evidence in courtroom situations. She has a longstanding interest in violent behaviour in childhood and adolescence and has published widely in the field. Her most recent publications include *'School Violence' as a Social Problem: Charting the*

Rise of the Problem and the Emerging Specialist Field (co-authored with P. Munn, Routledge, 2008) and '"They are just like caged animals": surveillance, security and school spaces' (*Surveillance and Society*, 2010). She has been based at the Faculty of Education, University of Edinburgh, for the past 8 years and is currently leading a review of violence in mainstream primary and secondary schools in the UK.

Helen Cowie is Research Professor and Director of the UK Observatory for the Promotion of Non-Violence at the University of Surrey in the Faculty of Health and Medical Sciences. She has published widely in the field of child development, specialising in bullying, violence in schools, mental health and young people, and peer support as an intervention to promote non-violence. Her textbook, *Understanding Children's Development* (co-authored with P.K. Smith and M. Blades, and first published by Blackwell in 1988), is now into its 5th edition and has become one of the major undergraduate developmental psychology texts in the UK. Her most recent books (both co-authored with J. Dawn) are *Managing Violence in Schools: A Whole-School Approach to Best Practice* (Sage, 2007) and *New Perspectives on Bullying*, Open University Press, 2008). Major European projects include 'Violence in schools training action (VISTA)', 'CyberTraining' and the creation of an online education centre to address school violence.

Jane Ellis is currently an NSPCC Senior Research Officer. Previously she worked as a consultant on prevention work in schools for WOMANKIND Worldwide, the Scottish Government, Westminster Domestic Violence Forum and Birmingham Women's Aid. Her PhD, undertaken at the University of Warwick, was a study of school-based work to prevent domestic violence where the role of young people as evaluators was explored. She has a background of working with children and young people in formal and non-formal educational settings, as both a teacher and community education worker. She has been a member of the DCSF Advisory Group on Violence Against Women and Girls.

Carlie Goldsmith is a Lecturer in Criminology at the University of Kingston. Her main criminological research interests have included community safety, neighbourhood policing and young people. As part of this work for her PhD thesis, she has been particularly interested in utilising ethnographic and qualitative research methods to explore the strategies adopted and developed by young people attempting to stay safe in their communities. Her core concern has been to examine the impact of contemporary criminal justice policies on young people's experience of community. Articles from this work have already been published – for example, in *ASBO Nation* (Policy Press, 2008).

Simon Hackett is Professor and Head of the School of Applied Social Sciences at Durham University, UK. He has published widely in relation to sexual abuse and sexual aggression. With Professor Helen Masson, he is involved in a multisite study of desistance, recidivism and life course trajectories of young people 10 years after the initial identification of their sexually abusive behaviours. Simon's practice base with children and young people with harmful sexual behaviours extends back to the early 1990s and he was previously a programme director of G-MAP, a leading UK community-based specialist service.

Simon Hallsworth is Professor of Social Research in the Department of Applied Social Science at London Metropolitan University and Director of the University's Centre for Social and Evaluation Research. He has advised a range of statutory agencies on issues relating to crime and community safety, and has written extensively concerning street-related violence and penal change and development. He is author of *Street Crime* (Willan, 2005) and co-editor of *The New Punitiveness: Trends, Theories, Perspectives* (Willan, 2005).

Veronica M. Herrera is an Assistant Professor in the Department of Criminal Justice at Indiana University. Her research focuses on examining the long-term effects of exposure to family violence on adolescent risk behaviour. Her work examines gender differences in pathways to delinquency, psychopathology stemming from histories of victimisation, predictors of dating violence, and influence of partner effects on young adult offending patterns. She is particularly interested in the ways in which girls' routes to delinquency differ from boys'. She has published articles in *The Journal of Youth and Adolescence, Violence and Victims, Child Abuse and Neglect* and *The Journal of Family Violence*.

Andrew Kendrick gained his PhD in social anthropology from the London School of Economics in 1984. He was a Lecturer and Senior Lecturer in Social Work at Dundee University before he took up the post of Professor of Residential Child Care with the Scottish Institute for Residential Child Care at Strathclyde University. Andrew became Head of Department of the Glasgow School of Social Work in 2006. He has carried out a wide range of research related to child care and welfare, with a particular focus on residential child care. He recently edited the book *Residential Child Care: Prospects and Challenges* (Jessica Kingsley Publishers, 2007).

Paul B. Naylor is a Senior Research Fellow in the Institute for Health Services Effectiveness, Aston Business School, Aston University. Since taking up a research career 12 years ago, he has published, in total, more than 20 book chapters, web articles, and peer-reviewed journal articles. Most of this work has been on bullying among children and anti-bullying peer support systems in school, but also on workplace bullying and interpersonal racism.

Sharon L. Nichols is an Assistant Professor of Educational Psychology at the University of Texas at San Antonio. She is Chair of the Adolescence and Youth Development Special Interest Group of the American Educational Research Association, and co-author of two books: *Collateral Damage: How High-Stakes Testing Corrupts America's Schools* (with D.C. Berliner, Harvard Education

Press, 2007) and *America's Teenagers – Myths and Realities: Media Images, Schooling and the Social Costs of Careless Indifference* (with T.L. Good; Erlbaum, 2004). Her current work focuses on the impact of test-based accountability on adolescent motivation and development.

Laurie Petch works as a practitioner–researcher in the area of applied existential child psychology. He is currently practising as an educational/school psychologist in Regina, Saskatchewan, Canada, where he also has a training role. Simultaneously, he is working to complete his PhD in ScHARR in the University of Sheffield, UK. He is a member of the British Psychological Society, the Canadian Psychological Association, the Society for Phenomenology and the Human Sciences, and the International Collaborative of Existential Counsellors and Psychotherapists. His research interests focus on renewing child and educational psychology practice through an approach underpinned by existential philosophy.

Emma Renold is a Reader in Childhood Studies at the School of Social Sciences, Cardiff University. She is the author of *Girls, Boys and Junior Sexualities: Exploring Children's Gender and Sexual Relations in the Primary School* (RoutledgeFalmer, 2005) and co-editor of the international journal *Gender and Education*. Working at the intersection of queer and feminist poststructuralist theory she has published widely on the gendering and sexualisation of children and childhood across diverse institutional sites and spaces. Her current research project, 'Young people and place' foregrounds locality, bodies and movement in a participative multi-modal ethnography of girls' and boys' negotiations of urban and semi-rural public space.

Jessica Ringrose is a Senior Lecturer at the London Institute of Education. Her current research is on young people's sexual identities and hierarchies on social networking sites, available in *New Femininities: Postfeminism, Neoliberalism and Identity* (Palgrave, 2010). Her research on intersectional femininities and competitive, heterosexualised aggression and bullying appears in *Feminism and Psychology*, *Feminist Theory*, *Girlhood Studies* and *The British Journal of Sociology of Education*. Her writing on postfeminism, neoliberalism, class and feminine 'success' can be found in *Gender and Education* and *Feminist Media Studies*. Jessica is currently writing a book: *Postfeminist Education? Girls and the Sexual Politics of Schooling* (Routledge).

Ian Rivers is Professor of Education at Brunel University, West London. He is a chartered health psychologist and has held Chairs in Applied and Community Psychology at York St John College and Queen Margaret University. He is the recipient of the British Psychological Society's 2001 Award for Promoting Equality of Opportunity through his work as a psychologist in the UK, and in 2007 was elected a Fellow of the American Psychological Association for his contribution to lesbian, gay, bisexual and transgender (LGBT) psychology internationally.

Peter Squires is a Professor of Criminology and Public Policy at the University of Brighton. His work has included the fields of policing, youth crime and anti-social behaviour, and firearm-involved crime. Recent projects on young people, gangs and the use of weapons, in conjunction with the Centre for Crime and Justice Studies at King's College, London, have been the basis of his recent work exploring the street life of young people, 'gangs' and what has been referred to as the 'weaponisation' of youth violence. His book *Shooting to Kill?: Policing, Firearms and Armed Response* was published by Wiley-Blackwell in early 2010.

Nicky Stanley is Professor of Social Work at the University of Central Lancashire. She researches in the fields of domestic violence, parental mental health and child welfare, young people's mental health and inter-agency work. Commissioned research includes studies of domestic violence initiatives, social work practices, the mental health of young people, teenage pregnancy and student suicide. Her study of service responses to children and families experiencing domestic violence has been published by NSPCC (2010). She is co-editor of *Child Abuse Review* and has published books on domestic violence and child protection, mothers' mental health needs and inquiries in health and social care.

Jeff Stuewig is a Research Assistant Professor in the Psychology Department at George Mason University in Fairfax, Virginia. His research interests include developmental psychopathology, aggression, shame, guilt and risky behaviour over the life course. Recently, he has been involved in a study examining the moral emotions and their relationship to future recidivism and rehabilitation among a sample of jail inmates. He has published articles in *Addictive Behaviors*, *Child Maltreatment*, *Development and Psychopathology*, *The Journal of Interpersonal Violence*, *Criminal Behaviour and Mental Health*, and *The Journal of Social and Clinical Psychology*.

Jenna V. Williams is an Assistant Psychologist in the Mineral Hospital's Neuro-Rehabilitation Service in Bath, UK. She graduated from the University of Bristol in 2006 with a first-class honours degree in experimental psychology. Jenna joined the University of Sheffield in 2007 as a Research Assistant where she worked on projects focusing on the social relationships of adolescents and young adults with Asperger Syndrome (high-functioning autism); interdisciplinary team working in community rehabilitation settings; evaluating the use of telehealth in chronic obstructive pulmonary disease; and a European partnership implementing secondary school anti-bullying peer-support systems. Jenna has publications in the evolutionary psychology of relationships and the social psychology of bullying of adolescents with Asperger Syndrome.

Tara Young is Senior Research Fellow at the Centre for Social and Evaluation Research at London Metropolitan University. Tara obtained a first-class degree in sociology from the University of the West of England, Bristol, and a Master's degree in criminology from the London School of Economics and Political Science. She is now working towards a PhD by publication. Tara has worked on a number of research projects focusing on group delinquency and gang membership. Her work on gangs in the UK (with Professor Simon Hallsworth) has influenced policy at local and national levels. She has co-authored several journal articles on street-based youth groups and *Girls and Gangs – 'Shemale' Gangsters in the UK?* Her current projects include understanding multiple perpetrator rape.

Acknowledgements

We would like to thank our publisher, Wiley-Blackwell, and particularly the project editor Karen Shield, for their support, patience and commitment to this book. We owe a large debt of gratitude to Annabel Lander and Melanie Turner for all their administrative support and hard work over the duration of this project. We would also like to thank the NSPCC, especially Lorraine Radford and Phillip Noyes, for their continuing support and funding for our work in this important area of child welfare. Last but not least, our chapter authors have been a rewarding group to work with and we thank them for their efforts and patience.

1 Introduction

CHRISTINE BARTER AND DAVID BERRIDGE

BACKGROUND

Children behaving badly are a national scandal, a crisis never before seen, where children are out of control and dangerous. The streets are filled with hooded gangs of feral youths, while children routinely intimidate, attack and stab each other. Adults are no longer respected, their authority, values and laws disregarded. The rule of the street, governed by delinquent sub-cultures, has replaced the comfort of family values, with ever younger children being initiated. Or so we are led to believe. This represents, it has been argued, nothing less than a contemporary moral panic (Blackman and Walkerdine, 2001).

It is unclear what facts are submerged in this mist of rhetoric. How great a social problem is violence between children and young people? Has there been an unprecedented escalation in children's violence, or has such violence always been present but lain unrecognised and hidden, as with child abuse and domestic violence? Who are these child perpetrators and their victims, and what can we do to safeguard all children and young people's welfare in this area?

This book was conceived as a dispassionate and considered response to these questions, and to challenge some of the erroneous beliefs that surround children's violence or, as one author describes the problem, 'toxic childhoods' (Palmer, 2007). Such ideologies around violent and out-of-control childhoods not only pervade public attitudes and prejudices towards children and young people, but also influence how policy makers and practitioners respond to these problems through, for example, social welfare settings, education and the criminal justice system, including the courts.

Not all forms of peer violence receive equal recognition or concern. Although we acknowledge that professional and public attention, mediated though a moral panic agenda, can be unhelpful and counter-productive, some aspects of peer violence fail to reach public or policy consciousness. Indeed, a common form of violence between young people occurs on the battlefield, where the UK and the US have deployed 18-year-olds in armed conflicts – for example, in Iraq and Afghanistan. Perhaps the only form of peer violence to

Children Behaving Badly? Peer Violence Between Children and Young People
Edited by Christine Barter and David Berridge
© 2011 John Wiley & Sons Ltd.

come under sustained public and policy scrutiny, apart from, unsurprisingly, young offenders, has been school-based violence, generally conceptualised as bullying. Why some areas receive unparalleled attention while others remain concealed is open to interpretation.

However, a plausible explanation surrounds wider power inequalities. Children's violence that directly challenges societal norms or institutions, such as that involving young offenders or some forms of school-based violence, is perceived as necessitating intervention, whereas peer violence that reflects wider power structures, especially inequalities based on gender, sexuality and 'race', continue to be tolerated (see Chapters 7, 10 and 13). In reality this has meant that little shared understanding has developed concerning the similarities and differences between different forms of peer violence, including the messages each can bring to best practice. There is an urgent need to inform understanding and professional responses in this complex and contested area of child welfare.

OVERVIEW OF OUR WORK ON PEER VIOLENCE

Both of us have wide experience in the field of child welfare research. Over the past 15 years our joint work, funded by the National Society for the Prevention of Cruelty to Children (NSPCC), a large UK children's charity, has focused mainly on under-recognised and under-researched areas of peer violence. Initially this interest started with our research on NSPCC investigations into children's allegations of institutional abuse (Barter, 1998). The analysis revealed that young people's allegations concerned abuse by *peers* as well as staff. Yet many of the NSPCC investigators interviewed felt that their recommendations concerning peer abusers were often viewed with less importance by the commissioning authority than those relating to staff.

Our interest in peer violence was further intensified in our subsequent work on young people's experiences of racism and racial harassment (Barter, 1999). This review showed that *peers*, rather than adults, were the main instigators of racism. However, from a child protection perspective, the review also found a lack of social work awareness regarding the impact of racial harassment and violence on children and young people, and an absence of practice guidance in the area.

These findings led to our research, funded by the Economic and Social Research Council under its Violence Research Programme, on peer violence in residential children's homes (Barter *et al.*, 2004). The research was the first UK study to focus exclusively on peer violence in this context. The level of peer violence we found in children's homes was a major cause of concern. It is important to acknowledge that settings with very similar resident groups exhibited very different levels of violence, indicating that violence is socially determined and not simply an individual preoccupation. The conceptual framework developed from this research, based on young people's narratives, is used in this volume by Andrew Kendrick (Chapter 6) to look at peer violence across all out-of-home settings.

While the aim of the research was to explore violence between children's homes' residents, it also exposed another form of peer violence: teenage partner violence. Many of the girls interviewed spoke about their boyfriend's use of violence and control. A subsequent review of this area (Barter, 2006, 2009) showed that, although a body of evidence existed in the US, very little research had been undertaken in the UK. Similarly, policy understanding and professional awareness of this form of intimate violence, as distinct from adult experiences of domestic violence, was also disconcertingly absent. The editors have since undertaken two studies on partner violence in teenage intimate relationships, one of which is reported in Chapter 8 of this volume (Barter *et al.*, 2009; Wood, Barter and Berridge, forthcoming).

We have therefore explained our interests and credentials for embarking on this book. Similar themes were taken up in other related work (e.g. Berridge *et al.*, 2008; Kilpatrick *et al.*, 2008). But undoubtedly a main driving force for undertaking this book was the children and young people who have shared their experiences with us over the past 15 years. Throughout our work on peer violence, the most consistent and powerful findings have been children's and young people's own testimonies on how peer relationships, and especially those involving violence, are among the main causes of anxiety and unhappiness in their lives; and that these concerns remain largely unacknowledged by, and unreported to, adults. For example, when we explained our current research on violence in teenage relationships to participants, the response below was common:

Zoe: That's cool, someone's fighting our corner.

DEFINITIONS AND MEANINGS

Violence is a disputed concept. In this book we have adopted a wide definition of violence that incorporates physical, sexual, emotional and verbal forms. We use Kelly's (1988) conceptualisation of a 'violence continuum', in which different forms of violence can have a similar impact. Thus we do not impose a pre-determined hierarchy of harm in which, for example, physical violence is given priority above other forms. This reflects children's and young people's own evaluations where non-physical forms of violence can be seen as damaging as violence involving physical force, as illustrated below:

Having names called is worse ... because it hurts you more ... If you have a fight ... the pain goes and it heals, but having been called whatever is always at the back of your head.

Fiona, 14, quoted from Barter *et al.*, 2004, p. 29

We have used a definition of childhood that spans birth to 18 years. As much previous writing on peer violence has focused on older children and adolescents, we wanted to ensure that we compensated for this by including work on younger children's experiences, especially preschool children (see Chapter 2).

The age of 18, in many respects, legally defines the end of childhood in the UK. Some ambiguities to this threshold exist – for example, the state's responsibility for children 'looked after' can extend, at least in theory, into the early 20s. Nevertheless, reaching the age of 18 is generally seen as marking the final transition from childhood to adulthood. Unfortunately, the signifiers of adulthood, in terms of employment, housing and independence, are often severely restricted (Elliot, 1994). Thus, delimitations between childhood dependency and adult autonomy may be more theoretical than practical, especially for disadvantaged groups. While acknowledging this inconsistency, we have attempted to retain the age of 18 as the upper age limit for this book. Violence from young adults, especially men, has attracted considerable attention in research and policy, and we wanted to ensure that our focus remained on children's experiences.

VIOLENT CHILDHOODS – PROTECTION TO PUNISHMENT

Violence between children is a complex and controversial area and one where media-fuelled trepidation about an epidemic of violent children has come to dominate public perceptions and debate. Often such concern is based on appalling and therefore high-profile, although exceptionally rare, events. Major public concern in the UK can probably be traced back to 1996, when two 10-year-old boys abducted and murdered the two-year-old toddler James Bulger. The coverage of the murder, and the representation of the two 10-year-old boys in the press, by police and the courts as 'born evil' and demonic, were a watershed for how childhood deviancy in the UK has come to be perceived (Holland, 2004). The public was especially shocked by the very young age of the murderers. The imagery of a moral collapse prevailed where children, who are supposed to be innocent and protected, turned into killers. This case led to an intense and continuing scrutiny concerning the meaning of childhood, and especially the duality of the innocent/evil child. In this discourse, the innocent and therefore pure, angelic and uncorrupted child, who is in need of our protection, is juxtaposed against the evil, wilful and demonic child, who is in need of constraint for the protection of society (Higonnet, 1998). As Scraton warns:

> The conception of 'evil' within the aberrant child has long traditions … It resides permanently beneath the surface which presents a veneer of tolerance and understanding in direct contrast to the forces released once a child or young person steps out of line.
>
> Scraton, 1997, p. 167

Children quickly transgress from protection to punishment with little regard for the wider factors that may influence their actions. Once a child transcends one state to another there is little chance of redemption – through their actions they have relinquished the right to their own childhood. Again, this is illustrated in the Bulger case where the children were put on trial as adults, not juveniles. Owing to public outcry against these children, the then Home Secretary attempted to increase the 10-year sentence given by the courts to 15 years (although this was overruled by the Court of Appeal and criticised by the European Court of Human Rights).

Following this, as argued by Brown (2007), a new consensus emerged on the way in which children have come to be viewed by the state, where their own vulnerability and victimisation have been replaced by a more pronounced concern directed at curbing their anti-social and deviant behaviour. This is put succinctly by the following quotation from a young person:

> Some kids get left out of being seen as victims. They don't seem vulnerable, but just because they don't seem vulnerable doesn't mean they aren't. Often the worst behaved are the most vulnerable.
>
> Evans, 2004, p. 15

A comparable media and public outcry occurred more recently in 2009 when two brothers, aged 10 and 11, abducted, tortured and sexually humiliated two boys aged 9 and 11 in South Yorkshire (Doncaster Safeguarding Children Board, 2010). The boys, who were in the care of Doncaster social services at the time of the attack, were convicted in an adult court in January 2010 of causing grievous bodily harm. They were given indeterminate sentences, although they would be eligible for release in five years. Since 2004 the same authority has seen seven children die in suspicious circumstances, leading to a number of serious case reviews (Bennet, 2009), but these deaths failed to receive the same degree of media and public anger and condemnation that was directed at the brothers, who had not killed.

It is important to remember that not all countries view their children in this way. A year after James Bulger was murdered in Liverpool, England, a similar murder occurred in Trondheim, Norway – the Raedergard case. The response could not have been more different. Whereas in the UK the child murderers were represented as evil and in need of punishment, in Norway they were seen as innocent, in need of protection and rehabilitation (Franklin and Larsen, 2000). We should perhaps ask why some countries, including the US (Elliot, 1994), have so readily embraced such malevolent depictions of their young, while others question what their society has done to fail their children so terribly and how this can be amended? In the UK some commentators have argued for a similar approach to be adopted – for example, Johnston (2007) reported Professor Sir Al Aynsley-Green, the then Children's Commissioner for England, as saying:

There is a crisis at the heart of our society and we must not continue to ignore the impact of our attitudes towards children and young people and the effect that this has on their well-being.

The recall to prison of one of James Bulger's killers in 2010 has re-ignited the debate. Jon Venables, amid huge media publicity, was recalled to prison aged 27 as a result of breaching the licence under which he was released with a new identity in 2001. According to the Justice Secretary, Jack Straw, an 'extremely serious allegation' had been made against him (Walker, 2010).

Following the recall of Venables, the current Children's Commissioner, Maggie Atkinson, stated that serious reconsideration should be given to raising the age of criminal responsibility, and that we needed to reconsider how we respond to children who offend (quoted in Thomson and Sylvester, 2010). She continued that James Bulger's killers should not have been prosecuted because children under 12 do not fully understand the consequences of their actions. In England, Wales and Northern Ireland the age of criminal responsibility is 10-years-old, while in Scotland it is soon to be raised to 12 from 8 (Broadbridge, 2009). These represent the lowest ages of criminal responsibility in Europe, where young people are criminally responsible from between 12- and 18-years-old (Broadbridge, 2009).

Atkinson argued that we should look to other European countries' methods of dealing with young offenders that are 'more therapeutic, more family- and community-based, more about reparation than simply locking somebody up' (Thomson and Sylvester, 2010). James Bulger's mother responded by calling for Atkinson to be sacked for her 'twisted and insensitive' remarks. In response Atkinson apologised for any 'hurtful' comments while reiterating her belief that a serious discussion about increasing the age of criminal responsibility to 12 years old still had to take place (BBC, 2010).

The Commissioner also called for a debate regarding to what extent victims of crime should influence policy and practice in criminal justice and child welfare services (BBC, 2010). This is a concern that both editors agree requires attention. Although the abhorrent and tragic circumstances of individual cases require recognition, and lessons need to be learnt regarding what may have prevented a tragedy occurring, the voices of individual victims should not determine policy and practice. The continuing rights of victims and their relatives, therefore, require further debate. We need as a society to put aside our anger and examine instead, calmly and with compassion, how such children can be helped and rehabilitated. There is a risk that politicians and the media can respond to such tragedies in a way that makes matters worse. Policy in this sensitive area needs to be underpinned by a measured and robust debate, in which children's rights and the United Nations Convention on the Rights of the Child are upheld, and the needs of both the victims and their assailants are recognised. This may not occur when individual victims, however devastating their situation, have the ability to stifle debate and determine policy.

UNITED NATIONS CONVENTION ON THE RIGHTS OF THE CHILD

The following articles of the United Nations Convention on the Rights of the Child, and the corresponding obligations of governments to safeguard these rights, are of particular importance in relation to peer violence:

Article 3

1. In all actions concerning children, whether undertaken by public or private social welfare institutions, courts of law, administrative authorities or legislative bodies, the best interests of the child shall be a primary consideration.
2. States Parties undertake to ensure the child such protection and care as is necessary for his or her well-being, taking into account the rights and duties of his or her parents, legal guardians, or other individuals legally responsible for him or her, and, to this end, shall take all appropriate legislative and administrative measures.

Article 19

1. States Parties shall take all appropriate legislative, administrative, social and educational measures to protect the child from all forms of physical or mental violence, injury or abuse, neglect or negligent treatment, maltreatment or exploitation, including sexual abuse, while in the care of parent(s), legal guardian(s) or any other person who has the care of the child.
2. Such protective measures should, as appropriate, include effective procedures for the establishment of social programmes to provide necessary support for the child and for those who have the care of the child, as well as for other forms of prevention and for identification, reporting, referral, investigation, treatment and follow-up of instances of child maltreatment described heretofore, and, as appropriate, for judicial involvement.

As argued by Yiasouma (2007) with regard to children's rights, a potential conflict of interest occurs when the aggressor is also a child; however, under the United Nations Convention a duty of care exists both for the victim and the child or young person who has harmed. The first priority must be to protect the former from further harm, and to seek appropriate services and support. But it is equally imperative that the child or young person who has caused the harm is provided with appropriate help and support to meet his or her needs. Applying a children's rights perspective does not entail letting violent children simply get away with it. It does, however, require a commitment to providing the services that will enable these children to reflect on their actions, understand the hurt they have caused, learn from their experiences and work towards building a positive future (Yiasouma, 2007; Garside, 2010). This will inevitably be a difficult process, and one that will not be helped by invoking the adult criminal justice system, or a society that views such children and young people as inherently evil and unredeemable. Violence between children is clearly a highly charged topic. We need to remind ourselves that more children are *victims* of violent crimes than they are perpetrators (Elliot, 1994; Commission on Children and Violence, 1995).

CHILDHOOD EXPERIENCES

A study by UNICEF (2007), the United Nations children's organisation, looked at the position of children and young people in 21 industrialised countries. The researchers used 40 indicators to analyse the quality of childhoods in each country. The UK was ranked *bottom* of these developed countries in its ability to bring up children successfully. In relation specifically to children's family and peer relationships, the UK again came last of all 21 countries.

The research also showed that the proportion of children who report that their peers are 'kind and helpful' varied considerably across countries, from 80 per cent in Switzerland and Portugal to only just over 40 per cent in the UK. The World Health Organisation report (Currie *et al.*, 2004) stated that being liked and accepted by peers was a crucial factor in the health and development of children and young people, and that those who were not socially integrated were far more likely to exhibit difficulties with their physical and emotional health. The above findings are particularly worrying when we look at young people's exposure to violence from their peers. This is illustrated in Cawson *et al.*'s (2000) large, representative survey of nearly 3,000 young adults on the prevalence of all forms of childhood maltreatment. This study showed, as have others, that the most common source of distress to the sample during their childhood had been bullying and discrimination by other young people. Another recent school-based survey of 1,353 young people showed that approaching 1 in 6 of the total sample, equally for boys and girls, reported that their friends used aggression towards peers (Barter *et al.*, 2009). Elliot (1994) argues that the strongest cause of peer violence is being attached to a delinquent peer group where violence is encouraged and reinforced. The UNICEF (2007) study also positioned the UK bottom for young people's risky behaviours, such as smoking, drinking and under-age sex.

Thus, it is not surprising that research by Margo and Dixon (2006) argues that Britain's youths are the worst-behaved in Europe. However, work by Barter *et al.* (2009) provides evidence regarding the prevalence and possible influence of violence from *adults* on young people's lives. Disconcertingly, 13 per cent of girls and 9 per cent of boys reported that they had experienced violence from an adult family member, and 20 per cent of girls and 10 per cent of boys witnessed domestic violence. For these, violence could seem a normal part of everyday life.

The 2007 UNICEF report also highlighted that young people's subjective sense of personal well-being was rated second to bottom. Rankin (2006) showed that around 1 in 10 UK children aged 5–16 had a mental health problem, one of the highest incidence rates in Europe. Worryingly, longitudinal research shows that young people's mental health in the UK has been in decline over the past 30 years. This deterioration has not occurred to the same degree in many other developed countries including the US (Collishaw *et al.*, 2004), nor with any other age group (Rutter and Smith, 1995).

Layard (2005) states that it is important to recognise that mental health problems and poverty are intrinsically linked. This may help to explain the high relative level of mental health problems for UK children. The 2007 UNICEF report showed the UK to have one of the highest levels of relative child poverty and deprivation of all 21 countries. No consistent relationship between a country's wealth and the well-being of its children was found. However, it did reveal that children who grew up in areas of deprivation were more vulnerable and significantly more likely to be exposed to multiple hardships. Given these findings, we may conclude that UK childhoods are not something to be envied; and there seems to be something seriously amiss in the UK in what we are doing to children's lives.

CHILD WELFARE POLICY AND PRACTICE – AMBIGUITY AND DISCORD

Perhaps the single most recognised form of peer violence, at least in educational policy and practice, is bullying. In the 1970s bullying began to emerge as an area for study and policy attention. Since then, awareness and policy developments have become widespread and now every UK school is inspected by the national inspection agency OFSTED on their response to bullying. Anti-bullying policies have become an integral part of the official school agenda, although commentators have argued that in the past only certain forms of bullying have received official recognition (see Chapters 10 and 13). A wide range of policy and practice initiatives, aimed at stopping or reducing school bullying, have been developed in the UK and internationally.

Over the last decade the government has issued a range of new guidance for schools under its Safe to Learn initiative (Department for Children, Schools and Families, 2007a). This covers different aspects of bullying including homophobic bullying (ibid., 2007b), cyber bullying (ibid., 2007c), bullying involving pupils with special educational needs and disability (ibid., 2008), bullying in the community (ibid., 2009a), bullying in children's homes (ibid., 2009b), and also sexist, sexual and transphobic bullying (ibid., 2009c). This is in addition to the existing guidance on tackling bullying related to race, religion and culture (Department for Education and Skills, 2006). The Safe to Learn initiative (Department for Children, Schools and Families, 2007a) defines bullying as 'behaviour by an individual or group usually over time, which intentionally hurts another individual or group either physically or emotionally' (p. 11).

It is still too early to determine the impact of these new guidelines on levels of school bullying, although evaluations concerning the effectiveness of other strategies and initiatives have been mixed (see Chapter 3).

Although school-based bullying has become an established area for policy development, other forms of peer violence have not benefited from this heightened recognition. Indeed, child welfare policy has often failed to acknowledge the significance of peer violence on the lives and well-being of children and young people. Much child welfare research and practice focuses exclusively on *adult–child* interactions, be they neglectful/abusive or in a professional context (Barter, 2009). Only recently has social work attention moved to incorporate other aspects of peer violence – for example, in relation to sexually harmful behaviours. Regrettably, other areas of peer violence and abuse still remain largely neglected in social work research, despite the fact that young people themselves have repeatedly identified peer relationships, and especially those involving violence, to be one of their main concerns (Utting, 1997; Barter *et al.*, 2004).

Consequently, professional practice may not be reflecting young people's own concerns and wishes regarding the impact of peer violence. A number of obstacles have been presented to explain this omission, including viewing peer violence as experimental; fear of stigmatisation; a mistaken view that peer abuse is less harmful than abuse by adults; lack of awareness of adolescent abuse generally; and low reporting levels (Hird, 2000; Barter, 2009). The omission to respond to peer violence in current safeguarding responses may reflect a limitation of the system itself:

> In many respects the UK child protection system, its tools and current practices, are poorly equipped to protect a young person whose problems do not necessarily revolve around the quality of parenting at home, but may be created or exacerbated by their own behaviours.
>
> Children's Society response to the *Paying the Price* consultation,[1]
> November 2004, quoted in Evans [2004], p. 16.

Reforms through the government's 'Every Child Matters' (2003) agenda were designed to improve life for all children and young people, which should include peer relationships. Five outcomes were presented, which all children should achieve:

- be safe;
- be healthy;
- enjoy and achieve;
- achieve social and economic well-being;
- make a positive contribution.

---

[1] *Paying the Price* was a consultation paper on commercial sex in the UK, published by the Home Office in July 2004. It provided information and opinions on a wide variety of problems associated with on- and off-street prostitution.

The reforms included new duties to cooperate with, and to consider, safeguarding and the promotion of welfare for all children. It was argued that the outcomes would be achieved through meeting the needs of the most vulnerable through high-quality, inclusive, universal services. It may be asked, for example, if it is possible for children and young people to 'make a positive contribution' to their community or society given the very negative and stigmatising ideologies around aspects of childhood that currently prevail.

Alongside these reforms the previous government instituted a programme to decrease the level of anti-social activity, including violence, through its 'Respect' agenda. Although this agenda incorporated both prevention and enforcement, in practice the main emphasis was on enforcement to the detriment of prevention. Thus support for parents, youth activities and Individual Support Orders, configured into the Respect agenda, received far less emphasis than did enforcement measures, such as Anti-Social Behavioural Orders (ASBOs), which have been widely perceived as a central mechanism to combat youth delinquency (see Chapter 14).

This is a complex area and there is a need for greater clarity. While on the one hand government has been committed to meeting the needs of all children and young people through its Every Child Matters programme and its endorsement of children's rights and the UN Convention on the Rights of the Child, on the other hand it has demonised children and young people through its support of harsh, punitive measures, such as the high recent use of youth custody and ASBOs. In addition, and for too long, both social work practice and research have disregarded violence and abuse perpetrated between children and young people. This inconsistency leaves children and young people unprotected.

THEORETICAL STANDPOINT OF THE BOOK

This is the first UK publication, as far as we are aware, to directly address the complexity of peer violence from a range of perspectives and disciplines, including sociology, psychology, criminology, education, social work and child welfare. Any reliance on a single theoretical standpoint is likely to be inadequate in explaining the complexity of our social world, and especially in understanding violence. Empirical work needs to understand the ways in which complementary theoretical standpoints can help unravel multifaceted social problems (Layder, 1998). By adopting a multi-disciplinary approach, this book sets out to provide useful insights into theoretical understandings of the issues, and to highlight their implications for policy and practice developments.

Although diverse disciplines and perspectives are represented, the importance of understanding and responding to children's and young people's own views and experiences is a common theme of the book. Many of the contributors, either overtly or covertly, use conceptualisations associated with the sociology of childhood. This sociological framework has, over the past two decades, become a well-acknowledged theoretical standpoint that juxtaposes children's own experiences of being a child and the institutional form that childhood takes (e.g. James, Jenks and Proud, 1998; Mayall, 2002, 2004). Within this literature, children are seen as being actively involved in the construction of their own social lives, the lives of those around them and the societies in which they live. This enables children to be viewed as significant actors in, and interpreters of, a complex social world (Brannen and O'Brien, 1996):

> The nature of children's childhood is not simply the outcome of the particular structural conditions in which children happen to find themselves ... Neither is it solely the outcome of sets of discourses produced by adults ... Nor is it yet simply a function of the cultural determinates associated with, for example class or kin relations. It is also a product of the everyday actions of children themselves.
> James and James, 2004, p. 23

To avoid the danger of simplistic accounts of a homogeneous childhood, the plurality of children's experiences must be acknowledged, according to gender, class, disability, ethnicity and age (James *et al.*, 1998). Much work, for example, has been undertaken on the gendered nature of childhood and the ways in which constructs of masculinity and femininity shape young people's realities (McRobbie, 1990; Holland *et al.*, 1998; McCarry, 2003; Sieg, 2007), including their experiences of peer violence (Chung, 2005; Barter *et al.*, 2009).

RATIONALE FOR INCLUSION

All the following chapters are based on up-to-date research evidence; some present previously unpublished findings. Our contributors are experts in their field and we are grateful for their participation. A strength of the book, in our view, is that for the first time it brings together international research and commentary on a wide range of peer violence areas, which provide new insights and messages for child welfare understanding and practice. The collection spans the childhood spectrum developing a unique comprehension of peer violence from early childhood through to late adolescence. Contributors were invited so as to provide a diversity of perspectives and a combination of well-recognised and researched areas, such as school bullying, and less known areas, as with UK teenage partner violence and peer violence in out-of-home care. The collection directly addresses issues of diversity through consideration of wider power inequalities based on gender, 'race' and homophobia.

As editors, we wanted to report not only empirical and theoretical under-standing but also to identify possible implications for practice. We therefore asked authors to conclude their chapter with a list of points or issues for prac-tice. It is important to recognise that the diversity of authors contributing to this collection means that some contributors work in a more directly applied manner, in relation to policy and practice, than others. Nonetheless we feel that the differences between chapters are part of the appeal of an edited volume.

LAYOUT OF BOOK

The 16 chapters of the book are divided into four sections. Part 1 includes five chapters, which address peer violence in very different contexts. In Chapter 2, Jane Brown focuses on peer violence among preschool children. Initially she revisits the contentious debates about the definition of violence and asks to what extent this term can be applied to very young children. The influence of attitudinal factors, including ideas of childhood innocence, is elaborated upon. She concludes by examining the challenges associated with interpretation of childhood aggression, including how physically aggressive and 'superhero' play in preschool settings is mediated by expectations about gender and social class. Chapter 3 by Helen Cowie explores the underlying causes of school bullying, its impact and the associated outcomes for the quality of peer relationships. She considers the ways in which professionals can work with young people to counteract bullying and understand more about the nature of their relationships with others. In the next chapter (4), Paul Naylor, Laurie Petch and Jenna Williams outline research on violence between siblings. They begin by clarifying what constitutes sibling violence and abuse. Findings from a recent systematic review are used to explore the prevalence, correlates and causes of sibling violence. The authors explore the effects of such violence on children and discuss what future research is required.

Chapter 5 looks at the controversial area of violent crimes by young people, including an analysis of 'gangs'. Using testimonies derived from research on violent street crime, Tara Young and Simon Hallsworth document the processes by which young men become immersed in violent street worlds. They explore the factors that lead young men to engage in 'a life on road', examining the violence they conduct and the street collectives in which they are immersed. Through this, the populist image of the 'gang' is challenged. Lastly in this section, Andrew Kendrick (Chapter 6) addresses the issue of peer violence in out-of-home settings. He adopts Barter *et al.*'s (2004) framework of peer violence from children's residential care and applies it across a broader range of out-of-home settings, including foster family care, secure accommodation and young offender institutions. He outlines the ways in which carers are responding to issues of peer violence in out-of-home settings, and identifies 'good practice' messages.

Part II of the book introduces the reader to different forms of peer violence. In Chapter 7, Les Back recounts the murder of Stephen Lawrence to provide a detailed exploration of the links between youth crime and the legacy of violent UK racism. He provides a powerful and moving account of how the brutal stabbing provided a tragic watershed in the history of racism in Britain. The chapter draws on the struggle of the Lawrence family and their supporters to bring the murderers to justice, a struggle which, according to the author, lays bare the institutional failure and injustices of the British criminal justice system. Following this, Christine Barter (Chapter 8) focuses on one of the least recognised forms of peer violence in the UK: teenage partner violence. This chapter, based on an original UK research project, documents the incidence rates for physical, sexual and emotional forms of teenage partner violence, and addresses the associated factors that may increase a young person's suscepti- bility, either as recipient or assailant. The dynamics of teenage partner vio- lence, including frequency, development over time and help-seeking, are explored. Young people's own testimonies are presented throughout. The find- ings of this research led directly to the government's launching of a £2 million media awareness campaign on teenage relationship abuse.

Simon Hackett, in Chapter 9, is concerned with the problematic, abusive and harmful sexual behaviours perpetrated by children and young people. Official statistics, probably an underestimate, show that children and young people account for a significant proportion of reported sexual abuse. The chapter provides a concise analysis of the existing research in this sensitive area and looks at who these children and young people are, their family context and the risk of recidivism. The final chapter of Part II is by Ian Rivers and looks at homophobia and peer violence. The author argues that among adolescents, homophobic violence has a number of significant characteristics that distinguish it from other forms of peer aggression, particularly in schools. He reminds us that not all victims of homophobic violence are lesbian, gay or bi-sexual, because children and young people who are deemed to be somehow 'different' may also experience homophobic violence. He questions why young people use sexuality above any other mark of individuality to determine who is a target and who is unaffected.

Part III seeks to develop a more in-depth and critical understanding of certain aspects of peer violence. In Chapter 11, Veronica Herrera and Jeffrey Stuewig consider how child maltreatment and domestic violence have an impact on peer violence. Using longitudinal data, they examine the impact of three forms of child maltreatment – marital violence, child physical abuse and child sexual abuse – on children and young people's aggression, bullying and peer victimisation. Previous research in this area has largely failed to incorporate gender as a mediating factor. In response, the authors position this as a central component in their analysis and discussion. Following this, Sharon Nichols (Chapter 12) reviews the current theoretical and empirical literature on the media portrayal of youth violence. She explores, through various theo- retical lenses, how instigators and victims of violence are depicted, and the ways in which race, gender and age intersect with media portrayal. She addresses how US and European media compare, especially around how youth violence is depicted and contextualised. Furthermore, she explores how prevalence rates of youth violence contrast to media representations. Chapter 13 then returns to the issue of bullying as Jane Ringrose and Emma Renold provide a challenge to how bullying is currently perceived and responded to in anti-bullying policies. Using a feminist post-structural framework, and drawing on recent ethnographic and qualitative data, they explore how the concept of 'bullying' works to simplify and individualise highly complex power relations embedded in girls' and young women's school-based peer group cultures. They contend that policy continues to ignore gendered and sexualised violence in schools. It will be interesting to see, given the authors' arguments, how the new guidance for schools on preventing sexist, sexual and transphobic bullying (Department for Children, Schools and Families, 2009c) has an impact on this form of gendered peer violence.

In the final section, we have two chapters that directly address responses to peer violence in two very different contexts. Chapter 14 by Peter Squires and Carlie Goldsmith is an exploration of the ambiguity regarding the police and criminal justice responses to young people. The authors draw on research evidence to determine whether 'new youth justice' has actually helped or hindered marginalised children and young people. In Chapter 15, Nicky Stanley, Jane Ellis and Jo Bell consider the role and effectiveness of school-based preventive programmes aimed at reducing teenage partner violence in intimate relationships. They draw on two independent evaluations of UK programmes to consider the achievements of such programmes and the challenges they encounter. Gender differences emerge as a key factor, which needs to inform both the delivery of these programmes and their content.

Finally, in the concluding chapter, the editors draw together some of the key messages and common themes from the book.

The book is aimed at policy makers, academics, practitioners and advanced students from a wide range of social welfare disciplines. It should be of both UK and international interest, and has important implications for safeguarding children's and young people's welfare. *Children Behaving Badly?* sets out to challenge populist and harmful representations of youth violence, and the associated narratives of modern children as essentially 'evil' and out-of-control. We hope you will feel that the book achieves its aims.

REFERENCES

Barter, C. (1998) *Investigating Institutional Abuse of Children: An Exploration of the NSPCC Experience*, NSPCC, London.

Barter, C. (1999) *Protecting Children from Racism and Racial Abuse: A Research Review*, NSPCC, London.

Barter, C. (2006) Teenage dating violence: new DfES guidance for sexually active children – an evidence based response? *ChildRight*, July/August, 22–5.

Barter, C. (2009) In the name of love: exploitation and violence in teenage dating relationships. *British Journal of Social Work*, **39**, 211–33.

Barter, C., McCarry, M., Berridge, D. and Evans, K. (2009) *Partner Exploitation and Violence in Teenage Intimate Relationships*, NSPCC, London.

Barter, C., Renold, E., Berridge, D. and Cawson, P. (2004) *Peer Violence in Children's Residential Care*, Palgrave Macmillan, Basingstoke.

BBC (2010) *Children's Chief Apologises for Bulger Killers Comment*, BBC News, 17 March, http://news.bbc.co.uk/1/hi/uk/8572028.stm (accessed 19 March 2010).

Berridge, D., Dance, C., Beecham, J. and Field, S. (2008) *Educating Difficult Adolescents: Effective Education for Children in Public Care or with Emotional and Behavioural Difficulties*, Jessica Kingsley Publishers, London.

Bennet, R. (2009) *Doncaster Social Services Facing Inquiry After Seven Suspicious Deaths*, Timesonline, 13 January, www.timesonline.co.uk/tol/news/uk/crime/article5505375.ece (accessed 8 March 2009).

Blackman, L. and Walkerdine, V. (2001) *Mass Hysteria: Critical Psychology and Media Studies*, Palgrave, London.

Brannen, J. and O'Brien, M. (1996) *Children in Families: Research and Policy*, Falmer Press, London.

Broadbridge, S. (2009) *The Age of Criminal Responsibility in England and Wales*, Standard Note SN/HA/3001, House of Commons, Home Affairs Section, www.parliament.uk/briefingpapers/commons/lib/research/briefings/snha-03001.pdf (accessed 2 April 2010).

Brown, J. (2007) Time, space and gender: understanding 'problem' behaviour in young children. *Children and Society*, **21** (2), 98–110.

Cawson, P., Wattam, C., Brooker, S. and Kelly, G. (2000) *Child Maltreatment in the United Kingdom: A Study of the Prevalence of Child Abuse and Neglect*, NSPCC, London.

Chung, D. (2005) Violence, control, romance and gender inequality: young women and heterosexual relationships. *Women's Studies International Forum*, **28**, 445–55.

Collishaw, S., Maughan, B., Goodman, R. and Pickles, A. (2004) Time trends in adolescent mental health. *Journal of Child Psychology and Psychiatry*, **45**, 1350–62.

Commission on Children and Violence (1995) *Children and Violence*, Calouste Gulbenkian Foundation, London.

Currie, C., Roberts, C., Morgan, A. *et al.* (eds) (2004) *Young People's Health in Context. Health Behaviour in School-aged Children (HBSC) Study: International Report from the 2001/2002 Survey*, World Health Organisation, Geneva.

Department of Children, Schools and Families (2007a) *Safe to Learn: Embedding Anti-Bullying in Schools*, DCSF, London.

Department of Children, Schools and Families (2007b) *Homophobic Bullying, Safe to Learn: Embedding Anti-Bullying in Schools*, DCSF, London.

Department of Children, Schools and Families (2007c) *Cyber Bullying, Safe to Learn: Embedding Anti-Bullying in Schools*, DCSF, London.

Department of Children, Schools and Families (2008) *Bullying Involving Children with Special Educational Needs and Disability, Safe to Learn: Embedding Anti-Bullying in Schools*, DCSF, London.

Department of Children, Schools and Families (DCSF) (2009a) *Safe from Bullying: Guidance for Local Authorities and Other Strategic Leaders on Reducing Bullying in the Community*, DCSF, London.

Department of Children, Schools and Families (2009b) *Safe from Bullying in or Children's Homes, Safe to Learn: Embedding Anti-bullying in Schools*, DCSF, London.

Department of Children, Schools and Families (2009c) *Guidance for Schools on Preventing and Responding to Sexist, Sexual and Transphobic Bullying, Safe to Learn: Embedding Anti-Bullying in Schools*, DCSF, London.

Department for Education and Skills (DfES) (2006) *Bullying around Racism, Religion and Culture*, DfES, London.

Doncaster Safeguarding Children Board (2010) *A Serious Case Review 'J' Children: The Executive Summary*, January, Doncaster Safeguarding Children Board, http:// news.bbc.co.uk/1/hi/uk/8300034.stm (accessed 12 January 2010).

Elliot, D. (1994) Youth violence: an overview, paper presented at the Aspen Institute Children's Policy Forum, Centre for the Study and Prevention of Violence, 18–21 February, Queenstown, Australia.

Evans, K. (2004) *Mixed Messages: Can Anti-social Behaviour Measures and Every Child Matters Match Up?* Children's Society, London, www.lga.gov.uk/lga/aio/34822 (accessed May 2006).

Franklin, B, and Larsen, G. (2000) *The Murder of Innocence*, www.communitycare.co.uk/ Articles/2000/06/06/8245/The-murder-of-innocence.htm (accessed 27 June 2010).

Garside, R. (2001) *From Criminal Justice to Social Justice: Rethinking Approaches to Young Adults Subject to Criminal Justice Control*, Centre for Crime and Justice Studies, King's College, London, www.crimeandjustice.org.uk/t2asocialjustice structure.html?search_string=From%20criminal%20justice%20to%20social%20 justice (accessed 27 June 2010).

Higonnet, A. (1998) *Pictures of Innocence: The History and Crisis of Ideal Childhood*, Thames and Hudson, London.

Hird, M.J. (2000) An empirical study of adolescent dating aggression. *Journal of Adolescence*, **23**, 69–78.

Holland, J., Ramazanoglu, C., Sharpe, S. and Thompson, R. (1998) *The Male in the Head*, Tufnell Press, London.

Holland, P. (2004) *Picturing Childhood*, I.B.Tauris, London.

James, A. and James, A.L. (2004) *Constructing Childhood: Theory, Policy and Social Practice*, Palgrave Macmillan, London.

James, A., Jenks, C. and Proud, A. (1998) *Theorising Childhood*, Polity Press, Cambridge.

Johnston, P. (2007) *Crisis Point over Britain's Disaffected Youth, The Telegraph*, 15 February, www.telegraph.co.uk/news/uknews/1542725/Crisis-point-over-Britains-disaffected-youth.html (accessed 18 February 2007).

Kelly, L. (1988) *Surviving Sexual Violence*, Polity Press, Cambridge.

Kilpatrick, R., Berridge, D., Larkin, E., Lucas, P. and Sinclair, R. (2008) *Working with Challenging and Disruptive Situations in Residential Child Care: Sharing Effective Practice*, Knowledge Review 21, Social Care Institute for Excellence, London.

Layder, D. (1998) *Sociological Practice: Linking Theory and Social Research*, Sage, London.

Layard, R. (2005) *Happiness: Lessons from a New Science*, Penguin, London.

Margo, J. and Dixon, M. (2006) *Freedom's Orphans: Raising Youth in a Changing World*, Institute for Public Policy Research, London.

Mayall, B. (2002) *Towards a Sociology for Childhood: Thinking from Children's Lives*, Open University Press, Buckingham.

Mayall, B. (2004) Sociologies of childhood, in *Developments in Sociology 20: An Annual Review* (ed. M. Holborn), Causeway Press, Ormskirk.

McRobbie, A. (1990) *Feminism and Youth Culture*, Macmillan, Basingstoke.

McCarry, M. (2003) 'The connection between masculinity and domestic violence: what young people think', unpublished PhD thesis, University of Bristol.

Palmer, S. (2007) *Toxic Childhood: How the Modern World is Damaging our Children and What We Can Do About it*, Orion Publishing Group, London.

Rankin, J. (2006) Mental health in the mainstream. *Criminal Justice Matters*, **61** (1), 10–11.

Rutter, M. and Smith, D. (eds) (1995) *Psychosocial Disorders in Young People: Time Trends and their Causes*, Wiley, London.

Scraton, P. (1997) *Child in Crisis?* UCL Press, London.

Sieg, E. (2007) What you want, or what you get? Young women talking about the gap between desired and lived heterosexual relationships in the 21st century. *Women's Studies International Forum*, **30**, 175–86.

Thomson, A. and Sylvester, R. (2010) *Even Bulger killers were just children, says Maggie Atkinson, Children's Commissioner*, The Sunday Times online, 13 March, http://women.timesonline.co.uk/tol/life_and_style/women/families/article7060162.ece (accessed 13 March 2010).

UNICEF (2007) *Child Poverty in Perspective: An Overview of Child Well-being in Rich Countries*, Innocenti Report Card 7, UNICEF Innocenti Research Centre, Florence.

Utting, W. (1997) *People Like Us. The Report of the Review of the Safeguards for Children Living Away from Home*, Department of Health, London.

Walker, P. (2010) *Jon Venables back in Prison 'over child pornography offences'*. www.guardian.co.uk/uk/2010/mar/07/jon-venables-alleged-child-porn-offences (accessed 7 March 2010).

Wood, D., Barter, C. and Berridge, D. (forthcoming) *Teenage Partner Violence and Disadvantaged Groups*, NSPCC, London.

Yiasouma, K. (2007) *Peer Abuse – Appropriate Responses*, Peer Abuse Conference Report, Belfast, Northern Ireland, 19 June, www.docstoc.com/docs/23409757/Peer-Abuse-Conference-Report (accessed 8 March 2009).

Part I Peer Violence in Different Contexts

Part I   Peer Violence in
          Different Contexts

2 Understanding Dimensions of 'Peer Violence' in Preschool Settings: An Exploration of Key Issues and Questions

JANE BROWN

INTRODUCTION

The broad aim of this chapter is to identify central debates and explore key issues regarding 'peer violence' in younger, preschool children. Inevitably, it will address the thorny issue of conceptualisations of violence, and consider the advantages and disadvantages of applying the term 'peer violence' to the life stage of early childhood. The significance of ideologies of childhood innocence and 'taken-for-granted' assumptions regarding the gendered nature of physically active play in young children will be highlighted.

Two key areas of debate are identified. First, the relevance of adult interpretations of what constitutes unacceptable peer aggression in young children remains an important area, often articulated in terms of the 'eye of the beholder' in empirical research on the topic (Farver, 1996). Second, this chapter also considers the implications of 'zero tolerance' practices towards gun and aggressive play in nursery settings and, therefore, takes an inclusive approach to the nature and forms of peer violence in young children. In keeping with this standpoint, the chapter draws on a constructionist paradigm in order to consider peer violence in early childhood. In conclusion, implications and suggestions for practice will be addressed. Unless otherwise specified, the exploration focuses on children aged between 3 and 5 years who, in the UK, represent the upper age-band of children catered for in nursery and day care settings.

Children Behaving Badly? Peer Violence Between Children and Young People
Edited by Christine Barter and David Berridge
© 2011 John Wiley & Sons Ltd.

CHANGING CHILDHOOD, AND CONTEMPORARY
CONCERNS ABOUT VIOLENT CHILDREN

Theories of childhood construct 'the child' in distinctively different ways
(Burman, 1994; Danby and Yelland, 1998) and sociological approaches to
childhood view 'the child' as constituted socially (Jenks, 1996, 2004). In the
early 1990s, James and Prout (1990) set out a paradigm for the study of childhood, which advocated that childhood should be analysed as a social construction. So, rather than confirming the characteristics of childhood to be a
universal phenomenon, comparative analysis reveals the multiplicity of experiences of children. As a result, the idea that childhood is both culturally and
temporally specific is now well established in the multi-disciplinary and rapidly
expanding field of childhood studies (Hall and Montgomery, 2000; Thorne,
2004). This approach provides a useful basis for not only understanding binary
tensions evident in conceptualisations of children (i.e. the child as inherently
bad/evil versus good/innocent), but also in illuminating current anxieties about
violence perpetrated by children.

As one would expect, norms and expectations about childhood behaviours
change over time, which means that activities once viewed as 'natural' and
'normal' are evaluated very differently in the contemporary ideological and
discursive context. Illustrative examples of this phenomenon can be readily
found in the seminal work of Iona and Peter Opie, the British folklorists who
from the 1950s onwards charted the territory of childhood by recording children's games in schools and streets across the UK. In the context of pretend
games such as the then popular 'Cowboys and Indians', it is of note that gun
play is construed as a perfectly acceptable childhood activity (Opie and Opie,
1959). Opie and Opie also describe a game known as 'divie daggers' where the
player, notably a boy in the photograph that depicts this game, aims a knife at
the ground between his parted legs. The object of this game is to insert the
knife in the ground, successfully avoiding the player's feet. Today, in the
context of the intensified policing and monitoring of the behaviour of children
(James and James, 2001), parents who permitted such play would be subject
to criticisms of lax and negligent parenting (Parsons, 2005) and even 'pathologisation discourses' (Walkerdine, 1999). The Opies' innocent and carefree
portrayal of an independent and autonomous play culture in childhood provides a noteworthy contrast with the current risk-averse climate that legitimises adult surveillance and intervention in children's peer group interactions.
Today, an important theme in the professional discourses of early years' specialists are the dangers posed by physically lively and aggressive play in young
children (Tannock, 2008). Physically active and exuberant play is deemed to
require social control by nursery staff, and channelling into more acceptable
learning opportunities (e.g. Harbin and Miller, 1991; Sandseter, 2007).

Current anxieties regarding children as perpetrators of violence have been
shaped by a complex range of factors, including extraordinary and rare cases

of violence committed by children. Such incidents have been the focus of intense media scrutiny, most notably the murder of young Jamie Bulger in 1993. This tragic case, where two boys abducted the 2-year-old from a shopping centre, caught poignantly on a CCTV camera, provided a symbolic reference point for an intensified focus on childhood criminality and deviance (Holland, 2004). Some argue that there has been a pendulum shift in public and professional attitudes towards children, certainly fuelled by the media, from widespread concern about the abuse and victimisation of children, which gathered momentum from the beginning of the 1980s onwards (see Stainton Rogers and Stainton Rogers, 1992), to a more recent public and policy interest in antisocial activity in increasingly younger children (Brown, 2007). This focus is to some extent misplaced, as the Commission on Children and Violence (1995) pointed out: children are far more likely to be the victims of violence than the perpetrators of violent acts.

PEER VIOLENCE, YOUNG CHILDREN AND NURSERY SETTINGS

A fundamental issue in a consideration of peer violence relates to the definition of violence employed. Clearly, how violence is conceptualised and understood has important implications for how violent acts are addressed and the types of behaviour strategies adopted by schools. 'Violence', however, is widely recognised as a 'slippery' and problematic concept (Parkes, 2007). Ongoing disputes about the meaning of violence are debated around the following key distinctions:

• narrow conceptualisations;
• broad conceptualisations.

Narrow conceptualisations tend to stress individual behaviour, physicality and interpersonal forms of violence. However, a weakness identified in this approach is the over-emphasis on visible and tangible types of violence at the expense of institutional and symbolic forms (Herr and Anderson, 2003). Broader conceptualisations, by contrast, encompass a wider variety of types as well as symbolic forms including institutional practices. While the latter broad-based approach is more commonly applied to peer violence in adolescence, it can usefully be applied to younger children, as we shall see. This is important given that the perceptions and practices of early years' specialists have significant implications for evaluating peer conflict in nursery settings (Broadhead, 1992; Holland, 2003; Tannock, 2008). In this chapter, the topic of peer violence will be understood in the wider context of everyday play, as well as aggressive forms and relatively rare and extreme types of behaviour in early childhood. Furthermore, this position would also cover what some researchers label 'verbal violence' where expressions such as 'Bang! Bang! You're dead' (see Harbin and Miller, 1991) are defined as 'violent play behaviour'. However, disentangling the 'objective' status and nature of such talk is problematic given that specific kinds of aggressive play in children can provoke emotive and strong reactions in nursery staff (Holland, 2000, 2003; Jones, 2001).

From the point of view of parents and early years' specialists, examples of everyday problematic behaviour relate to the act of sharing, conflict over toys, and orderly and fair 'turn taking' on play equipment (Corsaro and Eder, 1990; Taylor, 2007). Contrary to sensationalist media reports, physical incidents between children, including fighting and striking other children, appear to be comparatively rare in nursery settings, as are extreme acts of physical violence (Brown and Burman, 2002).

PEER CULTURES AND THE SOCIAL WORLDS OF YOUNG CHILDREN

Peer violence and conflict in early childhood take place within the wider context of children's socialisation, and encompass their peer cultures and play. In Corsaro's (Corsaro and Eder, 1990; Corsaro, 1997) analysis of young children's socialisation, he found that there were two central themes in children's everyday lives:

- participating socially;
- challenging and gaining control of adult authority.

Corsaro and Eder, 1990, p. 202

In a series of observational studies undertaken in American and Italian pre-school settings, Corsaro and Eder (1990) demonstrate how integration into play groups can be particularly challenging for individual children. Gaining entry into groups is difficult because peer groups are inclined to identify with and defend shared spaces and objects in nursery settings, and they therefore tend to guard their ongoing play activities from the intrusion from others (Gallacher, 2005). However, when children attend elementary school, social differentiation becomes observable in children's peer groups (Corsaro and Eder, 1990). Significantly, social hierarchies are more likely to be established in peer groups that enjoy ongoing contact. Moreover, some researchers have found that children's awareness of their status within pecking orders of socially cohesive groups helps to lessen peer conflict (Farver, 1996).

Psychologically orientated observational studies, however, have indicated that particular boys identified as violent and physically aggressive are drawn to other like-minded males and play in small, single-sex groups of three to four children. Other characteristics of these particular boys are that they tend to disrupt the play of other nursery children, and their own play is prone to escalate into hostile and intimidating behaviour (Farver, 1996; Dunn and Hughes, 2001). In terms of younger children's use of racist insults, Connelly's

(1998) ethnographic study of younger primary-aged children showed how verbal abuse among boys was more likely to arise in threatening, competitive situations and in the context of games such as football. Connelly maintained that it is when masculine status and identity are at risk that peer relations tend to become racialised and 'race' is used by young children to 'make sense of their success or ... failure' (Connelly, 1998, p. 134).

Boys' physical and auditory dominance of playroom space has been found to be a salient issue in preschool settings (Brown, 2007). Small cliques of physically active and aggressively inclined boys were observed to take control of micro-spaces in the playroom such as the home corner and reading corner (Brown, 2007), and displayed what has been conceptualised as a hegemonic and ritualised version of masculinity (see Davies, 1989; Thorne, 1993). As Davies (1989) explained, hegemonic masculinity refers to a dominant and powerful form of masculinity practised by particular boys and some men. Similar patterns of male behaviour were also found in primary and secondary school settings, where older boys colonised and dominated recreational spaces such as playgrounds and locker areas (see Thorne, 1993; Mills, 2001), in addition to harassing girls and invading their private, marginal spaces (Connelly, 1998). An embryonic form of hegemonic masculinity has been observed in young boys in nursery settings, as well as studies undertaken in the infant classroom (Keddie, 2003).

ENERGETIC PLAY: ROUGH AND TUMBLE PLAY, SUPERHEROES AND WARRIOR DISCOURSES

Play is popularly conceived as 'the work' of the child and an important way in which children acquire competencies and learn experientially about managing social relationships. Importantly, it also provides the opportunity for young children to experiment with and explore risk (Tannock, 2008). The benefits of physically active play for young children are therefore multifaceted and undisputed.

So what are the key dimensions of energetic and physically exuberant play? There exist a number of overlapping categories of energetic peer play identified and studied in early childhood. These include what is termed 'rough and tumble' play (Jarvis, 2007; Sandseter, 2007), the more specific 'play fighting' (Broadhead, 1992) and imaginative play that involves superhero narratives (Thorne, 1993; Jordan, 1995; Marsh, 2000). In relation to rough and tumble play, detailed observational studies highlight the skills required and its intricate nature:

> Rough and tumble play lends itself to extended play bouts involving moving around, although not always running, often crawling, hiding, manoeuvring accompanied by interaction and planning.
>
> Jarvis, 2007, p. 174

According to Jarvis (2007), a distinguishing feature of rough and tumble play, which involves play fighting, is that it appears fun and enjoyable, as confirmed by laughter and prolonged eye contact between participating children. Similarly, studies that focus on educators' views found that 'displays of a cheerful face' was a main component of teachers' assessments of rough and tumble play (Tannock, 2008, p. 359). This contrasts with an aggressive and threatening type of play, which was characterised by facial shows of anger, as well as shorter, more intense bouts of child-to-child contact (Jarvis, 2007).

In contrast, superhero play draws on action stories widely promoted through popular culture, such as TV programmes, cartoons and action figure toys. Well-liked and common superhero play scenarios observed in nursery settings include Superman, Batman, X-man, Action man and Power Rangers, where the powerful male protagonists dominate and control the action. These storylines are especially attractive to some young boys. This is not surprising given that 'the superhero discourse is primarily produced by men for men and boys' (Marsh, 2000, p. 211).

Marsh's observational study carried out in an infant classroom found that, when interested girls were permitted to join superhero cliques, they were assigned to helping and minor roles by participating boys. However, when circumstances were conducive – namely, when staff were supportive and positively encouraged such play in all children – superhero play became strongly attractive to young girls. According to Marsh, staff endorsement of this activity has an impact on the self-esteem of all children but has particular implications for young girls. Encouraging girls to engage in lively play is crucial because some girls can be especially sensitive to teachers' social cues, particularly adults' expectations regarding acceptable behaviour (Broadhead, 1992; Sims, 1998; Holland, 2003). While Marsh found that the style of girls' superhero play was rather different from that of boys, she regarded such play opportunities as essential for girls because it allowed them to experiment with being 'agents of action', rather than being on the margins of lively group activity. As a result, Marsh concluded that, in order to encourage girls to assume more assertive and central roles in heroic discourses, teachers need to be proactive and help create the circumstances in which this can happen.

GIRLS AND BOYS, LIVELY PLAY AND THE PERSPECTIVES OF NURSERY STAFF

Early years specialists' ideas about young children's behaviour in nursery settings are highly gendered, because girls have been viewed consistently as better behaved in comparison to boys (Hartley, 1993; Yelland and Grieshaber, 1998; Walkerdine, 1999). Importantly, young girls are also more likely to be associated with sedentary and stationary activities (see Holland, 2003), opting for desk-bound activities in playroom settings (Brown, 2007). This contrasts with the tendency to normalise and naturalise boisterous and physically active behaviour in boys. As a result, managing lively play scenarios in the confines of institutional settings presents a number of challenges for early years' specialists, especially in relation to managing the play of 'noisy, boisterous boys'.

A series of studies have indicated that nursery teachers can be too controlling of lively play in children, and tend to overestimate the extent to which children's pretend fighting develops into actual fighting (Thorne, 1993; Schafer and Smith, 1996). Other observational studies have found that adults tend to underestimate children's competence and ability to find their own solutions and self-regulate fantasy play (Broadhead, 1992; Walkerdine, 1999).

Holland (2003) has questioned the value of pursuing corrective practices in nursery settings, specifically the negative disapproval of the play preferences of aggressively inclined boys. She argues that the constant policing of boys' behaviour, through repeatedly sanctioning and redirecting their aggressive activity, is counter-productive and a waste of staff energy. Other studies have found that early educators held ambivalent attitudes towards vigorous types of play. While acknowledging the many benefits of physically active play, Tannock (2008) found that nursery staff assessed physically exuberant play as particularly risky and potentially dangerous in nursery settings. A key concern for nursery staff was the fear that a child in their care might be hurt. As a consequence, they assessed rough and tumble play as an inappropriate activity for the physical confines of the nursery environment.

'ZERO TOLERANCE' AND THE SOCIAL CONTROL OF GUN PLAY IN NURSERY SETTINGS

In 1982 the European Parliament ratified a resolution that highlighted concerns about the growing popularity of war toys, especially replica weapons (Commission on Children and Violence, 1995). Sweden and Norway now have in place successful voluntary restrictions on the sale of war toys, while Malta prohibits their import and Greece bans all television advertising of them. The European Parliament recommends that its member states ban advertising of war toys and support action to reduce their sale. According to the Commission on Children and Violence (1995), play with 'aggressive toys', including replica weapons, could have a detrimental impact on children's well-being:

> It may even contribute to the general desensitisation of children to violence and that they may inhibit more pro-social and non-violent play.
>
> p. 213

Concern about gun and war play are not solely confined to professionals who work with young children, yet evidence for the desensitisation hypothesis remains unsubstantiated. Research findings indicate that it is the wider context of childrearing and especially particular parenting styles (e.g. lax or too harsh) that are inter-related to later aggression and anti-social activity (Haapasalo and Pokela, 1999; Morrison, MacDonald and Leblanc, 2000).

Zero tolerance of gun and aggressive play is an established practice, not only in preschool establishments across the UK (Holland, 2003), but elsewhere in Europe (Wegener-Spohring, 1989). According to James and Freeze (2006), the political slogan of zero tolerance emerged in the US in the early 1990s, quickly became synonymous with 'tough on crime policies' and the criminal justice system, and was later taken up by the education system (p. 583). In the UK, zero tolerance has its origins in the feminist movement of the 1980s and 1990s, and the successful campaigns to raise awareness of male violence against women and children in domestic settings (Holland, 2003).

A substantive critique of zero tolerance is that the policy is based on a positivist framework (i.e. there is an objective reality that can measured and predicted), which encourages inflexible responses to a range of low-level and extreme behaviours (James and Freeze, 2006). When applied to educational settings and young children, it takes little account of the fact that children will be exposed to a variety of childrearing practices and beliefs, which are likely to support a number of ways of dealing with peer conflict (Brown and Burman, 2002; Rourrou et al., 2006). Significantly, Canadian research, which investigated the views of Latino parents, found that mothers viewed zero tolerance practised in their children's preschools as particularly harsh and punitive (Bernhard et al., 2004). Mothers also felt that adherence to the practice encouraged an overreaction to everyday misdemeanours, thus prompting what they regarded as unnecessary adult involvement in the peer interactions of young children. Consequently, the interventionist practices of nursery teachers were at odds with Latino mothers' beliefs regarding children's need to develop autonomy, and the fact that children were capable of resolving disagreements between peers.

Favoured conflict resolution styles in children have also been linked with social class backgrounds of parents. In Brown and Burman's small-scale study in 2002 (unpublished final report for the Calouste Gulbenkian Foundation), including four types of preschool provision in Scotland, they found that parents residing in areas of socio-deprivation were more inclined to advise their children to 'hit first' and 'hit back' in disputes with other children. Importantly, the use of physical force was regarded as a rational and pragmatic solution to the day-to-day reality of peer and parenting cultures in their locality. As a result, children 'being able to look after themselves' was viewed as a basis for successfully coping with everyday life in their community. In contrast, some professional parents expressed strong anti-violence views, arguing that there were a number of preferable ways in which their children could be assertive and 'get their own way' in disputes with other children.

Young children's creative resistance to the social control of gun-making and war play in nursery settings is well documented as an ongoing fascination for children, especially males (Levin, 2003). A number of studies have reported that young children are generally adept at circumventing adult prohibitions (Corsaro and Eder, 1990; Gallacher, 2005). In relation to gun play, children found using 'make-believe' guns – commonly fashioned with Lego or improvised with sticks – tend to claim it is a more non-controversial and acceptable object such as a camera, fishing-rod (Wegener-Spohring, 1989) or iron (Brown, 2007).

From the perspective of nursery staff, gun play is undoubtedly a sensitive issue, raising ethical dilemmas for some teacher educators (Harbin and Miller, 1991; Holland, 2003). For example, Broadhead (1992) found that some female staff associated gun play in nursery settings with violence perpetrated by males in adulthood:

> Several women in the group felt totally opposed to gun play and felt that they could not allow it under any circumstances. For them it represented an undesirable aspect of male behaviour.
>
> Broadhead, 1992, p. 49

It is not surprising, therefore, that gun play tends to be met with disapproving and emotive comments from staff working in preschool settings, such as 'guns hurt people', 'we don't play with guns at school' (Jones, 2001; Holland, 2003).

FINAL COMMENTS

This chapter has taken a broad-based, inclusive approach to understanding the nature and forms of peer violence in younger children, placing the topic firmly within an understanding of young children's everyday lives and their play. Inevitably, this involves the recognition of children's socially differentiated peer cultures, and how they are acted out and controlled within the spatial confines of preschool settings. However, it could be argued that the notion of peer violence sits very uneasily with the category of young children and the life stage of early childhood. Powerful ideologies of childhood innocence are inextricably bound-up with cultural beliefs regarding age and immaturity, as well as ideas about the innate goodness of vulnerable and dependent young children. Moreover, it could also be argued that, by applying the term 'peer violence' to very young children, it inadvertently contributes to the 'widening of the net' and the increased social control and surveillance of childhood (see James and James, 2001).

There is no doubt that continued debate about how war, weapon and aggressive play are dealt with in nursery settings remains highly pertinent to discussions regarding the early years, in addition to debates about the nature of modern childhood. As we have seen, children and especially young boys display an enduring fascination with superhero play scenarios. Exploring and debating the ways in which such play is constructively tackled in preschool settings, as Holland (2003) has persuasively argued, is as relevant now as it has ever been, especially if we consider the broader backdrop of young children's day-to-day lives and their unprecedented access to violent images of war and armed conflict.

The following poses some questions for practitioners:

- To what extent is intervention in children's energetic and lively play necessary? How practical is experimenting with 'wait time'?
- Are there workable alternatives to zero tolerance of gun play in nursery settings?
- To what extent do the personal beliefs of those working with young children influence professional responses to gun play?
- Does the organisation of space and equipment optimise children's engagement in cooperative play?
- Do girls need more encouragement to participate in rough and tumble play in nursery settings?

REFERENCES

Bernhard, J.K., Freire, M., Bascunan, L., Arenas, R., Verga, N.R. and Gana, D. (2004) Behaviour and misbehaviour of Latino children in a time of zero tolerance: mothers' views. *Early Years*, **24** (1), 49–62.

Broadhead, P. (1992) Play-fighting, play or fighting? From parallel to co-operative play in the pre-school. *Early Years*, **13** (1), 45–50.

Brown, J. (2007) Gender, time and space understanding problem behaviour in young children. *Children and Society*, **21** (2), 98–110.

Burman, E. (1994) *Deconstructing Developmental Psychology*, Routledge, London.

Corsaro, W.A. (1997) *The Sociology of Childhood*, Pine Forge Press, Thousand Oaks, CA.

Corsaro, W.A. and Eder, D. (1990) Children's peer cultures. *Annual Review of Sociology*, **16**, 197–220.

Commission on Children and Violence (1995) *Children and Violence*, Calouste Gulbenkian Foundation, London.

Connelly, P. (1998) *Racism, Gender Identities and Young Children's Social Relations in a Multi-Ethnic, Inner-City Primary School*, Routledge, London and New York.

Danby, S. and Yelland, N. (eds) (1998) The serious and playful work of gender: talk and social order in pre-school classroom, in *Early Childhood Gender* (eds S. Danby and N. Yelland), Routledge, London.

Davies, B. (1989) *Frogs and Snails and Feminist Tails: Pre-school Children and Gender*, Allen and Unwin, London.

Dunn, J. and Hughes, C. (2001) I've got some swords and you're dead: violent fantasy, anti-social behaviour friendship and moral sensibility in young children, *Child Development*, **72** (2), 491–505.

Farver, J.A. (1996) Aggressive behaviour in pre-schoolers' social networks: do birds of a feather flock together? *Early Childhood Research Quarterly*, **11**, 333–350.

Gallacher, L. (2005) The terrible twos: gaining control in the nursery? *Children's Geographies*, **3**, 243–64.

Haapasalo, J. and Pokela, E. (1999) Child rearing and antecedents of criminality. *Child Abuse*, **4**, 107–27.

Hall, T. and Montgomery, H. (2000) Home and away: 'childhood', 'youth' and young people. *Anthropology Today*, **16** (3), 13–15.

Harbin, J. and Miller, D. (1991) Violent play behaviour and language of four year old boys: the significance of teacher mediation. *Early Child Development and Care*, **75**, 79–86.

Hartley, D. (1993) *Understanding the Nursery School*, Cassell, London.

Herr, K. and Anderson, G.L. (2003) Violent youth or violent schools? A critical incident analysis of symbolic violence. *International Journal of Leadership in Education*, **6** (4), 415–33.

Holland, P. (2000) Spoiled for a fight: war play in the nursery. *The New Therapist*, **7**, 13–17.

Holland, P. (2003) *We Don't Play with Guns Here: War, Weapon and Superhero Play in the Early Years*, Open University Press, Buckingham.

Holland, P. (2004) *Picturing Childhood*, I.B.Tauris, London.

James, S. and Freeze, R. (2006) One step forward, two steps back: immanent critique of the practice of zero tolerance in inclusive schools. *International Journal of Inclusive Education*, **10** (6), 581–94.

James, A. and Prout, A. (eds) (1990) *Constructing and Reconstructing Childhood*, Falmer Press, Basingstoke.

James, A.H. and James, A. (2001) Tightening the net: children, community, and control. *British Journal of Sociology*, **52** (2), 211–28.

Jarvis, J. (2007) Monsters, magic and Mr Psycho: a biocultural approach to rough and tumble play in the early years of primary school. *Early Years*, **27** (2), 171–88.

Jenks, C. (1996) *Childhood*, Routledge, London.

Jenks, C. (2004) A sociological approach to childhood development, in *Blackwell Handbook of Childhood Social Development* (eds P.K. Smith and C.H. Hart), Blackwell, Oxford.

Jones, L. (2001) Trying to break bad habits in practice by engaging with post structuralist theories. *Early Years*, **21** (1), 25–32.

Jordan, E. (1995) Fighting boys and fantasy play: the construction of masculinity in the early years of school. *Gender and Education*, **7** (1), 69–86.

Keddie, A. (2003) Little boys: tomorrow's macho lads. *Discourse: Studies in the Cultural Politics of Education*, **24**, 290–306.

Levin, D.E. (2003) Beyond banning war and superhero play: meeting children's needs in violent times. *Young Children*, **58** (3), 60–4.

Marsh, J. (2000) But I want to fly too! Girls and superhero play in the infant classroom. *Gender and Education*, **12**, 209–20.

Mills, M. (2001) *Challenging Violence in Schools – An Issue of Masculinities*, Open University Press, Buckingham.

Morrison, M., MacDonald, G. and Leblanc, T. (2000) Identifying conduct problems in young children: developmental pathways and risk factors. *International Social Work*, **43**, 467–80.

Opie, I. and Opie, P. (1959) *The Lore and Language of School Children*, Clariden Press, Oxford.

Parkes, J. (2007) The multiple meanings of violence: children's talk about life in South African neighbourhood. *Childhood*, **14**, 401–14.

Parsons, C. (2005) School exclusions and the will to punish. *British Journal of Educational Studies*, **53** (2), 187–211.

Rourrou, A., Singer, E., Bekkema, N. and De Haan, D. (2006) Cultural perspectives on peer conflicts in multicultural Dutch child care centres. *European Early Childhood Education Research Journal*, **14** (2), 35–51.

Sandseter, E.B.H. (2007) Categorising risky play – how can we identify risk taking in children's play? *European Early Childhood Education Research Journal*, **15** (2), 237–52.

Schafer, M. and Smith, P.K. (1996) Teachers' perceptions of play fighting and real fighting in the primary school. *Educational Research*, **38**, 156–66.

Sims, M. (1998) Gender segregation in young children's behaviour in child care settings. *Child Study Journal*, **28**, 1–16.

Stainton Rogers, R. and Stainton Rogers, W. (1992) *Stories of Childhood: Shifting Agendas of Child Concern*, Harvester Wheatsheaf, Hemel Hempstead.

Tannock, M.T. (2008) Rough and tumble play: an investigation of the perceptions of educators and young children. *Early Childhood Education*, **35**, 357–61.

Taylor, T. (2007) Managing unwanted behaviour in pre-school children. *Community Practitioner*, **80** (4), 30–5.

Thorne, B. (1993) *Gender Play: Girls and Boys in School*, Open University Press, Buckingham.

Thorne, B. (2004) Editorial: theorizing age and other differences. *Childhood*, **11** (4), 403–8.

Walkerdine, V. (1999) Violent boys and precocious girls: regulating childhood at the end of the millennium. *Contemporary Issues in Early Childhood*, **1**, 3–23.

Wegener-Spohring, G. (1989) War toys and aggressive games. *Play and Culture*, **2**, 35–47.

Yelland, N. and Grieshaber, S. (1998) Blurring the edges, in *Gender in Early Childhood* (ed. N. Yelland), Routledge, London.

3 Understanding Why Children and Young People Engage in Bullying at School

HELEN COWIE

INTRODUCTION

Oliver and Candappa (2003), in their survey of UK pupils, found that half of primary school children and over one in four of secondary school children reported that they had been bullied in the previous term. The Children's Commissioner (Aynsley-Green, 2006), in his consultation with children and young people throughout the UK, found that they mentioned bullying as one of the most common difficulties that they faced in their lives. Similar findings have been reported internationally and there is a growing body of research to document the nature of bullying in different countries, its incidence in each country and the range of intervention strategies that have been developed to counteract and prevent it.

For a useful summary, see the work of the EU-funded Violence in School Training Action (VISTA) project (Cowie *et al.*, 2006), in which a team of educators from across Europe integrated research findings and documented good practice in the field. They concluded that, despite cultural differences in the nature and incidence of bullying, there was consistent evidence that the most effective way of addressing the issue of school bullying was to develop a whole-school approach involving consistent policies, collective action, shared responsibility and interventions derived from a systematic needs analysis of each particular school or community. They also recommended that such action should be embedded within the whole school's practices, and regularly monitored and evaluated by representatives of all sections of the school community, including the students.

Recent research evidence confirms that there are extremely damaging outcomes for children who are bullied by their peers, especially when the bullying

Children Behaving Badly? Peer Violence Between Children and Young People
Edited by Christine Barter and David Berridge
© 2011 John Wiley & Sons Ltd.

is long term, indicating a complex multi-directional process. The bullied child's self-esteem is likely to be adversely affected by these relationship difficulties – a situation which, in turn, increases the likelihood of mental health problems. Bullies too are at risk. Children who bully have learned to use their power and aggression to control others, a mode that is not conducive to healthy relationships either in the present or in their future lives. Furthermore, there is evidence from longitudinal studies that children who bully are more likely in adult life to be involved in criminal activity or domestic violence. This chapter explores some of the underlying causes of school bullying and also the outcomes for the quality of peer relationships. We end the chapter with some suggestions on interventions to tackle the issue.

WHAT IS BULLYING?

The phenomenon of bullying is not confined to schools but, unfortunately, continues throughout the lifespan. Our focus here is on school bullying but it is helpful to consider the definition by Bowie (2000) of workplace bullying as 'a perceived or actual verbal, emotional threat or physical attack on an individual's person or property by another individual, group or organisation' (p. 2). This definition takes account of the individual adult experience of being bullied as well as the real-life nature of the bullying behaviour or actions. It recognises that bullying can come from an individual or a work team, and that it can also be embedded in the social systems of an organisation.

Olweus (1996) proposed that bullying is a sub-set of aggressive behaviour and that a child or young person is being bullied or victimised when he or she is deliberately exposed, repeatedly and over time, to negative actions on the part of one or more other students, with the intention to harm. Olweus (1993) also indicated that bullying is not necessarily physically violent but can involve psychological aggression, so making a crucial distinction between direct and indirect bullying. Direct bullying includes hitting, kicking, pushing, name-calling, using insulting expressions or rude gestures, or making verbal threats. Indirect bullying includes such behaviour as deliberately excluding a person from a social group, spreading nasty rumours about a person, disclosing another's secrets to a third person and, most recently, anonymous cyber bullying through text messages, telephone or the internet.

Olweus (1993) had already distinguished between *passive* and *provocative* victims. Passive victims often show characteristics of insecurity and helplessness, sensitivity, nervousness and submissiveness. By contrast, provocative victims are anxious and defensive, often hyperactive, and apt to irritate and annoy other children to such an extent that they appear to provoke aggressive behaviour. Other researchers (e.g. Egan and Perry, 1998; Ma, 2004) identified a third category, the *bully–victim*, who is typically trapped in a cycle of rejection through being aggressive towards peers, but is also the target of peer aggression; these children appear to be the most emotionally disturbed and are most likely to be chronically involved in bullying for long periods of time.

Early researchers tended to take the Olweus definition (or one very similar) and measure rates of bullying against the criteria that he had identified. More recent studies (e.g. Smith *et al.*, 2002; Naylor *et al.*, 2006), however, found that teachers and pupils do not necessarily define bullying in the same way as researchers, because they may not always acknowledge the damaging impact of psychological forms of aggression, and they are less likely to refer to the 'imbalance of power', 'repetition over time' or 'intention to harm' aspects that are central to the Olweus definition. Younger children's conceptions of bullying, for example, often include fights between equals (which Olweus specifically discounts as bullying) and it is only as they get older that children begin to include the more indirect and psychological forms that bullying can take. Additionally, research suggests that psychological bullying is perceived by teachers as less severe than other forms of bullying (Hazler *et al.*, 2001; Bauman and Del Rio, 2006).

The social context plays a critical role in the emergence of bullying behaviour. Salmivalli *et al.* (1996) identified a number of participant roles in addition to *bullies* and *victims*. These roles that children adopt – *assistants* to the bully, *reinforcers* of bullying, *outsiders* and *defenders* – can each have a profound impact on whether bullying continues or whether members of the peer group intervene to stop it. (The participant roles refer to members of the peer group so, while they could apply to adults in workplace bullying contexts, in the research literature on school bullying the roles are confined to other children.) *Assistants* actively help the bully (e.g. by keeping a look-out for the approach of a teacher) and *reinforcers* provide positive feedback to a bully by shouting encouragement or laughing at the victim's plight. *Outsiders* contribute indirectly to a bullying situation simply by taking no action against the bully, even though they are likely to be aware of what is happening. Outsiders constitute the silent majority who keep their heads down and mind their own business. *Defenders* actively defend victims, for example, by running for help or by offering support to the victim, either at the time of the incident or afterwards.

Taking account of the social context in which bullying takes place offers essential insights into why it happens and why substantial numbers of children and young people can take part, whether influenced by their families, their communities or the immediate peer group. This can be illustrated by the example of *gender bullying* in which both boys and girls engage in objectionable behaviours focused on physical development during and after puberty, such as sexual name-calling by boys; rumour-spreading and destruction of sexual reputations by boys or girls; sexual assaults perpetrated by gangs of boys; and beating-up of girls by cliques of girls motivated by sexual jealousy. Duncan (1998) found that the older girls in his sample observed an increased use of sexualised verbal abuse as they progressed through secondary school, and that this peaked at around 14 years of age.

Pupils perceived as 'different' by their peers are especially vulnerable to attack. Retrospective studies of lesbian, gay and bisexual adults provide extensive evidence of bullying at school. In a three-year questionnaire survey of 190 lesbian, gay, bisexual and transgendered adults, participants reported long-term and persistent experiences of homophobia (Rivers and Cowie, 2006). The bullying tended to be perpetrated by groups of peers, usually all males or groups of males and females, rather than by individuals. The most frequent forms of bullying were verbal in nature, including name-calling (mostly names that were sexual in nature or specifically related to their actual or perceived sexual orientation) and being ridiculed in front of others (82% and 71% respectively). A large number of participants also reported indirect bullying, in the form of being teased (58%) and having rumours spread about them (59%). A majority of participants reported physical bullying (60%), and a minority reported being sexually assaulted either by peers or by teachers at school (11%).

Other minority groups may be symbolically excluded from peer group networks through the marginalisation of their histories and cultures, so leading to disaffection and underachievement (Wright et al., 2005; Hayden, 2007), or directly attacked with reference to their appearance, characteristics, beliefs and behaviour, resulting in self-exclusion and poor attendance. For example, in a study of gypsy traveller children (Derrington and Kendall, 2004; Derrington, 2005), 80 per cent had experienced some form of racial abuse as they made the transition to secondary school. Similarly, children with emotional and behavioural difficulties may also be at risk of being bullied. Norwich and Kelly (2004) examined the views of 101 children, aged 10–11 and 13–14 years with moderate learning difficulties, regarding their experiences in mainstream and special schools. Overall, 83 per cent of the sample reported that they had experienced some form of bullying, with 68 per cent experiencing a mixture of types of bullying, 24 per cent experiencing mainly verbal bullying, 5 per cent experiencing mainly physical bullying and 3 per cent experiencing mainly teasing.

RELATIONSHIPS IN THE PEER GROUP

In order to understand why bullying happens, we need to know about the dynamic nature of children's peer relationships and the important role that both friendship and the social contexts of friendship play in enhancing the quality of young people's lives and protecting them from harm. We cannot underestimate the power of the peer group in teaching young people about how to navigate their social worlds and, more specifically, in influencing whether or not a group member is bullied. Through forming relationships with others, children potentially learn on a daily basis about the happiness and fun to be derived from playing and working with friends and classmates; they learn how to express and when to control their feelings; they learn about sharing and cooperation; they discover that friendships are mutually satisfying; they learn that sometimes people fall out or have disputes and that dealing with these setbacks can be difficult but also satisfying. In fact, it is often at the point of difficulty that children discover the true value of friendship because it is then that they discover the role of friends as supporters when things go wrong (Dunn, 2004).

At the same time, if children experience sustained difficulties over time in their peer group relationships, as they do when they are bullied, then their emotional health and well-being are at risk of being undermined. In the context of our focus in this chapter on bullying, we first consider research findings that document the serious impact that the experience of bullying or being bullied can have on young people's lives.

WHY ARE SOME CHILDREN BULLIED?

Hawker and Boulton (2000) found that loneliness was positively associated with the experience of being bullied. Both social and generalised anxiety were significantly related to bullying, although the effects were not as strong as those for depression. Bullied children were also found to have significantly lower self-esteem than non-victims, in the sense that they had negative attitudes towards themselves, did not feel themselves to be in control of their lives and often experienced feelings of helplessness and powerlessness. On the basis of their findings, Hawker and Boulton concluded that mental health difficulties and low self-esteem appeared to be clear outcomes of being bullied. In addition, they proposed that some of the emotional and social difficulties demonstrated by victims of bullying may also have pre-dated the bullying, in the sense that these children could have been vulnerable already and so made easy targets for aggressive peers.

An opportunity to test this hypothesis arose from a number of longitudinal studies. Arsenault *et al.* (2006), as part of their longitudinal UK study of 2,232 twins from infancy onwards, were able to identify the children in their sample who had experienced bullying between the ages of 5 and 7 years. They found that a significant number of the children identified in this study as victims of bullying had come to school with pre-existing problems and were less happy than non-bullied peers during their first year at school, and that these bullied children reported more adjustment difficulties and unhappiness at school than children who had not been bullied. The researchers also identified two types of victim in their sample: 'pure' victims – that is, those who had not provoked the aggression – and those who were 'provocative' victims (sometimes known as bully–victims). They found that the children with a higher reported rate of mental health difficulties were to be found among the bully–victims.

This research suggested that young children with existing mental health difficulties appeared to have an increased chance of being bullied. Further insights were offered by a large-scale US study of adolescents by Bosacki *et al.* (2007) investigating whether self-esteem might be a protective factor for victims of bullying, particularly in its role as a mediator between social isolation on the one hand and, on the other, the 'internalising problems' of both depression and social anxiety. In their sample of 7,290 adolescents, aged between 13 and 18 years, they found that social isolation and friendship alienation were significantly related to low self-esteem and to depression and social anxiety. Low self-esteem was also significantly related to depression and social anxiety, independent of peer relationship difficulties. The direct association between peer relational difficulties and depression and social anxiety was significantly reduced when the researchers took account of the level of self-esteem. In other words, young people in this sample who, despite their interpersonal difficulties within the peer group, still scored highly on measures of self-esteem, were less likely to suffer from depression or social anxiety.

As well as documenting the damaging outcomes for young people's mental health from the experience of being bullied, these findings confirmed the supportive role of friendship. They also indicated the protective strengths of positive feelings of self-worth, confirmed by qualitative material in the study that showed quite wide variations in the extent to which the young people were emotionally affected by being bullied. This corresponds with research showing that those low in self-esteem are more likely to perceive an incident as peer victimisation and to interpret events more negatively than do more resilient peers (Verkuyten and Thijs, 2001).

Egan and Perry (1998), who measured the self-reported victimisation and global self-worth of 189 schoolchildren in the course of a school year, concluded that those low in self-esteem possibly lack the resilience afforded by higher levels of self-esteem. So being bullied may further reduce their self-esteem, thereby perpetuating a vicious cycle and making these individuals even more susceptible to the effects of victimisation. Therefore, not only do victims report low self-esteem, possibly as a direct result of being victimised, but also their low self-esteem primes them to view events negatively, making it more likely that they will construe a particular incident as deliberate 'bullying' and therefore, quite understandably, suffer emotionally from the humiliation and hurt of being targeted in this way by a peer. The findings of Egan and Perry (1998) confirm that some young people react more emotionally than others when they are having friendship difficulties or are being bullied, possibly because of their temperament or as a consequence of experiences of rejection or loss earlier in their lives. In other words, the same event will be experienced differently depending on the young person's emotional make-up, their history of friendship and intimate attachments or some inner strength that emerges despite the suffering that they are experiencing.

Unfortunately, although other more resilient children might successfully brush the episode aside with the help of friends and a range of personal protective strategies, research indicates that, even when some bullied children take action to defend themselves – for example, by seeking social support from other pupils – the peer group may still reject them. In 2008 Escobar (unpublished PhD thesis) found that coping strategies that are usually effective for resilient children with a network of friends become dysfunctional for those in greatest need of support, possibly where these children are perceived by peers as being too emotionally demanding or, in the case of the marginalised, as being 'unworthy' of support. Understandably, young people suffer lowered self-esteem when they are having difficulties in relating positively with members of the peer group. When coping strategies fail to protect such individuals or groups from being bullied, it is unsurprising that they show signs of depression or social anxiety, or become disaffected and drop out of school.

Research and practice, however, indicate that there are ways to intervene to help bullied pupils. As Egan and Perry (1998) discovered, for those young people who maintain their sense of self-worth, despite being bullied, and who work out a coherent set of strategies to solve the problem, there seems to be less likelihood that the bullying will continue. Useful information has also been retrieved from bullied children themselves. Smith *et al.* (2004) found that 'escaped victims' reported a number of useful strategies, such as telling someone, actively trying to make new friends and even befriending the bully – strategies which the 'continuing victims' (those who had been bullied for more than two years) were less likely to utilise. The continuing victims were also more likely to blame themselves for being bullied.

WHY DO SOME CHILDREN BECOME BULLIES?

There is a growing literature on the mental health of children and young people who bully their peers (Kaltiala-Heino *et al.*, 2000). Kumpulainen and Räsänen (2000) found that children involved in bullying, in particular those who were bully–victims at early elementary school age, had more psychiatric symptoms at the age of 15 years. The probability of being deviant at the age of 15 years was higher among children involved in bullying at the age of 8 or 12 years than among non-involved children.

However, other studies place more emphasis on the bullies' capacity to use social skills to manipulate others in order to increase their status within the peer group (Sutton, Smith and Swettenham, 1999). Bullies often show excessive lack of empathy for their victims and a capacity to justify their aggressive actions – for example, by blaming the victim, exacting 'just revenge' for an insult or slight, or feeling angry (Owens, Shute and Slee, 2000). Low fear reactivity seems to be a strong risk factor for becoming a bully because it prevents the development of a sense of conscience about harming others, undermines the quality of empathy for another's suffering and acts against the internalisation of pro-social norms of behaviour (Terranova, Sheffield Morris and Boxer, 2008).

Another characteristic that has been identified by studies of bullies is narcissism – a preoccupation with the self and over-sensitivity to any form of actual or perceived criticism (Salmivalli et al., 1999). Narcissistic individuals tend to be self-focused, highly competitive, exhibitionistic and aggressive people who lack empathy and who tend to be manipulative and self-seeking in their interpersonal relationships. Researchers such as Baumeister, Smart and Boden (1996) proposed that aggression is related to high self-esteem through what they define as defensive egotism – a tendency to hold favourable self-appraisals that may be not grounded in reality or may be exaggerated, combined with difficulty in accepting any criticism. Threats to such self-appraisals are met with aggression. This type of self-focused person tends to be highly competitive, manipulative, lacking in empathy and self-seeking in their relationships with others; they also score highly on measures of narcissism. Daly in his 2006 study of 1,628 adolescents in six Australian schools (unpublished PhD thesis), found that adolescents who scored highly on measures of self-esteem and narcissism also scored highly on aggression. He recommended that interventions that focus on building the capacity for empathy among young people who bully may actually be more effective in reducing aggression than interventions that aim to boost self-esteem. He points out that such narcissistic aggressive children, unlike their victims, would benefit from interventions that help them to develop empathy for others' suffering and distress rather than interventions to boost their own existing self-esteem, which tends to be unrealistically high.

The research that we have explored on the characteristics of bullies gives useful insights into why they engage in such aggressive behaviour towards their peers. However, as Henry (2008) points out, it is not enough to view bullying behaviour as an individual set of personal characteristics without considering the social contexts in which it takes place, and without taking account of the child's perception and experience of the stressors that cause it, such as violence at home. She also advocates that we take account of the quality of caregiver relationships at home. Children who bully appear to have become desensitised to others' feelings because of their own experiences of insecure attachment within the family leading to the suppression of their own feelings of empathy. This process of desensitisation disrupts the development of helpful, pro-social feelings and values in children who bully when they interact with their peer group. Children who have developed insecure relationships characterised by inconsistent attention to their needs, rejection and insensitivity on the part of the parent or caregiver are more likely to become potential bullies or bully–victims.

The research that documents the personality characteristics of bullies must also be viewed in the wider social context in which children and adolescents are growing up, where there are strong peer pressures for both boys and girls to behave within the strictly regulated dominant behaviour patterns required by the culture. For example, Frosh, Phoenix and Pattman (2002) found that it was very difficult for the inner-city boys in his sample to experiment with alternative ways of being masculine outside the narrow stereotypes provided by the culture for fear of the sanction of being bullied or ostracised if they did not fit the masculine 'ideal'. Even boys who were willing to defend bullied peers had to be careful in case the group turned on them. From this perspective, it would appear that bullies take advantage of the social structures in their peer groups to exercise their skill at manipulating others, and that they also gravitate towards groups, such as gangs, in which displays of deviant and aggressive behaviour are highly valued and so reinforced by peers.

WHAT CAN SCHOOLS DO?

Just as the literature on workplace bullying places emphasis on the culture of the organisation as a factor in whether bullying behaviour is condoned or challenged (Bowie, 2000; Cowie et al., 2002), so the culture of the school itself can have a profound impact on bullying among its pupils. Within the context of the school, there can be a strong link between the culture of the school and the extent of bullying among the pupils, between staff and pupils and within the staff teams themselves. Cowie and Jennifer (2007, 2008) propose that, if bullying is to be effectively challenged, all members of a school community must learn about bullying, its social dynamics, its origins and the impact that it has on everyone's life, as well as the many forms that bullying takes. The school community, including pupils, teachers, parents and other adults involved, can then identify the interventions that are most appropriate for their particular setting. The school can play a significant part in addressing bullying by focusing on relationships between pupils, between pupils and staff, between staff colleagues and between staff and management, encouraging open, genuine communication, challenging racism, homophobia and other forms of prejudice, and by devising policies and practices that offer emotional and social support to all members of the school community. Perhaps the most powerful way of counteracting bullying is for the school as a community to offer constructive alternatives to the self-seeking, manipulative worlds where bullies dominate. The school can enhance peer relationships by creating an emotionally literate arena where positive steps are taken to promote emotional health and well-being for all within the overall social context of the school (Frey et al., 2005; Mavroveli et al., 2007).

Examples of such interventions include training in restorative practices, each of which works through the relationship to develop qualities such as respect for the other, a problem-solving approach to conflict and the experi-ence of active, empathic listening. Additionally, interventions such as the support group method (Maines and Robinson, 1997) work directly to enhance empathy and to foster pro-social attitudes within a group. When these methods are successful, they enhance a group ethos in which it is possible to make reparation for the emotional damage that arises from bullying, and to increase the repertoire of responses to situations of conflict.

Peer support systems are widely accepted as being an important part of a school's strategy to counteract bullying and to create an atmosphere of safety in school by giving young people a structure within which they can discover and implement ways of improving the emotional health and well-being of their own school community. There is consistent evidence that the practice of peer support appears to give direction to young people's altruistic wishes to address injustices such as bullying and deliberate social exclusion in their school community. As Cowie *et al.* (2008) indicate, it is the awareness that peer supporters are there to help that enables all pupils to create a social construction that school is a safer place to be. In other words, the observation (and in some cases the experience) of the helpfulness of sharing worries and anxieties with another has become an accepted method for coping with peer group issues of concern, notably bullying, and for changing the culture from one of indifference to others' suffering to one of shared concern.

The most successful solutions to the problem of bullying appear to be those that work with the relationship in a social context, reinforced by the support of key adults at school (teachers and other professionals), parents and caregiv-ers (at home), members of the peer group and, if possible, with the active support of the local community.

KEY PRACTICE POINTS

- School bullying takes different forms, including physical and psychological, direct and indirect. Both staff and pupils are more likely to view physical bullying as more serious and harmful than other forms of bullying.
- Bullying does not happen just between individuals but takes place in the context of a peer group; the majority of children can be placed in at least one of a range of participant roles in bullying: bully, victim, assistant to the bully, reinforcer of the bully, outsider or defender.
- A number of factors, such as race, religion or culture, disability, sexual ori-entation and gender, might be used by the peer group to justify bullying others.
- Bullying can have some very serious outcomes in terms of mental health and social functioning. Those who bully are at risk as well as those who are bullied.

- There are a number of well-documented interventions that have been shown to reduce or prevent bullying but constant vigilance is needed. Most effective are those interventions that involve the whole school as a community and that address the problem at several levels: individual, classroom, school and wider community.

REFERENCES

Arsenault, L., Walsh, E., Trzesniewski, K., Newcombe, R., Caspi, A. and Moffitt, T. (2006) Bullying victimization uniquely contributes to adjustment problems in young children: a nationally representative cohort study. *Pediatrics*, **118**, 130–8.

Aynsley-Green, A. (2006) *Bullying Today*. Office of the Children's Commissioner, www.ncb.org.uk/ncercc/ncercc%20practice%20documents/report_bullying_bullyingtoday_final_november2006.pdf (accessed 8 July 2010).

Bauman, S. and Del Rio, A. (2006) Pre-service teachers' responses to bullying scenarios: comparing physical, verbal and relational bullying. *Journal of Educational Psychology*, **98**, 219–31.

Baumeister, R.F., Smart, L. and Boden, J.M. (1996) Relation of threatened egotism to violence and aggression: the dark side of high self-esteem. *Psychological Review*, **103**, 5–33.

Bosacki, S., Dane, A., Marini, Z. and YLC-CURA (2007) Peer relationships and internalizing problems in adolescents: mediating role of self-esteem. *Emotional and Behavioural Difficulties*, **121** (4), 261–82.

Bowie, V. (2000) Current trends and emerging issues in workplace violence. *Security Journal*, **13** (3), 7–23.

Cowie, H. and Jennifer, D. (2007) *Managing Violence in School: A Whole-School Approach to Best Practice*, Paul Chapman, London.

Cowie, H. and Jennifer, D. (2008) *New Perspectives on Bullying*, Open University Press, Maidenhead.

Cowie, H., Hutson, N., Oztug, O. and Myers, C. (2008) The impact of peer support schemes on pupils' perceptions of bullying, aggression and safety at school. *Emotional and Behavioural Difficulties*, **13** (1), 63–71.

Cowie, H., Jennifer, D., Chankova, D. *et al.* (2006) *School Bullying and Violence: Taking Action*, www.vista-europe.org (accessed 26 June 2010).

Cowie, H., Naylor, P., Rivers, I., Smith, P.K. and Pereira, B. (2002) Measuring workplace bullying, aggression and violent behaviour. *Aggression and Violent Behaviour*, **7**, 33–51.

Derrington, C. (2005) Perceptions of behaviour and patterns of exclusion: gypsy traveler students in English secondary schools. *Journal of Research in Special Educational Needs*, **5** (2), 55–61.

Derrington, C. and Kendall, S. (2004) *Gypsy Traveller Students in Secondary Schools: Culture, Identity and Achievement*, Trentham Books, Nottingham.

Duncan, N. (1998) Sexual bullying in secondary schools. *Pastoral Care in Education*, June, 27–31.

Dunn, J. (2004) *Children's Friendships: The Beginnings of Intimacy*, Blackwell Publishing, Oxford.

Egan, S.K. and Perry, D.G. (1998) Does low self-regard invite victimization? *Developmental Psychology*, **34**, 299–309.

Frey, K.S., Nolen, S.B., Van Schoiack Edstrom, L. and Hirschstein, M.K. (2005) Effects of a school-based social-emotional competence program: linking children's goals, attributions, and behavior. *Applied Developmental Psychology*, **26**, 171–200.

Frosh, S., Phoenix, A. and Pattman, R. (2002) *Young Masculinities*, Palgrave, Basingstoke.

Hawker, D.S.J. and Boulton, M.J. (2000) Twenty years' research on peer victimization and psychosocial maladjustment: a meta-analytic review of cross-sectional studies. *Journal of Child Psychology and Psychiatry*, **41** (4), 441–55.

Hayden, C. (2007) *Children in Trouble*, Palgrave, London.

Hazler, R.J., Miller, D.L., Carney, J.L. and Green, S. (2001) Adult recognition of school bullying situations. *Educational Research*, **43**, 133–46.

Henry, S. (2008) *Bullying as a Social Pathology*, Edwin Mellen Press, Lewiston.

Kaltiala-Heino, R., Rimpela, M., Rantanen, P. and Rimpela, A. (2000) Bullying at school an indicator of adolescents at risk for mental disorders. *Journal of Adolescence*, **23**, 661–74.

Kumpulainen, K. and Räsänen, E. (2000) Children involved in bullying at elementary school age: their psychiatric symptoms and deviance in adolescence: an epidemiological sample. *Child Abuse & Neglect*, **24** (12), 1567–77.

Ma, X. (2004) Who are the victims? in *Bullying: Implications for the Classroom* (eds C. Sanders and G.D. Phye), Elsevier Press, San Diego, CA.

Maines, B. and Robinson, G. (1997) *Crying for Help: The No Blame Approach to Bullying*, Lucky Duck Publishing, Bristol.

Mavroveli, S., Petrides, K.V., Rieffe, C. and Bakker, F. (2007) Trait emotional intelligence, psychological well-being, and peer-rated social competence in adolescence. *British Journal of Developmental Psychology*, **25**, 263–75.

Naylor, P., Cowie, H., Cossin, F., de Bettencourt, R. and Lemme, F. (2006) Teachers' and pupils' definitions of bullying. *British Journal of Educational Psychology*, **76**, 553–76.

Norwich, B. and Kelly, N. (2004) Pupils' views on inclusion: moderate learning difficulties and bullying in mainstream and special schools. *British Educational Research Journal*, **30** (1), 43–65.

Oliver, C. and Candappa, M. (2003) *Tackling Bullying: Listening to the Views of Children and Young People*, Research Report RR400, DfES Publications, London.

Olweus, D. (1993) *Bullying: What We Know and What We Can Do*, Basil Blackwell, Oxford.

Olweus, D. (1996) *The Revised Olweus Bully/Victim Questionnaire*, Research Center for Health Promotion (HEMIL Center), University of Bergen, Bergen.

Owens, L., Shute, R. and Slee, P. (2000) Guess what I just heard! Indirect aggression amongst teenage girls in Australia. *Aggressive Behavior*, **6**, 67–83.

Rivers, I. and Cowie, H. 2006) Bullying and homophobia at UK schools: a perspective on factors affecting and recovery. *Journal of Gay and Lesbian Issues in Education*, **3** (4), 11–43.

Salmivalli, C., Kaukiainen, A., Kaistaniemi, L. and Lagerspetz, K.M.J. (1999) Self-evaluated self-esteem, peer-evaluated self-esteem, and defensive egotism as predictors of adolescents' participation in bullying situations. *Personality and Social Psychology Bulletin*, **25**, 1268–78.

Salmivalli, C., Lagerspetz, K., Björkvist, K., Österman, K. and Kaukiainen, A. (1996) Bullying as a group process: participant roles and their relations to social status within the group. *Aggressive Behavior*, **20**, 1–15.

Smith, P.K., Cowie, H., Olafsson, R.F. and Liefooghe, A.P.D. (2002) Definitions of bullying: a comparison of terms used, and age and gender differences, in a fourteen country international comparison. *Child Development*, **73**, 1119–33.

Smith, P. K., Talamelli, L., Cowie, H., Naylor, P. and Chauhan, P. (2004) Profiles of non-victims, escaped victims, continuing victims and new victims of school bullying. *British Journal of Educational Psychology*, **74**, 565–81.

Sutton, J., Smith, P.K. and Swettenham, J. (1999) Bullying and theory of mind: a critique of the 'social skills deficit' view of anti-social behaviour. *Social Development*, **8**, 117–27.

Terranova, A.M., Sheffield Morris, A. and Boxer, P. (2008) Fear reactivity and effortful control in overt and relational bullying: a six-month longitudinal study. *Aggressive Behavior*, **34** (1), 104–15.

Verkuyten, M. and Thijs, J. (2001) Peer victimization and self-esteem of ethnic minority group children. *Journal of Community and Applied Social Psychology*, **11**, 227–34.

Wright, C., Standen, P., John, G., German, G. and Patel, T. (2005) *School Exclusion and Transition into Adulthood in African-Caribbean Communities*, Joseph Rowntree Foundation, York.

4 Sibling Abuse and Bullying in Childhood and Adolescence: Knowns and Unknowns

PAUL B. NAYLOR, LAURIE PETCH AND JENNA V. WILLIAMS[1]

AIMS AND CONCEPTUAL BACKGROUND

The uncommon murder of Jackson Carr, a six-year-old boy, by his siblings in the US in 2002 provoked debate about the links between everyday sibling conflict and more sinister patterns of abuse (Aynesworth, 2002). Given the large amount of time that siblings typically spend together as children and adolescents, in spite of age differences, it is reasonable to infer that their relationships can include abuse. We begin by clarifying the relevant concepts before considering published evidence pertaining to such abuse. We conclude by reviewing what is implied for professional practice by this research as well as identifying directions for further study. Firstly, however, what is childhood and adolescent sibling abuse?

We take the term 'sibling' to refer to brothers and sisters who are genetically related (full and half-siblings), or are not genetically related (step-siblings) and who share the same home(s) for the majority of the time. This last criterion is important as it enables familiarity and generates possible opportunities for abuse to occur.

Abuse is defined here as an imbalance of power, such that it is difficult for the target to defend him- or herself physically, verbally or psychologically (Olweus, 1999). Such abuse is also often difficult to escape from or to avoid. Abuse consists of offensive action or behaviour by the perpetrator that produces a reaction in the target that he or she can identify, and which may be

[1] We are grateful to Emmy van Deurzen for providing the idea of researching sibling abuse, and to Digby Tantam for the many helpful discussions on the topic that Paul B. Naylor has had with him.

observed by a third party. The abusive behaviour may be physical (including sexual) and/or emotional in nature. Also, it may consist of a one-off event or it may be repeated over time. We therefore see abuse as a subset of aggressive behaviour, which may be perpetrated and experienced by people of all ages, not only children and adolescents. Abusive acts and behaviours that victimise targets repeatedly over time and/or whose negative effects persist over time, are defined in this chapter as bullying.

Physical abuse includes hitting; punching; pulling; pushing; shoving; and throwing objects at the target. Wiehe (1997) maintains that physical abuse also includes tickling when it becomes painful and when the target has little or no control over events. By comparison, consensus scarcely exists as to how emotional abuse should be defined, although Wiehe suggests that it often involves one or more of the following: rejection; coercion; erratic discipline; scapegoating; ridicule; and denigration. Emotional abuse also involves frightening behaviours that are not directed at the other's body (e.g. throwing or smashing objects). Wiehe extends emotional abuse to include teasing that belittles and ridicules its target excessively. More specifically, physical and sexual abuse between siblings is often accompanied by emotional abuse.

The broad term '*sexual abuse*' subsumes acts involving physical contact with intended or unintended non-contact acts such as indecent exposure, exposure to pornography, sexual exploitation and sexual teasing, taunting and belittling. We therefore define incest as a subset of sexual abuse. Sibling incest involves intentional physical contact of a sexual nature, which includes inappropriate fondling, touching or sexual contact; oral sex; anal sex; digital penetration; and attempted or completed sexual intercourse. Canavan, Meyer and Higgs (1992) suggest that incest may occur consensually when partners provide nurture and safety to one another in abusive and painful family conditions. It could, in theory, be argued that such incest may be non-abusive if the partners have equal access to resources of power. Typically, however, incest involves the repeated use of power, threats and force by the more powerful perpetrator as a precursor to, during or after the acts of abuse.

Bullying can be distinguished from one-off incidents of physical and/or emotional abuse in that it usually involves the repeated misuse of power over time. We suggest, however, that a one-off abusive event can be considered to be bullying if it induces long-term fears in the target that the event may recur. Bullying may be expressed physically (e.g. hitting, kicking or punching) or verbally (e.g. threatening, mocking or name-calling) including, nowadays, via electronic means (e.g. texting and emailing). In addition, the target of bullying is often socially isolated by the perpetrator. Such social seclusion may become extreme if a person is deliberately and systematically ignored in order to coerce him or her into compliance. Since most childhood siblings are of different ages and spend a significant amount of time together, we argue that there is ample opportunity for one to bully the other.

PREVALENCE, CORRELATES, CAUSES AND EFFECTS OF CHILDHOOD AND ADOLESCENT SIBLING ABUSE

The research findings we present and discuss here are based on a systematic review, which will be reported elsewhere (Naylor et al., in preparation). Each section reports on three categories of abuse:

* physical, verbal and emotional abuse (as a single category);
* bullying (repeated abuse);
* sexual abuse between siblings.

PREVALENCE

Many or all of the studies in the category of physical, emotional and verbal abuse also involve bullying as we define it. Regarding the prevalence of such abuse in community samples, roughly half of all participants in a study of 203 undergraduates in the US (Hardy, 2001) said that they had been physically abused by a sibling in childhood, with 11 per cent saying that this was a daily occurrence.

Compared with the number of studies of bullying (as we have defined it) among school children and adults in the workplace, studies of sibling bullying are limited. Our literature review retrieved only two quantitative studies of sibling bullying, both carried out in the US. Duncan's (1999) study of peer and sibling bullying in a community sample of early adolescents (194 males, 178 females) provides the only evidence of prevalence data. Of the 336 children who had siblings, one-third reported that they were frequently bullied by them, with boys more likely to say so than girls (36% and 25%, respectively). Around 40 per cent of both boys and girls also reported that they bullied their siblings, and 11 per cent said that they 'often or very often beat up' their siblings.

Similarly, the literature contains sparse data on the prevalence of sexual abuse and incest between siblings in community samples. Hardy's study (2001) found that of their 202 American respondents, 7.4 per cent (of whom 93% were women) reported incestuous behaviour ranging from 'kissing and fondling to attempted intercourse' (p. 262) while growing up. Clinical and forensic samples provide prevalence data on types of sexual abuse. The majority (approximately 89%) of abusers in two studies attempted or completed vaginal penetration (de Jong, 1989, $n = 35$) or another form of intercourse (attempted, vaginal, anal and/or oral; Pierce and Pierce, 1987). In contrast, this was true for only 21 per cent of Gilbert's 14 cases (1992). Some of the disparity in these findings can, in all likelihood, be explained by differences in behavioural categories used by the researchers.

CORRELATES: AGE, BIRTH ORDER AND GENDER PATTERNS

A number of North American studies suggest that first-born children are more likely to be physically aggressive during early and middle childhood than their younger siblings (Felson and Rosso, 1988; Martin and Ross, 1995; Howe *et al.*, 2002). Similarly, a related study carried out in the US found that younger siblings and many older siblings cite the older sibling as the typical victor in 'fights' (McGuire *et al.*, 2000). These findings would seem to point towards the power imbalance inherent in bullying. In contrast, Dunn and Munn (1986) found that British 2-year-olds were often physically aggressive towards their *older* siblings. Moreover, a study of 10 preschool abusive children in the US, compared with a group of non-abusive children (Rosenthal and Doherty, 1984), found that severe violence against their siblings (e.g. breaking a leg, fracturing the skull, wounding with knives) was most common when the siblings were of the same sex and less than 4 years apart in age.

Although gender may not be a factor in determining the *initiation* of physical abuse, Howe *et al.* (2002) found that girls, compared with boys, are more submissive during the *resolution* of physical aggression, which led these researchers to suggest that 'being male ... may carry additional status in sibling exchanges to the extent that it is permissible to challenge an older sister' (p. 1469). This suggests a power imbalance in favour of boys. Interestingly, sibling bullies compared with sibling non-bullies scored higher on measures of both depression and loneliness.

A rare example of relevant research on bullying was carried out by Updegraff, McHale and Crouter (2002), who considered adolescents' 'domineering control' (a form of bullying) of their peers and siblings. Through home visits, interviews and questionnaires, these researchers studied the relationships and interaction patterns of 179 pairs of 15-year-old first-born children and 13-year-old second-borns over their next 3 years. First-borns were found to be more controlling towards their younger siblings than they were towards their best friend, with boys and girls reporting similar levels of sibling control. Over the time period of the study, first-borns became less controlling of siblings and friends. This pattern of change was similar for second-borns.

Turning to sexual abuse, most of the reports considered here concern older brother perpetrators and younger sister targets, although two studies report brother-brother and sister-sister incest. This pattern could be seen as an example of double power imbalance (age and gender). Collectively, these studies are based on a broad range of evidence including outcomes of medical examinations, psychiatric and psychotherapeutic reports, social work reports, police files, court reports and interviews with family members, as well as self-report interviews and questionnaires. It should be noted that all these studies were conducted in North America.

The available evidence suggests that step-siblings are particularly at risk of sibling sexual abuse and incest. For example, Gilbert (1992) found that about half of her sample of 15 perpetrators were step-siblings, and Pierce and Pierce (1987) found that just over half of their 30 male perpetrators of abuse were step-, foster- or adoptive siblings. This issue is one that may be of particular interest to practitioners and policy makers. More specifically, Pierce and Pierce cite the example of a child who was placed in residential care after abusing his foster siblings and went on to act out sexually while in the children's home. The same researchers also found, however, that sibling sexual abuse occurred more frequently in foster care than in residential care (46% and approximately 24% out of a total of 37 cases respectively).

OTHER CORRELATES

None of the reviewed studies provides any causal evidence for physical, verbal or emotional abuse between siblings, yet several correlates are suggestive. For example, sibling physical abusers have often experienced physically abusive or neglectful parenting or caring (Green, 1984; Rosenthal and Doherty, 1984). These studies suggest that sibling abuse is related to parental disregard for aggressive behaviour and to inconsistent discipline. Moreover, three studies have found links between inter-adult family discord and aggression between siblings (Brody, Stoneman and Burke, 1984; Kratcoski, 1984; Bush and Ehrenberg, 2003). In contrast, a single case study in Germany of the severe physical injuries (suction and bite injuries of the head with loss of nose and lip tissue) inflicted by a 2-and-a-half-year-old boy on his 7-day-old brother found *no* evidence that parental aggression was a factor (Hein, Pannenbecker and Schulz, 1992). A similar conclusion was reached by Green (1984) in his study of five serious cases of sibling abuse. In addition, Hardy (2001) was unable to find any link between sibling physical maltreatment and other types of domestic violence, although her findings led her to suggest that family financial difficulties can be a stressor leading to physical abuse between related children.

Other studies have commented on the health and well-being of children who physically abuse their siblings and their families. Rosenthal and Doherty (1984) found that their abusive group had suffered a higher prevalence of physical illness than the non-abusive group, and also significantly greater feelings of 'unhappiness' and 'helplessness'. Finally, we have uncovered very few findings linking sibling abuse with ethnicity, family size or other related socio-cultural variables in the literature. We discovered no reportable findings on this topic in our review.

Conclusive findings on the causes of incestuous sexual abuse are missing from the literature, like those on physical abuse. Again, we found a number of studies, however, which suggest correlates that point towards causal factors. Most perpetrators have suffered long-term parental physical and verbal abuse. For example, this was true for 63 per cent of Pierce and Pierce's (1987) 37 perpetrators; 92 per cent of Adler and Schutz' (1995) sample of 12 adolescent abusers; for the three cases of blame-shifting brother-brother incest pairs reported by Johnson (1988); for the single case of a 15-year-old boy in Ascherman and Safier's (1990) study; for most of Laviola's (1992) 17 female targets; and for the sons of Charlotte's father in Canavan *et al.*'s (1992) case study. In contrast, only 22 per cent ($n = 6$) of the perpetrators studied by Kaplan, Becker and Cunningham-Rathner(1988) and by Becker *et al.* (1986) were identified as having suffered physical abuse by a father or other male relative.

Sibling perpetrators of sexual abuse have also often been found to have suffered from sexual exploitation by adults, typically in the family. For example, this was true of almost half of Pierce and Pierce's (1987) 18 targets, and many of Gilbert's (1992) 15 cases. In his study of 60 adolescent abusers, of whom approximately 53 per cent had perpetrated incest, Worling (1995) found that significantly more of the abusers had been sexually abused as children compared with non-abusers. Smith and Israel (1987) report that 'many' of their study of 25 sibling incest abusers had been sexually abused and Kaplan *et al.* (1988) found that 15 per cent of their sample ($n = 13$ males) reported having been sexually abused. Adler and Schutz (1995) found, however, that only 1 (8%) of their 12 abusers reported having been abused, and that this was by an uncle. We should conclude that the likelihood of sexual abuse occurring in the history of incest abusers is quite high.

Some support for the intergenerational transfer hypothesis regarding sexual abuse (e.g. Pizzey, 1974) is provided by the findings that mothers of sibling incest abusers were significantly more likely to have been sexually abused as children than mothers of non-abusers (Smith and Israel, 1987; Adler and Schutz, 1995; Cyr *et al.*, 2002). Further support for the hypothesis is provided by Laviola's (1992) finding that 94 per cent of her 17 abused women described their mothers as emotionally neglectful during their childhood.

Other dysfunctional aspects of families in which sibling sexual abuse and incest have occurred have been found, including parental marital discord (Canavan *et al.*, 1992; Adler and Schutz, 1995; Worling 1995; Hardy 2001); extramarital affairs (Smith and Israel, 1987); sexual dysfunction of mothers (Kaplan, Becker and Martinez, 1990); other contemporaneous incest relationships involving fathers, maternal grandfathers and, in one case, a mother (Laviola, 1992); and children observing sexual activity between their parents or other adults (Pierce and Pierce, 1987; Smith and Israel, 1987). On the basis of her evidence, Laviola concludes that most of her sample's families were 'dysfunctional in child-rearing practices, relational patterns among family members, family rules, and response patterns to family stressors' (p. 414). Regarding stressors, Adler and Schutz (1995) note that in 67 per cent of their sample of 12 families there was a significant psychosocial stressor (disability, long-term financial problems and/or illness).

Extremely repressive parental attitudes to sex have also been found to correspond with the occurrence of sibling sexual abuse and incest in families.

Smith and Israel (1987) described one-third of the parents in their study as having 'puritanical mores', which discouraged sexual expression in their children. Other studies (Kaplan *et al.*, 1988; Adler and Schutz, 1995) have found that there is a tendency for parents to deny that sibling sex abuse has occurred and for others to attempt to minimise its significance.

For sexual abusers, a number of correlates have been found that may point towards causative factors. These include school and emotional problems (Gilbert, 1992); psychiatric diagnoses of conduct disorder; attention deficit disorders; adjustment disorders; social phobia; dysthymia (chronic mild depression); post-traumatic stress disorder (PTSD) (Becker *et al.*, 1986); and having undergone other mental health interventions before the discovery of their sibling sexual abuse (Adler and Schutz, 1995).

In Hardy's (2001) community sample of 202 undergraduates, 7 per cent reported sexual behaviour or incest with a sibling, with only 20 per cent of these indicating that it had been non-consensual. For clinical samples, however, the picture is different. Adler and Schutz (1995) found that all their 12 perpetrator cases denied using verbal threats to maintain secrecy, but 75 per cent of the targets said that they had been threatened to remain silent. Similarly, half of Gilbert's (1992) eight targets reported that they were subjected to physical force and a further six were bribed to maintain secrecy. Johnson (1988) reports that his entire sample of 23 perpetrators threatened and coerced their targets. By comparison, other studies have found that around half of perpetrators use verbal and/or physical threats and force (Pierce and Pierce, 1987; de Jong, 1989; Laviola, 1992). Based on this evidence, we must therefore concur with Christensen (1990) that sibling incest often involves coerced, severe, repeated abuse.

EFFECTS ON TARGETS AND PERPETRATORS

Evidence on the short- or long-term effects on abusers or the abused tends to be restricted to studies of sexual abuse. For example, Laviola's study (1992) of 17 women incestuously abused in childhood found that long-term effects included mistrust of men and women, sexual response problems, and intrusive thoughts concerning the incest. Similarly, Canavan *et al.* (1992) reported that four women sexually abused by their older brothers in childhood all had low self-esteem.

RELEVANCE TO PROFESSIONAL PRACTICE

Perhaps the most striking finding for practitioners is that, if incest is discovered between siblings, it is probable that a degree of coercion and control has taken place. Between siblings, the power differential based on age or gender may be apparent or it may be more subtle, being based, for example, on parental favouritism. It appears relevant to assume that a child or adolescent perpetrator of sexual abuse is likely to have been abused, in turn, at some point and in some fashion by an older sibling or adult family member. The likelihood of physical abuse having happened to a child who acts violently towards a sibling appears to be less compelling.

In general, the research on physical, verbal and emotional abuse and bullying seems to be limited compared to that on sexual abuse between siblings. The possibility of physical abuse between same-gendered siblings should be explored as possibilities when the behaviour of children who exhibit aggression is being assessed by applied psychologists or other behaviour specialists, particularly when the siblings are close in age. As a corollary, where internalising behaviours (such as separation anxiety or school refusal) are investigated, particularly in younger girls, the possibility of physical abuse or bullying by an older sibling should be considered as a possible factor.

PROPOSALS FOR FURTHER RESEARCH

On the basis of this review, we suggest ideas for further research on sibling abuse. We need to know much more about the characteristics of non-abused siblings in incestuous families and about perpetrators regarding their histories of neglect and physical, sexual and emotional abuse. Related to these aetiological variables, familial context risk factors for sibling abuse such as family stress due to financial distress and the effects of parental illness or disability, marital conflict and pervasive family patterns of abuse also seem to merit further study.

As reflected in this review, a greater number of studies have been published on sexual abuse between siblings than on physical, verbal or emotional abuse. Presumably this pattern is due to the rarity and perceived greater seriousness of inter-sibling sexual abuse. Yet, it should be noted that the long-term developmental consequences of severe or repeated non-sexual mistreatment by siblings remain unknown.

Regarding methodology, rather than relying on self-reports as is often the case, we suggest that future studies should always attempt independently to verify targets' claims of sibling abuse. Such reports should be verified by data from respondents including siblings, parents, school teachers and counsellors, and from the records of medical practitioners. We recognise, however, that there are ethical concerns about obtaining such data.

Further studies might also strive to operationalise concepts of abuse more stringently than is the case in much published research. For example, in some studies the measures used did not relate closely enough to at least one of the concepts of abuse as we have defined them here. Similarly, the reviewed studies typically did not invoke the 'abuse of power' criterion. Moreover, the measures employed not only need to be valid, they also need to be demonstrably reliable. Furthermore, data from a number of measures (e.g. self-report questionnaires and semi-structured interviews) should be triangulated to give more complete and robust profiles of targets, perpetrators and their families. We also suggest that, in order to begin unravelling the causal mechanisms of sibling abuse, there is great need for additional longitudinal research on the issue.

A further issue that we believe warrants attention is the degree to which the existing findings generalise to other contexts. Most of the studies on sibling abuse so far conducted have used small clinical samples from which it is difficult to generalise and so, for example, we know little about the prevalence of the different types of abuse in the general population and those that we have are probably underestimates. We suggest this course of research for two reasons: sibling physical and verbal abuse are often thought of by parents as normal; and general population prevalence studies so far undertaken have tended to focus on undergraduate students. General population or community prevalence studies are urgently needed to inform policymakers and practitioners about the scale of problems that need to be confronted and dealt with. A related issue is that, so far, the field has been dominated by research conducted in the US and, to a lesser extent, Canada. We feel that cross-cultural studies on the prevalence of sibling abuse would illuminate the qualitatively differential impacts on sibling abuse of, for example, political and religious ideology; cultural values, beliefs, and attitudes; and socio-economic status.

Even granting the rarity of tragedies such as the murder of Jackson Carr, in view of these suggested shortcomings in the evidence base, it seems that sibling abuse merits far greater attention from researchers, child care professionals and parents than it has done up to now.

REFERENCES

Adler, N.A. and Schutz, J. (1995) Sibling incest offenders. *Child Abuse and Neglect*, **19**, 811–19.

Ascherman, L.I. and Safier, E.J. (1990) Sibling incest: a consequence of individual and family dysfunction. *Bulletin of the Menninger Clinic*, **54**, 311–22.

Aynesworth, H. (2002) Texas youths held in brother's slaying; sister leads police to victim's body. *The Washington Times*, 17 April.

Becker, J.V., Kaplan, M.S., Cunningham-Rathner, B.A. and Kavoussi, R. (1986) Characteristics of adolescent incest sexual perpetrators. *Journal of Family Violence*, **1**, 85–7.

Brody, G.H., Stoneman, Z. and Burke, M. (1987) Family system and individual child correlates of sibling behavior. *American Journal of Orthopsychiatry*, **57** (4), 561–9.

Bush, J.E. and Ehrenberg, M.F. (2003) Young persons' perspectives on the influence of family transitions on sibling relationships: a qualitative exploration. *Journal of Divorce and Remarriage*, **39**, 1–35.

56	CHILDREN BEHAVING BADLY?

Canavan, M.C., Meyer, W.J. and Higgs, D.C. (1992) The female experience of sibling incest. *Journal of Marital and Family Therapy*, **18**, 129–42.

Christensen, C.W. (1990) A case of sibling incest: a balancing act. *Journal of Strategic and Systemic Therapies*, **9** (4), 1–5.

Cyr, M., Wright, J., McDuff, P. and Perron, A. (2002) Intrafamilial sexual abuse: brother-sister incest does not differ from father-daughter and stepfather-stepdaughter incest. *Child Abuse and Neglect*, **26**, 957–73.

de Jong, A.R. (1989) Sexual interactions among siblings and cousins: experimentation or exploitation? *Child Abuse and Neglect*, **13**, 271–9.

Duncan, R. (1999) Peer and sibling aggression: an investigation of intra- and extra-familial bullying. *Journal of Interpersonal Violence*, **14**, 871–86.

Dunn, J. and Munn, P. (1986) Sibling quarrels and maternal intervention: individual differences in understanding and aggression. *Journal of Child Psychology and Psychiatry*, **27** (5), 583–95.

Felson, R.B. and Rosso, N. (1988) Parental punishment and sibling aggression. *Social Psychology Quarterly*, **51** (1), 1–18.

Gilbert, C.M. (1992) Sibling incest: a descriptive study of family dynamics. *Journal of Child and Adolescent Psychiatric and Mental Health Nursing*, **5**, 1, 5–9.

Green, A.H. (1984) Child abuse by siblings. *Child Abuse and Neglect*, **8**, 311–17.

Hardy, M.S. (2001) Physical aggression and sexual behavior among siblings: a retrospective study. *Journal of Family Violence*, **16**, 255–68.

Hein, P.M., Pannenbecker, J. and Schulz, E. (1992) Bite injuries upon a newborn. *International Journal of Legal Medicine*, **105**, 53–5.

Howe, N., Rinaldi, C.M., Jennings, M. and Petrakos, H. (2002) 'No! The lambs can stay out because they got cozies': constructive and destructive sibling conflict, pretend play, and social understanding. *Child Development*, **73**, 1460–73.

Johnson, T.C. (1988) Child perpetrators – children who molest other children: preliminary findings. *Child Abuse and Neglect*, **12**, 219–29.

Kaplan, M.S., Becker, J.V. and Cunningham-Rathner, J. (1988) Characteristics of parents of adolescent incest perpetrators: preliminary findings. *Journal of Family Violence*, **3** (3), 183–91.

Kaplan, M.S., Becker, J.V. and Martinez, D.F. (1990) A comparison of mothers of adolescent incest vs non-incest perpetrators. *Journal of Family Violence*, **5** (3), 209–14.

Kratcoski, P.C. (1984) Perspectives on family violence. *Human Relations*, **37**, 443–54.

Laviola, M. (1992) Effects of older brother-younger sister incest: a study of the dynamics of 17 cases. *Child Abuse and Neglect*, **16**, 406–21.

Martin, J.L. and Ross, H.S. (1995) The development of aggression within sibling conflict. *Early Education and Development*, **6** (4), 335–58.

McGuire, S., Manke, B., Eftekhari, A. and Dunn, J. (2000) Children's perceptions of sibling conflict during middle childhood: issues and sibling (dis)similarity. *Social Development*, **9** (2), 173–90.

Olweus, D. (1999) Sweden, in *The Nature of School Bullying: A Cross-National Perspective* (eds P.K. Smith, Y. Morita, J. Junger-Tas, D. Olweus, R. Catalano and P. Slee), Routledge, London and New York.

Pierce, L.H. and Pierce, R.L. (1987) Incestuous victimization by juvenile sex offenders. *Journal of Family Violence*, **2**, 351–64.

Pizzey, E. (1974) *Scream Quietly or the Neighbours Will Hear*, Ridley Enslow Publishers, Short Hills, NJ.

Rosenthal, P.A. and Doherty, M.B. (1984) Serious sibling abuse by pre-school children. *Journal of the American Academy of Child Psychiatry*, **23** (2), 186–90.

Smith, H. and Israel, E. (1987) Sibling incest: a study of the dynamics of 25 cases. *Child Abuse and Neglect*, **11**, 101–8.

Updegraff, K.A., McHale, S. and Crouter, A.C. (2002) Adolescents' sibling relationship and friendship experiences: developmental patterns and relationship linkages. *Social Development*, **11**, 182–204.

Wiehe, V.R. (1997) *Sibling Abuse: Hidden Physical, Emotional and Sexual Trauma* (2nd edition), Sage, Thousand Oaks, CA.

Worling, J. (1995) Adolescent sibling-incest offenders: differences in family and individual functioning when compared to adolescent non-sibling sex offenders. *Child Abuse and Neglect*, **19**, 633–43.

5 Young People, Gangs and Street-based Violence

TARA YOUNG AND SIMON HALLSWORTH

Drawing upon recent research we conducted into street-based violence among young people, this chapter examines their involvement in violence both as victim and perpetrator. By exploring the testimonies of those who, in the parlance of the street, live their life 'on road', it also explores the street collectives in which young people congregate, the forces that propel them into violence and the violence they do.

Public concern about youthful involvement in violent crime has risen in recent years. The findings presented here are an amalgamation of three research studies designed to examine the extent of gang membership in the UK and the use of weapons among young people (see Young and Hallsworth, 2006; Young et al., 2007). The studies were largely qualitative and utilised semi-structured individual interviews with 111 young people between the ages of 14 and 18. The majority of male participants were from black and ethnic minority populations and female respondents were primarily white. All the participants had direct experience of violence and most were currently living in areas characterised by multiple deprivation. The interviews focused on the issues of gangs, gang-related violence and the meaning violence had for young people as perpetrators and victims.

STREET ORGANISATION

The research was conducted against a backdrop of rising concerns about the alleged increase of armed and organised gangs within the UK, and the propensity of affiliated members to use weapons. In part, the research sought to explore whether this notion had evidence to support it. As there is no clear consensus on what constitutes a gang, defining one remains a contentious issue. To inform our enquiry, we employed a definition to which there appears to be some minimal consensus in the literature. To be classified as a gang, a group has to be relatively durable, street-based and serially involved in delinquency

Children Behaving Badly? Peer Violence Between Children and Young People
Edited by Christine Barter and David Berridge
© 2011 John Wiley & Sons Ltd.

and violent offending. The group may have adopted appropriated signifiers, such as a name or a uniform, and claim allegiance to a territory, but these referents need not be present to signify a gang. At a basic level, a group is a gang if it engages in collective offending and possesses the characteristics listed above.

Underpinning the popular construction of a gang is the pervasive idea that gangs are large, organised collectives with a structured hierarchy and complex divisions of labour. According to recent research, some gangs have clearly defined roles for members who occupy positions such as 'leaders', 'lieutenants', 'enforcers', 'soldiers' and 'runners' (Pitts, 2008). These groups are often associated with the illegal drug economy and known to engage in activities like recruitment strategies and violent initiation rituals.

When the young people we interviewed described the kind of street organisation to which they belonged, few described themselves as belonging to gangs (although 17 young people [including 2 females] did define themselves as gang members); most strongly resisted the label 'gang' being used to define their group. When pushed to define the kind of group to which they belonged, our respondents spoke instead of friendship groups or crews and were clear that these were not 'gangs'.

Irrespective of whether or not the respondents identified with the label 'gang member', the groups to which the young people belonged typically consisted of individuals with shared biographies and histories. These were people who came together on a regular basis for socio-psychological reasons that were primarily benevolent. These included the need to socialise, find emotional, financial and social support, and to find affection and sympathy not found in the home (Firmin, Turner and Gavrielides, 2007). While some individuals in these groups did engage in violence, this violence was not intrinsic to the identity and purpose of the group and, as such, most groups could be defined as peer groups, rather than gangs. While most resisted the gang label, the young people were aware that those in authority, and the wider community, were often using this label to describe their groups.

The streets on which these peer groups congregated were certainly experienced by young people as dangerous and violent. The violence they narrated, however, did not appear to be bound up with organised street gangs, as much media reporting appeared to suggest, but to be driven by and connected to the disorganised and potentially volatile nature of the peer groups to which the participants belonged.

LIFE 'ON ROAD' AND ENTRY INTO IT

Rather than speak of the gang or its affiliations, a number of participants spoke about 'life on road'. For the young participants, the streets they lived in, or near, signified the 'road'. It was the 'hood' or the 'ghetto' where young people, worn down by marginalisation and exclusion, struggled to survive in a society they believed did not care or cater for their needs. At its most extreme, the hood – and by extension 'the road' – was a place where young people adopted a 'hood mentality', a fatalistic attitude to life that held 'no dreams, no ambition, no drive; no nothing'. Being 'on road' signified entry into an alternative community or subculture that was external to wider society; it was a community they either joined or had to confront. The young participants associated life 'on road' with crime, violence and the informal drugs economy.

When asked to explain how young people ended up on 'on road', the respondents cited an array of propulsion and attraction factors. Some of the young people were raised in chaotic families and many had experienced neglect, poverty and domestic violence. Many had a poor and hostile relationship with formal institutions such as educational facilities and the criminal justice system. These were the forces of exclusion that drove people away from formal society and 'displaced' them away into life lived 'on road'. These factors also acted to propel young people deeper into street life and the subculture of violence that defined it.

Life 'on road' also had allure, particularly for the most excluded young men and women. For these disassociated young people, life 'on road' provided an alternative space, a sovereign space free from constraints imposed by parents or carers, or social institutions such as school. It was also a place where they had a possibility of accumulating the things they desired, but which material exclusion and neglect prevented them from acquiring; these included, but were not reducible to, the company of peers, respect, money and access to desirable material goods:

> My momma couldn't buy the things that I wanted. I grew up hard and that made me, at a certain age, think if I want these things then I've got to go and get them ... I got here ['on road'] by myself; nobody got me here!
>
> Male, 18

While some saw the advantages of being 'on road', few *chose* to be there. For many, it was the default position people came to occupy when they felt they had no other options:

> They ain't on the road because they wanna be. They're on the road because they are trying to pass the time ... If you look at when young people get sucked into gangs, it's 14 upwards ... if their mum's not making money, how are they getting money? So there's no other way to get money, but to turn to the streets.
>
> Female, 17

If exclusion created the basis for displacement, the street provided the space for an array of replacement strategies. Like most people in society, the respondents wanted respect. They were, however, aware that they were positioned in the bottom tier of an inherently inequitable society that had bequeathed them limited life chances and was, for many, disrespectful. While it could be the case that some internalised their predicament by resolving their powerless status into what is often referred to as 'low self-esteem', this was not always the case. Indeed, far from accepting that low self-esteem is what they experienced, it is perhaps more accurate to say that they fought and innovated to accumulate the social resources necessary to maintain a viable sense of self-esteem. They wanted to be considered people of honour to whom respect was due.

VIOLENCE 'ON ROAD'

Media reports of gangland violence typically paint a picture of hyper-violence directed against strangers and other innocents. As our research found, this is often not the case. Violence involving young people as victims and perpetrators typically occurred between people known to each other. Indeed much of the violence enacted and experienced by the young people was restricted to their peer group or people they knew. However, violent altercations with complete strangers, especially adults, were not unheard of and the young people talked of being attacked by, and attacking, strangers; but these incidences were relatively rare.

Violence performed an omnipresent role in the lives of those we interviewed. The young people provided accounts of being victimised (verbally and physically) in private settings by parents, carers and other young people, and in public places as they moved around the 'dangerous streets' and 'hoods' in which they lived. They were exposed to a plethora of violent situations ranging from verbal abuse to bullying, coercion, shootings and stabbings. In the case of a number of young women interviewed, victimisation also included serious sexual assault up to and including rape.

The frequency with which the young people were exposed to aggression and violence necessitated the development of some form of protective mechanism to help them avoid, or delay, potentially violent situations. Congregating in groups was the most common way in which the young people protected themselves from danger. Ironically, as gang research has also shown, young people are more likely to be victimised as a result of being in a group than not, because being affiliated, or associated, to a group or gang attracts attention from other violent street collectives (including law-enforcement agencies), thereby increasing, rather than decreasing, victimisation levels (Klein, 1971, 1995; Thornberry *et al.*, 1995, Battin-Pearson *et al.*, 1998; Thornberry, 1998). Because bonding with others entailed a commitment to 'have the back' of other members – that is, to support and protect them in the face of adversity – this meant being prepared to mobilise violence with the group in order to defend its collective honour, a situation which raised, as opposed to lowered, the chances of victimisation – a finding that supports American gang research (Klein, 1971, 1995; Hagedorn, 1988; Vigil, 1988; Spergel, 1990; Decker and Van Winkle, 1996):

... if he's fighting [referring to a more violent friend], I wouldn't just watch him fight, I'd join in...I'll get involved 'cos I'm not going to stand there and see my friend getting rushed by somebody and just stand there.

Male, 17

The violence in which many of the participants were engaged was primarily 'low-level' violence (e.g. swearing, pushing). This could, under certain circumstances, provoke a more violent response. Quite often violence was the consequence of 'play fights turned bad'; this happened in situations where young people, male and female, would 'square-up' to each other, posture, show strength, and assert dominance to consolidate their position within the group. The more serious violence that arose 'on road' typically centred on forms of interpersonal violence, territorial conflicts and violence associated with the illegal drugs market.

INTERPERSONAL VIOLENCE

The young people talked about fights occurring over 'silly things'. The sorts of situations that provoked violence by young people included rumours about an individual, teasing, name-calling and jealousies. Each of these could be read as constituting status challenges that had to be met with force. Violence could also occur as retribution for a previous infraction. This could include a bad business transaction, a perceived act of injustice, such as infidelity or flirting, or where someone has appropriated someone else's property. As one 17-year-old female participant explained:

Mostly girls don't fight unless another be starting 'screwing' and callin' them names. Most girls argue over man dem and over who's been lookin' at who and saying this and dat. This situation can sometimes get outta 'and.

For the majority of young people, such slights against a person had to be dealt with and this might easily, although not always, involve the use of violence. While the ability to be violent was a competence that all those immersed in life 'on road' had to master in some way, interpersonal conflicts were often managed in ways that prevented violence from escalating. While some young people would go looking for trouble, for most, violence was something they would take steps to avoid if they could; and, given a chance, they would seek to disengage from volatile situations.

The young people identified a variety of conflict avoidance mechanisms. Actions such as overt posturing, shouting, swearing and 'standing off' would often be deployed, which provided participants with a performative space which, while aggressive in nature, contained the violence in ways that delimited its potential to escalate. However, if these were unsuccessful, they would mobilise their potential for violence and fight those who were 'getting out of hand' or 'out of control'. In some instances, a fight would be instigated to reprimand those who 'needed to be taught a lesson', to 'be less mouthy' and more 'respectful' of their peers. Violence, in other words, was not only a means by which conflicts could be resolved: it also, in itself, became an ordering mechanism.

Some status challenges, however, were of a nature or severity that left the protagonists with no option but to retaliate violently, particularly against those whom they perceived to show them a lack of respect or had directly challenged their honour (Hagedorn, 1988; Jacobs and Wright, 2006). Personal integrity *had* to be protected and the young people talked of doing what was necessary to protect their respectability and status. Just looking at someone in the 'wrong way' 'on road' constituted disrespect and could instigate a violent reaction in a cultural climate where young people feel they cannot back down or appear to be weak in the face of threat:

> I'm not gonna lie to you, I've beefed girls for looking at my sister the wrong way. I've beefed on petty stuff, but it's your anger and you're used to it now.
>
> Female, 16

> If you look at someone for three seconds constantly in the eye, that's it! He's coming over to you to ask you what you are looking at. People have been shot over looking at people.
>
> Male, 17

TERRITORIAL CONFLICTS

One of the issues that consistently surfaced in the interviews was the issue of 'postcode loyalties'. Despite holding a grim view of the area in which they lived, the young people evinced a strong sense of allegiance to their 'hoods' and 'ghettos' as they defined them. In the parlance of the street these were their 'endz', their territories; this was their turf. Some young people took pleasure in 'reppin' their 'endz' – that is, affirming their attachment to a particular neighbourhood or estate – and often took it upon themselves to police these territories holding to account outsiders who were caught 'slippin' within the designated boundaries. Three (symbiotic) reasons were expressed for the 'rep'. The first was the importance of identifying where a person was from. As one young male explained:

> For me, it's like letting someone know who you are or what area you come from. Yeah, just showing everyone in [area] and other boroughs about where you live and what goes on here.
>
> Male, 15

The second reason was to demarcate an area as belonging to a particular gang or group and by so doing delineate its territorial boundary. In holding interlopers to account, a power relation was also being established. The message mediated by 'reppin' (and through graffiti) was that this was sovereign territory, was guarded and owned. As such, the 'rep' allows disenfranchised and relatively powerless young people to create a sacred, safe space in which they can impose their will and prevent the victimisation of themselves as individuals or as a group (Sanders, 2005).

'Reppin' also has a more instrumental purpose. The young people talked of others using the term 'what endz you from?' as a legitimation for instigating violence and engaging in street robbery. The 'rep', in this sense, was the verbal equivalent to the term 'whatchulookinat?' or the timely 'visual bump' Katz discusses in his study on the seductions of evil (Katz, 1990). As one young man observed, somewhat sceptically:

> It's not really an area thing. If a guy wants to cause trouble [to] that person he will trouble him. He will find any excuse and that's [what endz you from?] just the easiest excuse.
>
> Male, 15

As an activity, 'reppin' was a highly gendered practice and essentially a male preserve. Both male and female participants observed that older males (16+) were less likely to be involved in 'touting' their postcode than younger (10–15) ones, and females hardly ever engaged in such behaviour.

VIOLENCE AND THE DRUG ECONOMY

The absence of career opportunities for young, multiply deprived people led some to innovate and seek alternative ways of making 'P's' (money). In many of the deprived areas where we conducted our research, this involved the young people entering the illegal drugs market as drug dealers or 'runners'. While violence is often thought to express a breakdown in social relations within the illegal drug market, which has no formal control system, it is an occupational requirement. Violence is a regulatory force, a means by which group and individuals impose status, structure, rules and boundaries.

Violence from predators (street robbers) was an occupational hazard for a number of young participants who operated in the drugs economy. As dealers, they were targeted (or targeted others) for their 'stash' and/or the money they had obtained through selling, and so had to protect themselves from potential victimisation. Arming themselves with weapons such as guns and knives was the typical step they took to guarantee their safety, especially because they felt they could not turn to the police when they got into trouble. Reporting to the police was deemed to be unacceptable and contravened the street codes the young people felt beholden to. Speaking to the police or 'grassing' was considered to be an act of betrayal and serious violence could, and was, dispensed upon those who were thought to associate with them. For the drug dealers, violence was a resource that could be (immediately) utilised to stave off attack and protect self-interest. Projecting a competence to inflict harm was an essential characteristic to have in a social milieu that trades on fear and intimidation and denies individuals access to state protection (Katz, 1990; Pearson and Hobbs, 2001).

RETALIATION AND ESCALATION

For those heavily immersed in life 'on road', backing down from a fight or challenge was inconceivable. Not to act, for these young people, would be to lose face, to lose reputation. It was to be a 'pussy', a 'bitch' or a 'non-man'. Non-retaliation conveyed weakness; it showed others that you were a 'pushover', an 'easy touch' to be dominated and further victimised. The young participants, both male and female, were sensitive to the fact that they had to stick up for themselves. As one young woman described the situation:

> That's not how it is. That's. … it [not reacting] will haunt you like, like a gash! Like you walked away from that beef, yeah. [It's like] anyone could have her up, yeah. Certain things that's gonna slip and they will call you 'slipping'.
>
> Female, 15

and, as one young man explained:

> Retaliation is always a definite action that's always taken. We can't have them coming over here and doing that and we don't do anything.
>
> Male, 16

'On road' violence begets violence and the young people described a street environment with no limitations:

> The rules of the game are that there are no rules! The rules of the game are that you enter at your own peril. The rules are if you come into this game, no matter what age. … anything goes. There's no limits 'on road'. No limit on the extent of where you can go from and where you can't go; so there's nowhere to draw the line. You (therefore) never know when you've gone too far! The road is free, there is no-one slowing the road down so the boundaries get blurred.
>
> Male, 18

What came through from our interviews, specifically with those who were deeply immersed in life 'on road', was how violent events could escalate with fatal consequences. Numerous participants reported losing someone related or intimately close to them to violent crime perpetrated by young people 'on road'. One participant revealed that he had lost more than 10 of his family and friends.

Those heavily immersed in life 'on road' often spoke of 'taking things to the next level' in what could become an often uncontrollable retaliatory cycle:

> You have to remember people bear grudges so things don't always finish. They just stay for another time. [So] if I'm going to go for you then I might as well snuff you because I ain't having you come back at me.
>
> Male, 16

> It's an ongoing feud between the gang and my friends. Well, because every time they get us we get them and when we get them, they come back and get us and like it's an ongoing cycle.
>
> Male, 15

Violence is 'schismogenic' in so far as it can easily mutate into a cycle of retaliation and revenge that increases, if it is not prevented, in frequency and severity (Decker and Van Winkle, 1996, p.179). Violence is also inextricably linked to a person's sense of self-protection and self-esteem. Thus, if an individual (or group) resorts to violence, the victim will respond with more violence. In turn, this may elicit increasing levels of violence that may culminate in the use of lethal force. Because backing down is considered to be a failing, one that could leave you open to further victimisation, for some young people, not to respond is not an option. For the most heavily immersed young men, the *possibility* of future retaliation could itself provoke an ultra-violent response and help escalate an initial infraction into a cycle of violence. As one young man argued, things had to be settled or 'squashed'. As those 'on road' had a pervasive distrust of control agents, violence became the *de facto* system by which street level justice was enacted.

A VIOLENT SUBCULTURE

If we consider what kind of violence rules are being articulated, then these testimonies point to what we would define as a 'subculture of violence, which is the end game of life immersed "on road"'. This 'on road' is a subculture where violence is considered an appropriate reaction to threat where weapons may be used as means. It is a subculture where the street codes license and justify retaliation in response to honour slights, where retaliation can mean mobilising ultra-violence. Unlike other subcultures of violence that may regulate, ritualise and delimit the spaces (and occasions) where violence is mobilised (Kontos, Brotherton and Barrios, 2003; Brotherton and Barrios, 2004; Stephenson, 2006), there appear to be no breaking mechanisms in place 'on road' to delimit the explosive potential of violence to escalate once unleashed. Rather than attributing the violence of the street to the arrival of organised gangs, it was its anomic, disorganised and un-ritualised character that created the space for it to develop and escalate.

THE EMOTIONAL CONSEQUENCES

What also appeared to influence the level (and extent) of violence was the psychological well-being of the young men and women 'on road'. Psychological research shows that consistent and sustained exposure to extreme violence can have a detrimental effect on an individual's capacity to assess and control their emotions, which can, in turn, provoke volatile and explosive reactions. According to Batmanghelidjh (2007), the response of young people exposed to long-term abuse and neglect is to shut down emotionally and enter an emotional 'state of emergency'. In this state, young people become 'lone soldiers' who survive on adrenaline, wit and instinct. Research also shows that victims of violence often feel shame and humiliation that, in violent situations, is subconsciously projected onto other people (Firmin *et al.*, 2007). In undertaking violence, perpetrators attempt to rid themselves of painful and unwanted feelings of inadequacy brought about by their own victimisation. In this sense then, violence becomes a mechanism by which individuals seek to eradicate tension. As Gilligan (1996) notes in his assessment of the motivation to violence of men, the more impotent (thus vulnerable to shame) people feel the more they turn to violence, individual or collective, as the quickest way to regain a feeling of power.

The 'state of emergency' characterised well the mindset of some of those 'on road' whom we interviewed. Some participants spoke, for example, of 'taking their life in their own hands every day' and of 'boxing-up' emotions that were not useful. The alarming consequence of this situation was that a number of young people conveyed this 'survivalist mentality' and had shut down to the point where they appeared not to care about the consequences of their actions for anybody, *including themselves*. In the words of one ex-gangster:

[People are thinking] fuck life, fuck everybody...I don't care anymore! I don't care if I shoot you, I don't care if I rob this person. They are willing to take more and bigger risks. They're thinking, if this is what people think I am, then I'll give them something to talk about.

Male, 18

Consequently, this 'hollowed-out' self exists in an unprotected, unregulated social environment devoid of emotion, and is prepared to do what it takes to survive:

Whoever's 'on road', they know this. They've gone through thinking about life's messed up, so now they're like ... boom! They've come to terms with it and they're just adaptin' to the situation and will do whatever they need to get through it.

Male, 15

CONCLUSION

Street-based violence involving the use of weapons remains high on the public and political agenda. In this chapter, we have sought to contribute to an understanding of its defining features by investigating the violent street worlds of those who are immersed in it. Rather than begin with the gang as our point of reference, we have taken seriously the testimonies of our informants and studied their own self-definition of their situation, 'life on road'. In so doing, we have attempted to make sense of the violence attendant on it and the nature of the street collectives that are involved.

POINTS FOR PRACTICE

- Unable to draw upon alternative ways to redress challenges and threats to themselves, young people are unable to 'back down' without 'losing face' or inviting further victimisation. Practitioners need to provide young people with the skills to be able to back away from a violent altercation with dignity so that they can retain their self-respect.
- Practitioners need to understand the pedagogic nature of the street and street justice (Jacobs and Wright, 2006), and supply young people with alternative ways to redress the harm they experience.
- The more immersed in life 'on road' young people are, the more likely they are to become absorbed into its violent subculture. Addressing socio-economic factors that push/pull young people onto 'on road', and tackling the psychological mindset that can develop as a result of being entrenched there, will help young people return to a more orderly existence.

REFERENCES

Batmanghelidjh, C. and Walker, G. (2007) *Demons and Angels: Who Cares? Poor Care Structures and Moral Breakdown: The Science of Morality*, Royal College of Physicians, London.

Battin-Pearson, S.T., Thornberry, T., Hawkins, D. and Krohn, M. (1998) Gang membership, delinquent peers and delinquent behaviour, *Juvenile Justice Bulletin*, US Department of Justice, Washington, DC.

Brotherton, D. and Barrios, L. (2004) *The Almighty Latin King and Queen Nation: Street Politics and the Transformation of a New York City Gang*, Columbia University Press, New York.

Decker, S.H. and Van Winkle, B. (1996) *Life in the Gang: Family, Friends and Violence*, Cambridge University Press, Cambridge.

Firmin, C., Turner, R. and Gavrielides, T. (2007) *Building Bridges Project: Race on the Agenda: Empowering Young People through Human Rights Values, Fighting the Knife Culture*, Race on the Agenda, London.

Gilligan, J. (1996) *Violence: Reflections on a National Epidemic*, Vintage Books, New York.

Hagedorn, J.M. (1988) *People and Folks: Gangs, Crime and the Underclass in a Rustbelt City*, Lake View Press, Chicago, IL.

Jacobs, B.A. and Wright, R. (2006) *Street Justice: Retaliation in the Criminal Underworld*, Cambridge University Press, Cambridge.

Katz, J. (1990) *Seductions of Crime: Moral and Sensual Attractions of Doing Evil*, Basic Books, New York.

Klein, M.W. (1971) *Street Gangs and Street Workers*, Prentice-Hall, Inc., Englewood Cliffs, N.J.

Klein, M.W. (1995) *The American Street Gang: Its Nature, Prevalence, and Control*, Oxford University Press, New York.

Kontos, L., Brotherton, D. and Barrios, L. (2003) *Gangs and Society: Alternative Perspectives*, Columbia University Press, New York.

Pearson, G. and Hobbs, D. (2001) *Middle Market Drug Distribution*, Home Office Research Study 227, Home Office, London.

Pitts, J. (2008) *Reluctant Gangsters: The Changing Shape of Youth Crime*, Willan Publishing, Exeter.

Sanders, B. (2005) *Youth Crime and Youth Culture in the Inner City*, Routledge, London.

Spergel, I.A. (1990) Youth gangs – continuity and change. *Crime and Justice*, **12**, 171–276.

Stephenson, S. (2006) *Crossing the Line: Vagrancy, Homelessness and Social Displacement in Russia*, Ashgate Press, Farnham.

Thornberry, T.P. (1998) Membership in youth gangs and involvement in serious and violent offending, in *Serious and Violent Juvenile Offenders: Risk Factors and Successful Interventions* (eds R. Loeber and D.P. Farrington), Sage, Thousand Oaks, CA.

Thornberry, T.P., Krohn, M.D., Lizotte, A.J. and Chand-Wieschem (1995) The role of juvenile gangs in facilitating delinquent behaviour, in *The Modern Gang Reader* (eds M.W. Klein, C.L. Maxson and J. Miller (**1995**), pp 174–185. Los Angeles, Roxbury.

Vigil, D. (1988) *Bano Gangs: Street Life and Identity in Southern California*, University of Texas Press, Austin, TX.

Young, T. and Hallsworth, S. (2006) *Ealing: A Borough Profile*, a report for the Metropolitan Police Service and the Safer Ealing Partnership, Ealing, Ealing Borough Police.

Young, T., Fitzgerald, M., Hallsworth, S. and Joseph, I. (2007) *Groups, Gangs and Weapons*, Youth Justice Board, London.

6 Peer Violence in Provision for Children in Care

ANDREW KENDRICK

INTRODUCTION

Over recent years, there have been ongoing concerns about the experience and outcomes of children and young people in out-of-home care settings (Kendrick, 1998, 2008a). They are some of the most troubled and vulnerable children in society, yet their needs are often not well met. They will have entered care for a variety of reasons – including abuse, neglect, and offending behaviour; and it has long been recognised that there is a link between poverty and entry into care (Bebbington and Miles, 1989). In March 2007, there were some 65,000 children and young people looked after away from home in the UK: approximately 46,000 children were living in foster family care, 10,000 were in residential care and 9,000 in kin care with relatives or friends.

Entry into care can be alienating and traumatising in its own right (Kendrick, 2005). In this context, the fact that children may experience violence and abuse in their care settings is of particular significance. Over the years, there have been a number of enquiries that have focused on the abuse of children and young people in care (e.g. Utting, 1991, 1997; Kent, 1997; Waterhouse, 2000), although Goldson (2006) notes the same cannot be said for the mistreatment of children in custody. For the most part, these enquiries have focused on abuse by staff and carers rather than abuse by *peers*. Children and young people, however, have consistently raised the issue of bullying and peer violence, and its impact on their experience of care (Paterson *et al.*, 2003; Morgan, 2008). There has also been a tendency to focus on abuse and violence in residential care. There is evidence, however, that children are just as likely to be abused in foster care as in residential care (Hobbs, Hobbs and Wynne, 1999).

There are a number of factors that have implications for the consideration of the issue of peer violence in out-of-home care settings. As we have seen, the past histories of this group of young people may have included physical

Children Behaving Badly? Peer Violence Between Children and Young People
Edited by Christine Barter and David Berridge
© 2011 John Wiley & Sons Ltd.

and sexual abuse, either as victims or perpetrators (Kendrick, 2008a). Approximately half of children and young people entering residential care have been violent to other children prior to entry (Sinclair and Gibbs, 1998, pp. 20–1). In addition, children who have suffered abuse and neglect can experience difficulties in developing positive and supportive relationships with their peers (Price and Brew, 1999). Looked after children and young people may have experienced instability and discontinuity of care, involving several care placements. This disruption can have a further impact on peer relationships. Young people have experienced stigma linked to being in care and it is important to recognise that children in care have highlighted that the most usual place where they experienced bullying was not in the placement itself, but in school or college (Morgan, 2007).

Emergency and crisis placements, and lack of alternatives, can lead to children and young people being placed inappropriately. Sinclair and Gibbs (1998), for example, highlight the negative aspects of an inappropriate age-mix in residential care. Perpetrators of abuse may be placed alongside victims of abuse (Brogi and Bagley, 1998; Kendrick, 2004).

Peer relationships between children and young people, and most often the negative aspects of these relationships – bullying, sexual exploitation and negative peer group cultures – have been highlighted (Gwynn, Meyer and Schaefer, 1988). Barter et al. (2004) found that peer group hierarchies or 'pecking orders' were a central context in which violence was experienced by young people, and were seen as being most problematic when they were in flux (see also Brannan, Jones and Murch, 1993; Parkin and Green 1997).

Locating peer violence within broader social contexts is also crucial in order to take account of the gendered and racist nature of particular forms of peer violence (Green, 2005; O'Neill, 2008; Kendrick, 2008b). The abuse, particularly sexual abuse, of girls and young women in care by boys and young men in care reflects wider societal concerns, as does homophobic abuse (O'Neill, 2008). Residential staff have expressed concern at the extent of racial prejudice among the children and young people in residential care, and certain groups, such as unaccompanied asylum-seeking children, have been identified as being at particular risk of racial abuse (Berridge and Brodie, 1998). One research study, however, found a low level of expressed racism and racist insults and attacks were rare; young people were very conscious that racism was unacceptable and that it would be taken seriously by staff (Barter et al., 2004, p. 215).

While there has been a good deal of focus on negative aspects, Emond (2003) shows how the peer group can act as a positive source of support: 'the group operates to monitor and secure residents' safety and acts as means of maintaining group culture' (p. 334). She also describes a complex set of relationships where young people have 'no fixed roles or group positions and as a result all experienced moments of being the most and least powerful' (p. 334). Peer group dynamics are also important in relation to foster care, and it is not unusual for more than one child to be placed with a family. There is also the added dynamic of the relationship between foster children and the foster carers' own children (Part, 1993).

Research has shown that there is a strong correlation between being bullied or sexually harassed and the subjective well-being of children and young people (Sinclair and Gibbs, 1998; Gibbs and Sinclair, 2000). It is crucial, then, that peer violence is recognised and addressed in out-of-home care.

DEFINITIONS OF PEER VIOLENCE IN OUT-OF-HOME PROVISION

> ... anything that actually makes someone feel sad or uncomfortable counts as bullying.
>
> Morgan, 2008, p. 7

There have been varying definitions of peer violence and part of the problem of reviewing the research on this subject concerns these differences – and particularly the way in which the catch-all term 'bullying' is used to discuss a range of distinctive behaviours. In the context of residential child care, bullying has been defined as 'the behaviour of one person or group which causes distress to another person or group as a result of physical threat, assault, verbal abuse or threats' (Support Force for Residential Child Care, 1996, p. 63).

Barter *et al.* (2004) provided a useful categorisation of peer violence in the context of a study of children's residential care:

- Physical contact violence: included 'fighting', 'punching', 'leathering', 'kicking', 'pushing', 'slapping', being beaten with implements and being stabbed.
- Physical non-contact violence: harmed young people emotionally rather than physically and included intimidation by looks or gestures, written threats, forceful invasion of personal space and attacks on personal belongings, such as 'trashing' rooms.
- Sexual violence: experienced by young people as abusive and sexual, involving, for example, 'flashing', touching of sexual body parts, coerced sexual contact and rape.
- Verbal violence: primarily involved name-calling concerning gender, sexuality, ethnicity, family and appearance.

This is a useful framework for the analysis of this phenomenon, but the research and literature uses such a variety of definitions and terms that it is problematic to fit the evidence into this schema. The range of definitions, different protocols on reporting of abuse and the fact that much abuse goes undisclosed create major issues in the comparison of research findings.

THE EXTENT AND NATURE OF PEER VIOLENCE IN OUT-OF-HOME CARE

Research on the abuse of children and young people in out-of-home care has been limited but it provides some indication of the scale and extent of peer violence across different settings. Two studies from the US found that a significant proportion of the perpetrators of abuse in out-of-home care settings were other children. Rosenthal et al. (1991) provide information on 325 perpetrators identified from 261 reported incidents of abuse in out-of-home care in Colorado. Foster care siblings were identified in 4 per cent of physical abuse cases, 11 per cent of neglect cases and 21 per cent of sexual abuse cases. 'Residents at setting' were identified in 1 per cent of physical abuse cases, 1 per cent of neglect cases and 16 per cent of sexual abuse cases. Spencer and Knudsen (1992) gave information on the perpetrators of sexual abuse:

> Child perpetrators were involved in 6 per cent of the foster home cases; 70 per cent (88/126) of residential home cases; 50 per cent (21/42) of state institution cases; and 67 per cent (10/15) of hospital cases.
>
> Spencer and Knudsen, 1992, p. 54

In one study of referrals of abuse of children in foster and residential care in one city in England, 20 per cent of foster care incidents involved another child as the abuser. Of these, 53 per cent of the abusers were other foster children, 31 per cent were siblings and 16 per cent were children of the foster family or other unrelated children. For those children in residential care, 16 per cent were abused by another child within the home, and 52 per cent were abused by children out of the home (Hobbs et al., 1999).

Peer violence, then, may be perpetrated by other children in care settings or by children and young people outside the care placement. It occurs across the range of provision for children in care, and the next sections will look in more detail at some different types of care provision.

RESIDENTIAL CHILD CARE

> Bullying in residential care is really frightening for young people. I've tried to tell staff and they sort it out for you but sometimes they can't be there all the time and bullies find a way of getting you on your own.
>
> (Female 14) Paterson, Watson and Whiteford, 2003, p. 31

There has been growing evidence that peer violence in residential child care is of more concern than abuse by staff:

> Children in residential care are vulnerable to violence from their peers, particularly when conditions and staff supervision are poor. Lack of privacy and respect for cultural identity, frustration, overcrowding, and a failure to separate particularly vulnerable children from older, more aggressive children often lead to

peer-on-peer violence. Staff may sanction or encourage peer abuse amongst children – either for amusement or to maintain discipline.

Pinheiro, 2006, p. 189

One in six of the young people in residential care in one study stated that they had been bullied or ill-treated by other residents (Triseliotis *et al.*, 1995). Sexual abuse by other residents is also a serious concern (Farmer and Pollock, 1998; Green and Masson, 2002; Green, 2005; O'Neill, 2008). It is not, however, inevitable, as one young person in residential care explains:

> There's never really been any bullying in this house. Like you hear a lot like there's bullying in children's homes and stuff, but everyone's sort of equal here … There's no head dog in this house, do you know what I mean, everyone treats each other like they'd like to be treated.
>
> (Christine, 14) Barter *et al.*, 2004, p. 65

Two contrasting studies in England provide evidence of the extent and nature of peer violence in residential child care. Research on the quality and outcomes of residential child care included interviews with 223 children and young people in 48 residential children's homes (Sinclair and Gibbs, 1998; Gibbs and Sinclair, 2000). They were asked questions about whether they had experienced attempts at bullying from other residents or whether anyone had taken sexual advantage of them (Gibbs and Sinclair, 2000). Barter *et al.* (2004) studied in detail the nature of peer violence in residential child care, in order to gain the experiences of 71 children and young people – aged between 8 and 17 – and 71 staff members from 14 children's homes.

Gibbs and Sinclair (2000) found that a significant proportion of children and young people (44%) reported being bullied in their children's home. However, this was very similar to the proportion who reported that they were bullied before they moved into the children's home (41%). The researchers found that age and reason for admission seemed to be particularly important as factors in bullying:

> Seventy per cent of those aged 12 or under, nearly half of those aged 13 and 14, but only just over a third of the remainder said that someone had tried to bully them after arrival.
>
> Gibbs and Sinclair, 2000, p. 250

Children and young people who were in care for reasons of abuse were more likely to be victims of bullying.

Barter *et al.* (2004) used qualitative semi-structured interviews and vignettes to look in detail at the nature of peer violence in residential child care. We have seen that they distinguished between verbal violence; physical non-contact violence; physical contact violence; and sexual violence (see also Barter, 2008).

The research found a general culture of verbal abuse and nearly all young people had experienced some form of verbal violence. Young people felt that the worst cases of verbal attacks – impugning the victim's sexuality or insulting their families – were more emotionally damaging than some forms of physical attacks:

> ... it's mainly verbal. Verbal hurts more than hitting though ... with hitting it's like oh a punch, the pain is over in a few seconds, but when you get verbal you know it stays in ya for quite a few days yeah ...
>
> (Adrian, 16) Barter *et al.*, 2004, p. 42

Almost half of young people in the study experienced physical non-contact violence, frequently alongside verbal and physical violence. This mostly consisted of destruction of personal property, but it also included threats and intimidation. Over three-quarters of young people experienced physical contact violence, either as victims or perpetrators.

Low-level physical violence frequently took place within friendship or sibling groups, and 'attacks' were often conducted in the full view of staff who would immediately intervene, thus preventing serious harm. High-level physical violence, ranging from knife attacks to severe beatings, could be isolated incidents or routine and frequent. Such attacks were generally embedded in wider power dynamics, were often pre-planned and took place away from staff surveillance:

> It's like the same thing I done to Sherry when she wrecked my room, she ripped my pictures, my favourite pictures and so I got her and I pushed her and I stamped on her, I was like, 'cause she stamped on them and she ripped them so I said, 'You don't like it when I stamp on you so don't stamp on my stuff and throw my stuff around'.
>
> (Amy, 13) Barter *et al.*, 2004, p. 73

In relation to sexual violence, Gibbs and Sinclair (2000) asked young people whether anyone had tried to take sexual advantage of them, either before they had moved into the children's home or afterwards:

> Over a third of the female residents (37%) but only nine of the male ones said that this had happened before admission. Nearly a quarter (23%) of the females and 7 per cent of the males said that it happened after.
>
> Gibbs and Sinclair, 2000, p. 251

However, Gibbs and Sinclair also make the important point that the rate of sexual harassment is not greater for residents when they move into a children's home. Twenty-three per cent of residents were taken sexual advantage of before they moved into their home compared to 13 per cent after. Young people may generally live in a context of violence.

Barter *et al.* (2004) found that reports of unwelcome sexual behaviours were low. Girls were three times more likely to report these than boys, and they experienced the most serious abuse including rape. Most perpetrators were male and all the incidents of unwelcome sexual behaviours involved some degree of coercion. Half of these incidents were unreported to staff, although they were disclosed to other young people. The authors observed:

> Unlike physical violence, staff did not generally locate incidents of sexual violence in relation to wider power dynamics between the young people concerned.
>
> Barter *et al.*, 2004, p. 51

The lack of confidence expressed by staff in addressing issues of sexual abuse and violence contrasted with the systematic approach they took with racist abuse.

YOUNG OFFENDERS INSTITUTIONS

Research focused on locked facilities has identified high levels of peer violence: one study of records in a young offenders institution concluded that it 'seems that violence within the institution is widespread throughout the population' (Skett, Braham and Samuel, 1996, p. 12). Even so, other research gives an indication of the extent to which official records will be an underestimate of the level of violence because 'less than one in five of those who had been victimised said that they had informed an officer afterwards' (Edgar and O'Donnell, 1997, p. 16; see also Howard League, 1995; Palmer and Farmer, 2002):

> Everyone does it. If I don't someone else will. You've got to learn to stand up for yourself … I'm doing them a favour really. I don't hurt anyone … I usually only have to look at them.
>
> Howard League, 1995, p. 38

Edgar and O'Donnell (1997) found high levels of victimisation and, in the previous month, one in three young offenders had been assaulted; half had been threatened with violence; over half had received hurtful insults; a quarter had suffered cell theft; and one in ten had been the victims of robbery A quarter of young offenders were both victims and victimisers in the previous month. Assault, verbal abuse and threats of violence tended to be reciprocated. Robbery, exclusion and cell theft, however, tended to be hierarchical, with little overlap between victims and victimisers (Edgar and O'Donnell, 1997, p. 16; see also Challen and Walton, 2004).

Levels of peer violence appear to be particularly high in young offenders institutions compared to other residential settings.

FOSTER FAMILY CARE

There has been much less of a focus on the abuse of children and young people in foster family care and, consequently, less awareness of the issue of peer violence (Nixon, 2000):

Pressure to find foster placements may mean small groups of young people who are strangers to each other are placed in the same foster home. In such a context the difference between residential and foster care in matters such as bullying may begin to fade.

Gilligan, 2000, p. 53

In a survey of 626 children in care, a quarter of those in foster care (26%) felt they were treated unfairly or picked on, almost exactly the same proportion as in residential care (27%) (Fletcher, 1993). In some cases, they referred to bullying by the foster carers' own children:

There are two other children who are the foster parents' own who bully me because they don't want me here.

(Female, 14) Fletcher, 1993, p. 65

A US study found that, in cases of suspected sexual abuse in foster family care, foster siblings and others were the alleged perpetrators more frequently than foster parents (Benedict et al., 1994). Benedict et al. (1996) give details of substantiated cases of sexual abuse and '... other foster children in the home were the perpetrators in 20 per cent of the incidents' (Benedict et al., 1996, p. 563). Linares (2006) studied sibling-to-sibling relationships among foster children and found high levels of conflict and aggression. Morris and Wheatley (1994) found that foster carers' own children were the most common perpetrators of sexual abuse in foster care (11 out of 24 cases):

A significant factor seemed to be the age-difference between the predominantly male abusers and the foster child; the abusers were commonly two or three years older.

Morris and Wheatley, 1994, p. 38; see also Nixon and Verity, 1996

Foster carers' own children may themselves be at risk of peer violence. Part (1993) found that these children identified three main difficulties with fostering: difficult and annoying behaviour, and stealing; the attention given to foster children; and the lack of privacy. Most, however, liked fostering and only 5 per cent were clear that they did not like their family being a foster family (Part, 1993; see also Sinclair, Wilson and Gibbs, 2005). In a survey of 102 children of foster carers:

... 38 per cent answered that 'aggression' had become part of their lives ... Many have had to deal with children coming from violent homes. Others have suffered directly in the form of bullying from those children staying with them ...

Karim, 2003, p. 45

Farmer and Pollock (1998) describe the use of foster care for sexually abused and abusing children. Some of these children went on to abuse in the placements:

... the victims were younger siblings either in a shared foster care placement or on a contact visit, the younger sons of the foster carers and other children in either residential or foster care.

p. 131

Karim (2003) found that 'fighting with foster siblings' was one of the reasons for change of placement.

Farmer, Moyers and Lipscombe (2004) found a close link between placement outcome and the impact of the fostered adolescents on the carers' own children and other fostered children. Nineteen (28%) of the young people had been physically aggressive to other children or adults during the placement, and five (7%) had put others at risk due to their sexual behaviour, including other children in the foster placement.

There are complex relationships between children and young people in foster care: sibling relationships, relationships with the foster carers' own children and relationships with other foster children. Peer violence must be viewed in terms of the complexity of these relationships.

DEVELOPING PRACTICE TO ADDRESS PEER VIOLENCE

In order to address the issue of peer violence in provision for children in care, it is important that policies and methods of intervention are developed and good practice promoted. Research, however, has highlighted that work in addressing peer violence can be patchy and, even where policies have been developed, there is inconsistency in implementation (Farmer and Pollock, 1998; Barter *et al.*, 2004). National care standards for both residential and foster care now make explicit the need for policy and procedures and support for foster carers and residential staff. It is interesting to note, however, that the standards are much more explicit and detailed for residential care than for foster care.

Inter-agency guidance on working to safeguard children identifies children living away from home as particularly vulnerable (HM Government, 2006). It stresses that there are a number of essential safeguards that should be observed in all care settings. These include children feeling valued, respected and listened to; clear and effective complaints procedures; an openness to the external world and children having access to a trusted adult outside the care setting; and training for staff and foster carers in all aspects of safeguarding children:

Peer abuse should always be taken as seriously as abuse perpetrated by an adult. It should be subject to the same safeguarding procedures as apply in respect of any child who is suffering, or at risk of suffering, significant harm from an adverse source.

HM Government, 2006, p. 199

The guidance highlights that work needs to be undertaken to address the needs of those who abuse, as well as those who are abused. It sets out three key principles for work with children and young people who abuse others: a coordinated approach on the part of the different agencies; the needs of those who abuse others should be considered separately from the needs of their victims; and an assessment should be carried out in each case (p. 200). The guidance also stresses that all care settings should have in place rigorous anti-bullying strategies.

Beresford and Wade (2006) reviewed the general literature on anti-bullying interventions and concluded that:

- there is little evidence that punitive approaches change behaviour;
- problem-solving approaches can have a positive effect;
- assertiveness skills and other coping strategies are important in supporting victims;
- properly managed and age-appropriate peer support programmes can support children to support each other;
- carers should support the anti-bullying approach;
- flexible and child-centred approaches should be adopted;
- effective whole-school approaches need to be consistent and inclusive.

Beresford and Wade, 2006, p. 54

It is clear, then, that out-of-home care services should develop multi-dimensional approaches to peer violence. Children and young people should be involved in developing policy and practice to prevent peer violence. There is a need for the training and education of staff, carers, other professionals and young people, so that they understand and appreciate the issues involved in peer violence, particularly sexual violence, and are better able to manage aggression in the context of out-of-home care (e.g. South Lanarkshire Council Social Work Resources, 1998; Doorbar, 2002).

Supervision of children and young people is central in preventing peer violence. For this to be effective, it is important that there is effective communication about their backgrounds and previous behaviour to ensure that carers are adequately prepared (Farmer and Pollock, 1998; Kendrick, 2004). Staff vigilance is a potent deterrent against bullying, in that children and young people who bully will know that it will be dealt with, and the victims of bullying will have similar confidence (Support Force for Residential Child Care, 1996). Foster carers must also be in a position to put in place rules and routines for keeping children safe (Farmer and Pollock, 1998).

Direct work with aggressive young people, both group work and individual work, should be put in place to address specific social skills, anger management and, where appropriate, sexual aggression (Browne and Falshaw, 1996; Barter et al., 2004; Kendrick, 2004). Similarly, direct work with victims of bullying and sexual aggression should assess their needs and, where appropriate, help them to develop specific social skills and acknowledge their experiences.

The ethos or culture of a care setting is crucial in developing a context in which children and young people feel valued and safe (Sinclair and Gibbs, 1998; Davidson *et al.*, 2005). Millham *et al.* (1981) argued that it is the 'ethos' of the establishment that effectively controls '... by fashioning a system of mutually held expectations, values and norms of conduct which exercise restraint on members' (p. 48). Such a culture of care must form the basis of the response to peer violence.

CONCLUSION

Official inquiries have focused on the abuse of children and young people in out-of-home care settings by staff and carers. It is likely, however, that peer violence by other young people has more impact on children and young people's experience of care. It is, therefore, essential that all those involved in the care of children and young people fully appreciate the implications of peer violence. In addition, children and young people themselves must participate in the development and implementation of policies that address bullying and sexual aggression.

REFERENCES

Barter, C. (2008) Prioritising young people's concerns in residential care: responding to peer violence, in *Residential Child Care: Prospects and Challenges* (ed. A. Kendrick), Jessica Kingsley Publishers. London.

Barter, C., Renold, E., Berridge, D. and Cawson, P. (2004) *Peer Violence in Children's Residential Care*, Palgrave Macmillan, Basingstoke.

Bebbington, A. and Miles, J. (1989) The background of children who enter local authority care. *British Journal of Social Work*, **19**, 349–68.

Benedict, M.L., Zuravin, S., Brandt, D. and Abbey, H. (1994) Types and frequency of child maltreatment by family foster care providers in an urban population. *Child Abuse and Neglect*, **18** (7), 577–85.

Benedict, M.I., Zuravin, S., Somerfield, M. and Brandt, D. (1996) The reported health and functioning of children maltreated while in family foster care. *Child Abuse and Neglect*, **20** (7), 561–71.

Beresford, B. and Wade, J. (2006) Anti-bullying interventions: what is the evidence of their effectiveness? In *Bullying Today: A Report by the Office of the Children's Commissioner, with Recommendations and Links to Practitioner Tools*, Office of the Children's Commissioner, London.

Berridge, D. and Brodie, I. (1998) *Children's Homes Revisited*, Jessica Kingsley Publishers, London.

Brannan, C., Jones, J.R. and Murch, J.D. (1993) Lessons from a residential special school enquiry: reflections on the Castle Hill report. *Child Abuse Review*, **2** (4), 271–5.

Brogi, L. and Bagley, C. (1998) Abusing victims: detention of child sexual abuse victims in secure accommodation. *Child Abuse Review*, **7**, 315–29.

Browne, K. and Falshaw, L. (1996) Factors related to bullying in secure accommodation. *Child Abuse Review*, **5** (2), 123–7.

Challen, M. and Walton, T. (2004) *Juveniles in Custody: A Unique Insight into the Perception of Young People Held in Prison Service Custody in England and Wales*, HM Inspectorate of Prisons, London.

Davidson, J., McCullough, D., Steckley, L. and Warren, T. (2005) *Holding Safely: A Guide for Residential Child Care Practitioners and Managers about Physically Restraining Children and Young People*, Scottish Institute for Residential Child Care, Glasgow.

Doorbar, P. (2002) *Beat Bullying! Working with Looked After Children to Overcome Threatening Behaviour*, Pavilion Publishing, Brighton.

Edgar, K. and O'Donnell, I. (1997) Responding to victimisation. *Prison Service Journal*, **109**, 15–19.

Emond, R. (2003) Putting the care into residential care: the role of young people. *Journal of Social Work*, **3** (3), 321–37.

Farmer, E. and Pollock, S. (1998) *Sexually Abused and Abusing Children in Substitute Care*, John Wiley & Sons, Chichester.

Farmer, E., Moyers, S. and Lipscombe, J. (2004) *Fostering Adolescents*, Jessica Kingsley Publishers, London.

Fletcher, B. (1993) *Not Just a Name: The Views of Young People in Foster and Residential Care*, National Consumer Council, London.

Gibbs, I. and Sinclair, I. (2000) Bullying, sexual harassment and happiness in residential children's homes. *Child Abuse Review*, **9**, 247–56.

Gilligan, R. (2000) The importance of listening to the child in foster care, in *Issues in Foster Care: Policy, Practice and Research* (eds G. Kelly and R. Gilligan). Jessica Kingsley Publishers, London.

Goldson, B. (2006) Damage, harm and death in child prisons in England and Wales: questions of abuse and accountability. *The Howard Journal*, **45** (5), 449–67.

Green, L. (2005) Theorizing sexuality, sexual abuse and residential children's homes: adding gender to the equation. *British Journal of Social Work*, **35**, 453–81.

Green, L. and Masson, H. (2002) Adolescents who sexually abuse and residential accommodation: issues of risk and vulnerability. *British Journal of Social Work*, **32**, 149–68.

Gwynn, C., Meyer, R. and Schaefer, C. (1988) The influence of the peer culture in residential treatment, in *Children in Residential Care: Critical Issues in Treatment* (eds C.E. Schaefer and A.J. Swanson), Van Nostrand Rheinhold, New York.

HM Government (2006) *Working Together to Safeguard Children: A Guide to Interagency Working to Safeguard and Promote the Welfare of Children*, Stationery Office, London.

Hobbs, G.F., Hobbs, C.J. and Wynne (1999) Abuse of children in foster and residential care. *Child Abuse and Neglect*, **23** (12), 1239–52.

Howard League (1995) *Banged Up, Beaten Up, Cutting Up: Report of the Howard League Commission of Inquiry into Violence in Penal Institutions for Teenagers under 18*. Howard League for Penal Reform, London.

Karim, K. (2003) *Voices from Care*, The Fostering Network, Glasgow.

Kendrick, A. (1998) In their best interest? Protecting children from abuse in residential and foster care. *International Journal of Child and Family Welfare*, **3** (2), 169–85.

Kendrick, A. (2004) Managing children and young people who are sexually aggressive, in *Managing Sex Offender Risk* (eds H. Kemshall and G. McIvor), Jessica Kingsley Publishers, London.

Kendrick, A. (2005) Social exclusion and social inclusion: themes and issues in residential child care, in *Facing Forward: Residential child care in the 21st century* (eds D. Crimmens and I. Milligan), Russell House Publishing, Lyme Regis.

Kendrick, A. (ed.) (2008a) *Residential Child Care: Prospects and Challenges*. Jessica Kingsley Publishers, London.

Kendrick, A. (2008b) Black and minority ethnic children and young people in residential care, in *Residential Child Care: Prospects and Challenges* (ed. A. Kendrick), Jessica Kingsley Publishers, London.

Kent, R. (1997) *Children's Safeguards Review*, Scottish Office, Edinburgh.

Linares, L.O. (2006) An understudied form of intra-family violence: sibling-to-sibling aggression among foster children. *Aggression and Violent Behaviour*, **11**, 95–109.

Millham, S., Bullock, R., Hosie, K. and Haak, M. (1981) *Issues of Control in Residential Child-care*, HMSO, London.

Morgan, R. (2007) *Looked After in England: How Children Living Away from Home Rate England's Care*, Office of the Children's Rights Director, Newcastle upon Tyne.

Morgan, R (2008) *Children on Bullying: A Report by the Children's Rights Director of England*, Ofsted, London.

Morris, S. and Wheatley, H. (1994) *Time to Listen: The Experiences of Young People in Foster and Residential Care*, Childline, London.

Nixon, S. (2000) Safe care, abuse and allegations of abuse in foster care, in *Issues in Foster Care: Policy, Practice and Research* (eds G. Kelly and R. Gilligan), Jessica Kingsley Publishers, London.

Nixon, S. and Verity, P. (1996) Allegations against foster families. *Foster Care* (January), 11–14.

O'Neill, T. (2008) Gender matters in residential child care, in *Residential Child Care: Prospects and Challenges* (ed. A. Kendrick), Jessica Kingsley Publishers, London.

Palmer, E.J. and Farmer, S. (2002) Victimising behaviour among juvenile and young offenders: how different are perpetrators? *Journal of Adolescence*, **25**, 469–81.

Parkin, W. and Green, L. (1997) Cultures of abuse within residential child care. *Early Child Development and Care*, **133**, 73–86.

Part, D. (1993) Fostering as seen by the carers' children. *Adoption and Fostering*, **17** (1), 26–31.

Paterson, S., Watson, D. and Whiteford, J. (2003) *Let's Face It! Care 2003: Young People Tell it How it is*, Who Cares? Glasgow.

Pinheiro, P.S. (2006) *World Report on Violence against Children*, United Nations, Geneva.

Price, J.M. and Brew, V. (1999) Peer relationships of foster children: developmental and mental health services implications. *Journal of Applied Developmental Psychology*, **19** (2), 199–218.

Rosenthal, J., Motz, J., Edmondson, D. and Groze, V. (1991) A descriptive study of abuse and neglect in out-of-home placement. *Child Abuse and Neglect*, **15**, 249–60.

Sinclair, I. and Gibbs, I. (1998) *Children's Homes: A Study in Diversity*, John Wiley & Sons, Chichester.

Sinclair, I., Wilson, K. and Gibbs, I. (2005) *Foster Placements: Why They Succeed and Why They Fail*, Jessica Kingsley Publishers, London.

Skett, S., Braham, L. and Samuel, J. (1996) Drugs and violence in a young offender establishment. *Prison Service Journal*, **106**, 9–13.

South Lanarkshire Council Social Work Resources (1998) *Bully Proofing our Unit: Addressing Bullying in Children's Units*, South Lanarkshire Council Social Work Resources, Hamilton.

Spencer, J.W. and Knudsen, D.D. (1992) Out-of-home maltreatment – an analysis of risk in various settings for children. *Children and Youth Services Review*, **14** (6), 485–92.

Support Force for Children's Residential Care (1996) *Good Care Matters: Ways of Enhancing Good Practice in Residential Child Care*, Department of Health, London.

Triseliotis, J., Borland, M., Hill, M. and Lambert, L. (1995) *Teenagers and Social Work Services*, HMSO, London.

Utting, W. (1991) *Children in the Public Care: A Review of Residential Child Care*, HMSO, London.

Utting, W. (1997) *People Like Us: The Report on the Review of Safeguards for Children Living Away from Home*, Stationery Office, London.

Waterhouse, R. (2000) *Lost in Care: Report of the Tribunal of Inquiry into the Abuse of Children in Care in the Former County Council Areas of Gwynedd and Clwyd since 1974 – Summary of Report with Conclusions and Recommendations in Full*, Stationery Office, London.

Part II Different Forms of Peer Violence

7 Young Men, Violence and Racism

LES BACK

Understanding peer violence among young people is not simply a matter of scrutinising their patterns of behaviour and dissecting their morality. If violent behaviour among young people leads civic leaders to speak of a 'crisis', the first question we must ask is: for whom is it a crisis? The recent concerns about 'knife crime' and 'gun crime', and the so-called 'weaponisation of youth', are cases in point, discussed eloquently elsewhere in this volume (see Chapters 5 and 14). It is telling that no connection has been made between the current moral panic about knife crime and the bloody legacy of violent racism in Britain. In 2008, the 40th anniversary of Enoch Powell's notorious 'rivers of blood' speech garnered considerable media and journalistic reassessment. Powell, one-time icon of demotic racism, was recuperated in much of the reporting as a prophet who anticipated our present condition. Yet, as Gilroy (2008) pointed out, the blood foaming on British streets has largely been that of black and brown citizens who have been caught violently in racism's sights.

In this chapter I want to explore the ways in which violent racism has an impact on young lives, and specifically in relation to young men. More than this, I want to argue that these tragic incidents reveal the ways in which racism damages the capacity of the police, politicians and members of the wider adult community to comprehend peer violence. The chapter focuses on the murder of Stephen Lawrence on the night of Thursday, 22 April 1993, close to a bus stop on the streets of south-east London.[1] His brutal stabbing cut short a young life and exposed the nature of the racism that wounds British society as a whole. The Metropolitan Police's failure to catch and prosecute his killers exposed the colour-coded nature of the British criminal justice system. This case was a landmark in the history of racism in Britain, and the struggle for justice produced an unprecedented amount of documentation from witnesses, bystanders and those who were culpable not only in the crime itself, but also in the institutional failures and injustices of the criminal justice system.

---

[1] Some of the material that follows is included in a more extended discussion of this case in Back (2010).

Children Behaving Badly? Peer Violence Between Children and Young People
Edited by Christine Barter and David Berridge
© 2011 John Wiley & Sons Ltd.

Over 15 years after the murder, Stephen Lawrence's killers still walk free and this injustice haunts the streets of the city and indeed the nation as a whole. Yet, the name Stephen Lawrence has become synonymous with bringing out into the open both violent and respectable racisms. It is carried through time in memorials, art works, dedicated scholarships, educational trusts, and the art galleries and educational building that all bear his name. Remembering Stephen Lawrence involves reckoning with those who want to deepen the wound and equally those who want to heal it. That process is ongoing in a way the spectre of Stephen Lawrence hangs over the streets of London and indeed the whole nation.

Benjamin (1997) wrote that:

> Language shows clearly that memory is not an instrument for exploring the past but its theatre. It is the medium of past experience, as the ground is the medium in which dead cities lie interred.
>
> p. 314

The narratives, acts of commemoration and desecration reveal the character of whiteness in the theatre of racism. One of the many lessons of this case is that power and violence hide in silence and the past is entombed or concealed. More than this, racism raises the public's apprehension of violent crimes, derived from the way that police officers react at a murder scene, the response of local residents and journalists' attempts to explain the crime. None of this makes sense without an appreciation of the ways in which whiteness comes to feature within the actions of those involved. The discussion here draws not only on secondary sources but also ethnographic work, interviews and observations garnered over the last 15 years both as a resident of south-east London and through being active in anti-racist politics in the area.

The remaining parts of the chapter are divided into three sections. First, a brief chronology of events leading up to Stephen Lawrence's murder will be outlined along with a description of the social landscape in which it took place. Here the emphasis will be on understanding how to make sense of the role that racism played not only in relation to the murder but also in how racism and whiteness came to define those at the crime scene. Second, the chapter will focus on the botched investigation and the struggle to expose the whiteness and injustice that stifled the Lawrence family's struggle for justice for their son. Racial dominance involves patterns of behaviour, defined by whiteness, that are situated in specific social contexts and lead to ways of acting that are historically produced rather than an inherent quality in 'white people' (Ignatiev and Garvey, 1996; Hartigan, 1999; Ware and Back, 2002). Finally, I want to end by returning to the issues of central concern in this book and reflecting on how a critical assessment of this case might inform our understanding of peer violence. Before doing this, I will try to describe the place where the murder took place and its social history by inviting you to take a walk down Well Hall Road.

WHITE LOOKS[2]

On 5 March 1998, it was reported that the plaque that had been set in the pavement to commemorate the place where Stephen Lawrence had died had been defaced. An off-duty police officer had stumbled across the vandalism of the memorial. Someone had tipped a pot of white paint over the plaque on Well Hall Road. I decided that I was going to go over to Eltham, look at the plaque and take some photographs.

It wasn't the first time that this had happened and there is something deeply disturbing about the repeated violation and vandalism that is directed at this place where Stephen Lawrence fell. A memorial plaque was first set in the pavement on Sunday, 23 July 1995.[3] Well Hall Road was sealed off, 200 friends and supporters gathered and the Bishop of Croydon, Reverend Wilfred Wood, led a roadside service. Racist vandals immediately preyed upon the marble memorial. Doreen Lawrence – Stephen's mother – reflected in her memoir:

> The first plaque laid down in Well Hall Road was commissioned by black workers in Greenwich, who collected money for the purpose. It was a small tablet and it was vandalised so badly that you could not recognise Stephen's name. A company decided to replace it, and they paid for something the size of a small paving stone.
>
> Lawrence, 2006, pp. 219–20

Stephen's body had been taken to Jamaica by his parents and laid to rest. His father, Neville Lawrence, explained:

> We had fears about burying Stephen here [in London] because of the situation surrounding his death and also the fact that it was explained to us that [racists] were going to be able to go and dig his body after he was buried ... I did not wish that to happen to my son so the family sat down just before we knew we were going to have his body and came to the conclusion that the best thing to do was to take him home to Jamaica.
>
> The Stephen Lawrence Inquiry 1999b, Appendix 7

Shortly after the white paint incident in March 1998, I made the short drive from my home to Eltham. It was around 10am when I parked the car in a small side road called Downham Road in the middle of Well Hall Road. What was immediately striking about this part of south-east London was the suburban affluence that stood side by side with the working-class public housing. The road that I parked in was expensive and upmarket. I remember looking out of the window of the car as I pulled up to see the mock Tudor frontage of a four- or five-bedroomed house. I didn't realise at that time, but the spot where Stephen Lawrence was killed was just 50 yards from where I had parked the car. Well Hall Road is a very long road that leads from the top of Woolwich

---

[2] Here the notion of a 'white look' is inspired by bell hooks' influential collection (hooks, 1992).
[3] *The Mercury*, Thursday, 27 July 1995.

Common right down to the bottom of Eltham. It is close to the prized symbols of the Millennium Dome (now called the '02 Arena') and the Prime Meridian in Greenwich, which is the point from which time is measured and the cartography of empire was drawn. Greenwich Council boasted on its billboard advertisements that 'The Millennium Starts Here'.

There are a series of bus stops just after the roundabout where the Coronet Cinema is located. At 10.30 pm on 22 April 1993, Stephen Lawrence stood here in Dickson Road to see if a bus was coming. He had spent the evening with his friend Duwayne Brooks, who was standing part-way between Dickson Road and the roundabout. He saw a group of five or six white youths opposite where Stephen was looking for the next bus. Duwayne called to Stephen, who hesitated. One of the white youths called out: 'What, what nigger?' This first set of deadly white looks identified the two black boys as targets. The group crossed the road quickly and engulfed Stephen. The attack probably lasted less than 15–20 seconds. During this time, one or more of the attackers stabbed Stephen twice. Duwayne called to him to run and follow him. Stephen managed somehow to run over 250 yards to the point where he fell. Bleeding profusely, he lost consciousness. In a panic, Duwayne went into a phone box and called for an ambulance.

He called out to a white couple across the street; they looked at him suspiciously. The couple – Conor and Louise Taafe – had just come from a meeting at the local Catholic Church. Their first thought was that Stephen and Duwayne had been in a fight or that they were about to commit a mugging. A second set of white looks, albeit more ambivalent and more fearful. Sensing that something was wrong, the Taafes went to attend Stephen who had collapsed on the pavement. The police officers who had arrived did little to attend to him. Louise Taafe tried to speak to Stephen. Conor Taafe commented at the inquiry into Stephen's death that they feared he was mortally wounded:

> Louise and I both knew that hearing is one of the last things to go, and so, while he was there, she said: 'You are loved. You are loved.' I had some blood on my hands. When I went home ... and washed the blood off my hands with some water in a container, and there is a rose bush in our back garden, a very, very old, huge rose bush – a rose tree is I suppose more appropriate – and I poured the water with his blood in it into the bottom of that rose tree. So in a way I suppose he is kind of living on a bit.
>
> Norton-Taylor, 1999, p. 37

The care the Taafes demonstrated is deeply poignant, yet their initial reaction to Duwayne and Stephen was one of suspicion (Cathcart, 1999, pp. 11–12). Whiteness coloured what the Taafes saw – two young black boys in the street after dark, and viewed as an immediate threat.

The police officers' assessment at the crime scene amounted to a third set of white looks. Perhaps the most damning finding contained within the

Macpherson Report, the result of the public inquiry into the murder, is the account of the racism that the Lawrence family and Duwayne Brooks suffered at the hands of the police (The Stephen Lawrence Inquiry, 1999a). This is best represented in the words of their own statements. First Duwayne Brooks, who said of the attitude of the police at the scene of the crime:

> I was pacing up and down, up and down. I was desperate for the ambulance. It was taking too long. I was frightened by the amount of blood Steve was losing. I saw his life fading away. I didn't know what to do to help him. I was frightened I would do something wrong.
>
> WPC Bethel said, 'How did it start? Did they chase you for nothing?' I said one of them shouted, "What, what nigger?" She asked me if I had any weapons on me. She was treating me like she was suspicious of me, not like she wanted to help. If she had asked me for more details of the boys' descriptions or what they were wearing I would have told her. Those would have been sensible questions ...
>
> I was driven to Plumstead police station. I now know that in their statements the police said I broke a window in the front office. I didn't. I wasn't even in the front office. It just shows they were treating me like a criminal and not like a victim. They kept saying, 'Are you sure they said "What, what nigger?"'. I said, 'I am telling the truth.' A senior officer said to me, 'You mean you've done nothing wrong to provoke them in any way?' I said, 'No, we were just waiting for a bus.'
>
> Norton-Taylor, 1999, pp. 95–6

What comes through so powerfully in this testimony is the extent to which Duwayne and Stephen are viewed by the police as in circumstances of their own making. Two black boys being attacked spells – in the eyes of white police-men and women – 'gang violence', not a racist attack.

Doreen and Neville Lawrence's treatment at the hands of the police showed incredible insensitivity. They were seen to be the puppets of 'political agita-tors', being manipulated by 'outsiders'. In her evidence to the inquiry, Doreen Lawrence outlined this:

> Basically, we were seen as gullible simpletons. This is best shown by Detective Chief Superintendent Ilsey's comment that I had obviously been primed to ask questions. Presumably, there is no possibility of me being an intelligent, black woman with thoughts of her own who is able to ask questions for herself. We were patronised and were fobbed off ...
>
> The Stephen Lawrence Inquiry, 1999a, p. 11

and Neville Lawrence:

> It is clear to me that the police come in with the idea that the family of black victims are violent criminals who are not to be trusted.
>
> The Stephen Lawrence Inquiry, 1999a, p. 12

Figure 7.1 Bus stop Well Hall Road, Eltham
Source: photograph by author

Within these white looks, black victims of racist crime are defined as either gang members or simpletons being manipulated by political agitators. Whiteness here is a way of seeing that leads to a way of acting. In the case of racist perpetrators, it is the split-second glance from which black targets of violence are identified, attacked and ultimately killed. Equally, the fear and apprehension of the Taafes, the most sensitive and caring witnesses at the crime scene, are products of the association conjured-up by seeing two black boys in distress after dark. Finally, what the police saw was coloured by the damaged filter of white apprehension. Each of these white looks had different outcomes, but they shared some of the same qualities – that is, they marked out the presence of the two black boys in this neighbourhood either for attack, fear or suspicion. Racism murders, divides and inflicts brutal forms of harm. It also damages the ability of both victim *and* perpetrator to apprehend, make sense of and engage with the social world. Duwayne Brooks later said in his statement to the inquiry that Stephen didn't know how to read the signs, he didn't understand the danger.

There are three bus stops: two on the right-hand side and one on the left. As I walked up the right-hand side of the road, the first bus stop was covered with National Front (NF)[4] graffiti – some of it was in black marker pen, but most was actually etched into the paint of the bus stop. One said 'This is the NF bus stop.' Tens of NF emblems were scratched into the lamp-post and onto the bus shelter itself – there were a few things written on the seats and an NF sign on the rubbish bin, written in black 'magic marker' ink. I imagined the

Figure 7.2   Police incident board at the Stephen Lawrence memorial
Source: photograph by author

---

[4]The National Front is one of Britain's openly racist political parties. It had its political height in the 1970s and has been overtaken in terms of size by the British National Party. The NF emblem is however commonly used opportunistically as potent symbols for racists who have nothing to do with the official party.

many hands it must have taken to etch this defacement. Still other hands have tried to scribble over, scratch out and cover the fascist emblems. As I walked past, a black person was standing at the bus stop.

Still further up the road, I saw an orange police placard that referred to the incident where Stephen Lawrence's plaque had been defaced. I walked past the placard – this is about 15 yards before the second bus stop. On the ground a small plaque is set into the paving stones, which had clearly had white paint cleaned off it recently. The stone is a simple square granite tablet and written in gold lettering are the words: 'IN MEMORY OF STEPHEN LAWRENCE – 13.9.1974 – 22.4.1993 MAY HE REST IN PEACE.' The sight of the words puts a different inflection on Benjamin's (1992) famous ambulant invitation to go 'botanizing on the asphalt' (p. 36) (to humanise the urban environment).

This area had seen murderous racism before: Roland Adams had his life taken by a gang in neighbouring Thamesmead and Rohid Duggal was killed outside a kebab shop in Eltham (see Hewitt, 2006, pp. 44–9).[5,6] Almost immediately after Stephen Lawrence was killed, anti-racist activists and concerned ordinary Londoners laid flowers at the roadside where he collapsed.[7] It is as if the place where he fell has come to symbolise the wound of racism: people come to this place either to heal or deepen it.

'WALL OF SILENCE': SPEAKING AND SHOWING

After the attack 26 different people from within the area gave evidence implicating the five main suspects: Neil Acourt, Jamie Acourt, David Norris, Gary Dobson and Luke Knight. Information was also passed directly to the Lawrence family. Despite this, the police complained of a 'wall of silence' in the local community (Jeffrey, 1999). Doreen Lawrence commented later:

> Every time we tried to pass this information to the police, they just didn't seem interested. They kept insisting there was a wall of silence but the only wall of silence was around their ears.

The five suspects had a history of violence, a fixation with knives and vituperative racism. The Acourt brothers, self-styled gangsters, called themselves the 'Eltham Krays'.[8] It was not until 7 May that the police arrested the main suspects and made them appear in an identity parade. The police investigation

[5] Roland Adams, a 15-year-old black boy, was stabbed fatally at a bus stop on Friday, 21 February 1991.
[6] Sixteen-year-old Rohid Duggal was stabbed in the heart by a gang of white youths in June 1992.
[7] 'Kick Out the BNP', *Eltham and Greenwich Times*, Thursday, 29 April 1993.
[8] After Ronnie and Reggie Kray, the infamous east London gangsters who rose to prominence in London's gangland during the 1950s and 1960s.

was a complete mess: an appalling catalogue of mistakes, along with displays of ignorance and bigotry with regard to Stephen's parents, Neville and Doreen Lawrence, and Duwayne Brooks, Stephen's friend.

In April 1995, the family took out a private prosecution. It was heard a year later in the High Court but the case against Neil and Jamie Acourt and David Norris was dropped at the committal proceedings. It is here that the family first saw the surveillance tape that the police had recorded covertly at Gary Dobson's flat in Footscray over a 3-week period in December 1994. Doreen Lawrence (2006) reflected:

> It was clear that somehow the boys sensed that someone had been in the flat. As if they had an idea that someone was listening … But they did not realise that it was not just an audio-recording, that there would also be visual images. Since they were unaware that a camera was watching, their body language was unguarded and all the more shocking.
>
> p. 140

Doctor Stephen Shepherd described in court the way that Stephen Lawrence had been struck with a large knife from above, downward into his chest. The video evidence showed the young men's obsession with knives. Neil Acourt, the elder brother, rehearsed stabbing moves with a foot-long knife including a motion like the arc of a bowler's action. This dance of white violence was repeated over and over again. Stephen Lawrence's murderer used a similar motion to strike the fatal blow. Doreen Lawrence (2006) described it later as an 'obscene performance … It was truly impossible to comprehend how these boys' parents could watch that video without showing any sign of shame' (p. 145). The surveillance video also showed how the obsession with knives became part of the choreography of violence that was rehearsed and taught. It was sometimes directed playfully at members of the friendship group as a means to maintain a pecking order. While the boys were cocky and shameless in the courtroom, they did not look at the bereaved family. Their mothers did not try to hide their contempt and, from just a few feet away, appeared to glare openly and scowl at Doreen Lawrence.

The Lawrence family lodged a formal complaint against the police officers involved. After the inquest verdict, the Lawrence family met the then Shadow Home Secretary, Labour MP Jack Straw. Straw initially proposed a general investigation into the state of race relations, but was dissuaded by Doreen Lawrence who insisted that any inquiry should be into the events surrounding her son's murder. In July, after the May 1997 general election, the new Labour Home Secretary, Jack Straw, announced that a judicial public inquiry was to be set up and chaired by Sir William Macpherson. This was to be started after the Police Complaints Authority report into the investigation conducted by the Kent Constabulary. In December 1997, the report went to the Home Secretary and revealed that the handling of the Lawrence investigation showed 'significant weaknesses, omissions and lost opportunities in the conduct of the case' (Norton-Taylor, 1999, p. 12).

These are the events that led up to the Stephen Lawrence inquiry. It was a historic event. It sat for 59 days in Hannibal House in the Elephant and Castle. It called the alleged murderers to answer questions along with the key figures in the police force that had bungled the investigation. The first part of the investigation focused on 'the matters arising from the death of Stephen Lawrence.' In addition, the inquiry sat for a further day to 'identify the lessons to be learned for the investigation and prosecution of racially motivated crimes.' Eighty-eight people gave evidence; thousands of pages of transcription were produced. The report described Stephen's parents, Neville and Doreen Lawrence, as the mainsprings of the inquiry. They attended virtually all the hearings. Eugene McLaughlin and Karim Murji (1999) concluded:

> Anyone who attended the inquiry at the Elephant and Castle in London soon realised that something quite extraordinary and unprecedented was happening.
>
> p. 372

It was revealing to watch the five suspects and the police being brought to give evidence before the inquiry. It was not just the Acourts, Norris, Knight and Dobson who had hidden in silence. It had also been the police officers. Doreen Lawrence said in her statement after the coroner's inquest:

> The wall of silence was not only in the surrounding area where my son was killed, but with the officers who were supposed to be investigating the crime.
>
> The Stephen Lawrence Inquiry, 1999a, p. 300

The inquiry was a matter of reckoning with the perpetrators of the injustice suffered by the Lawrence family. This bringing to book was a daily spectacle in the news media.

Bourdieu (1977) once wrote that 'a whole system of values reappear in gesture and movements of the body …' (p. 94). Watching the police officers involved in the botched investigation walk into the inquiry, holding their papers tightly, symbolised the resistance on their part to admit to any wrong-doing. The fact that the inquiry took place in inner London was significant, because it meant that it was hosted in a profoundly multicultural and ethni-cally mixed environment. It was in many respects holding the inquiry there that forced the perpetrators to return to a world they had fled. One of the general patterns in south-east London is that white working-class communities have moved out of the inner city into the white suburbs like Eltham and Welling. This is often referred to as 'white flight'. The five suspects fought tooth and nail to avoid appearing. On 29 and 30 June, they appeared and ran the gauntlet of a hostile crowd. Their image of racism was not what our political culture has come to expect – that is, the Nazi, the shaven-headed skinhead with bovver boots. Rather, they were stylishly dressed in suits and wearing Ben Sherman shirts and Armani sunglasses. What was disturbing was how familiar they looked.[9] They could have been one of any number of friends or relatives. They swaggered and bowled into the inquiry,[10] embodying a form of masculine performance that announced readiness, an unrepentant mastery of their bodies as they moved through this hostile space. Only Dobson looked scared. The rest embraced the challenge. Neil Acourt was 'giving it', his hand in front of him, arms at 30 degree and his fingers twitched in invitation to his adversaries to 'come on'. Inside the inquiry they said nothing, admitted nothing and accepted nothing.

The Macpherson Report commented:

> All five suspects came into the witness box and answered questions under oath or affirmation. To say that they gave evidence would be to dignify their appearance. They all relied upon alleged lack of memory. They showed themselves to be arrogant and dismissive.
>
> The Stephen Lawrence Inquiry 1999a, p. 40

In particular, the five suspects were confronted with the video surveillance evidence recorded by the police in December 1994. The report referred to this material as 'prolonged and appalling words which sully the paper upon which they have been recorded'. The transcriptions of this material are truly appalling.

The suspects clearly thought they were only being listened to but their body language and facial expressions were also being filmed clearly.[11] They mocked the police with staged commentary on the murder and the investigation. Neil Acourt and David Norris were sneering and contemptuous. In one extract recorded on the evening of 7 December 1994, Acourt teased his invisible eavesdroppers:

> And they ain't got nothing still. We ain't done nothing that's what I mean, there's none of us done fuck all. But the thing that makes me laugh, Dave, they're gonna be doing it for the rest of our lives mate and I am just gonna be laughing all the way to Leeds.
>
> The Stephen Lawrence Inquiry 1999b, p. 21

A few moments later, Neil Acourt says of the victims:'I fancy they've had a crack deal me self I fancy.' Norris replies:'Probably had a bit of a toot or something or had a bit of crack it's all gone wrong, the coon's got knackered up and all of a sudden four innocent people are getting done for it.' Neil Acourt says:'Yeah, that's what I fancy has happened.' Norris continues:'That's definitely what's happened Neil. Every time it [Stephen's murder] comes on

---

[9] Doreen Lawrence commented: 'And though I might have expected to see evil-looking monsters, these seemed such ordinary young men – cocky, self-assured, threatening, certainly, but those were things that could be said of many young men on the street' (Lawrence, 2006, p. 143).

[10] 'The bowl' is a specific form of working-class masculine embodiment. See Garry Robson (2000, pp. 79–81).

[11] See *The Stephen Lawrence Inquiry*, 1999b, p. 19.

the news – the real people are sitting laughing their nuts off ...' 'What real people?', says Neil Acourt. Norris repeats: 'Yeah the real people are sitting laughing their nuts off.' Luke Knight adds: 'Think they've got away with it mate, fucking scot free.'

Unable to resist, but unaware that he is looking straight into the surveillance camera, Neil Acourt says, laughing: 'Yeah they're definitely doing that.' Doreen Lawrence commented in her autobiography: 'The look of gloating triumph on his face as he said that will live with me for the rest of my life' (Lawrence, 2006, p. 150).

The five suspects' apparent 'loss' of memory was revealed in other ways. Connerton (1989) has written that memory and history can be 'sedimented in the body', that in walks, gestures and bodily practices are stored an embodied history (p. 102). This could also apply to the ways in which we might interpret Neil Acourt's laughing into the face of the police surveillance camera, or his body language as he left Hannibal House. As they 'bowled' out of the inquiry to face a hostile crowd, their violence and aggression were manifest in every movement. The expressions on their contorted faces spoke volumes and left little doubt. Watching the scenes acted out on the walkway to the inquiry was like seeing a microcosm of racism in south London.

Gadd, Dixon and Jefferson (2005) have shown in their study of racist perpetrators in North Staffordshire that the accounts of race and racism from the sample of perpetrators were broadly the same as those offered in focus groups with members of the wider community. The profiles of the perpetrators were often complex, sometimes ambiguous and not hardened in terms of their commitment to racism:

> What their life stories did reveal were patterns of severe, occasionally extreme, material and emotional deprivation combined with, or compounded by, histories of other kinds of offending behaviour, criminalisation, domestic violence, mental illness, and the abuse of drugs and alcohol.
>
> Gadd et al., 2005, p. 9

In line with the broader argument within this chapter, this suggests the importance of developing close attention to the varied ways in which social actors are positioned in relation to racism, and the conditions – biographical, contextual and historical – that furnish the social stage for violent racism.

CONCLUSION

The Institute of Race Relations commented in 2006 that there have been 68 racist murders since Stephen Lawrence (Athwal and Kundnani, 2006). Violent racism continues to stain the streets of Britain with blood, while the public at large and the media in general have moved their attention and concerns to new moral anxieties about violent youth. In the summer of 2008, the Ministry of Justice reported record numbers of racist incidents in Britain, with more than 61,000 cases being reported in 2006–07.[12] The rise was uneven nationally with London actually registering a lower rate of increase compared to other parts of the country. In the years that followed Stephen's murder, violent racism has remained a strong feature of national life. However, the commitment to addressing racist violence seems to have waned. The Runnymede Trust concluded in a recent report:

> Current work to challenge attitudes to prevent racist violence is surprisingly scarce given the scale of the problem.
>
> Isal, 2005, p. 1

The news media has become less attentive to racist violence, often with the result that these cases pass only as local news items.[13]

In this final section I want to sum up the main argument, and also to reflect on some of the lessons contained in the Stephen Lawrence case concerning the cultural mechanisms of racist violence. The first and fundamental point is that racism thinks with its eyes. It is within the racist's look that black and brown people are identified as targets. The white look, as described here, identifies and marks the victim as a target and a presence 'out of place'. Beyond this though, these white looks involve making judgements too, so that the young victims of violent crime are defined as somehow implicated in these circumstances that are ultimately of their own making (that is, through the key motifs of black criminality: knife crime, gang conflicts, mugging). Here whiteness is best understood not as defined by the colour of the skin but by a particular pattern of seeing, acting and making sense of the world. While these social actors are positioned very differently in relation to a violent event, they can also share ideas about racial conduct, propriety, and patterns of political and criminal behaviour. These white looks can distort the apprehension of even the most sensitive and caring witnesses. This means that the way racial violence is defined, interpreted and evaluated becomes part of the problem itself, and in need of careful critical assessment.

Second, the perpetrators of racist violence as shown in this case can inhabit a life world in which racism and violence become habitual. Racist incidents, then, may not simply be one-off violent episodes but rather emerge from mundane rehearsals of violence to reactions to the TV and banter between friends. The knife here becomes a part of everyday life, not just a tool of self-defence (see Chapter 14), and acts as a symbol of masculine power, command and status. The surveillance material of the five main suspects in the Lawrence case showed how this works within the embodied, habitual realm, where violent actions are rehearsed and choreographed playfully within the group

---

[12] Nigel Morris 'Huge rise in number of racist attacks', *The Independent*, 9 July 2008.
[13] I am thinking here, in particular, of the case of Tarsen Nahar who was beaten to death by a white teenager in Hayes, Middlesex, in April 2007. See *Ealing Times*, Wednesday, 25 June, 2008.

itself. A related point here is that power hides in silence – within the unspoken, the assumed, the taken for granted. In a sense, the inquiry into Stephen Lawrence's murder attempted to name this process in defining institutional racism as 'unwitting' or tacit acts that have racism outcomes. Read sceptically, this way of understanding unintentional racism can appear to divert attention from institutional responsibility. It is suggested that such active inactions are directly implicated in racism in ways that are sometimes premeditated and disparaging, sometimes ignorant and negligent, sometimes self-exculpating.

Third, racism draws maps of belonging within the physical and social land-scape; it is ultimately a territorial form of power that seeks to define who belongs and who is 'out of place'. These maps are not consistent or stable: they are implicit within the stories people tell about a place, or they are drawn and marked through practices like racist graffiti. This is one way of defining com-munity and writing over the landscape. However, they do not simply emerge as the result of some natural order within the city. They are written, made and projected on to the landscape as a way of claiming the meanings of a locality and who can belong to it.

Finally, the inquiry into the failure to bring Stephen Lawrence's killers to justice was a historic moment in the development in the history of anti-racism in Britain. However, the sense of urgency about tackling violent racism has been replaced by other concerns about youth violence, gangs and weaponry. It is important to remember that the knife has also been a staple weapon within the arsenal of violent racism. Politicians and journalists commenting on the current 'crisis of knife crime' or the 'weaponisation of youth' have over-looked this fact. Virtually all the moral panics about youth since the war contain elements of historical amnesia. However, it is particularly important in the context of a hardening in attitudes to difference that a commitment to understand racism – both violent and demotic – is placed more centrally within the public agenda on young people and violence.

REFERENCES

Athwal, H. and Kundnani, A. (2006) Sixty-eight racist murders since Stephen Lawrence. *Institute of Race Relations News*, April, Institute of Race Relations, London.

Back, L. (2010) Whiteness in the dramaturgy of racism, in *Handbook of Race and Ethnic Studies* (eds P. Hill-Collins and J. Solomos), Sage, London.

Benjamin, W. (1992) *Charles Baudelaire: A Lyric Poet in the Era of High Capitalism*, Verso, London.

Benjamin, W. (1997) *One-way Street*, Verso, London.

Bourdieu, P. (1977) *Outline of a Theory of Practice*. Cambridge University Press, Cambridge.

Cathcart, B. (1999) *The Case of Stephen Lawrence*, Viking, London.

Connerton, P. (1989) *How Societies Remember*, Cambridge University Press, Cambridge.

Gadd, D., Dixon, B. and Jefferson, T. (2005) *Why Do They Do It? Racial Harassment in North Staffordshire*, The Centre for Criminological Research, Keele University, Staffordshire.

Gilroy, P. (2008) *There Ain't No Black in the Union Jack: The Cultural Politics of Race and Nation*, Routledge, London.

Hartigan, J. (1999) *Racial Situations: Class Predicaments of Whiteness in Detroit*, Princeton University Press, Princeton, NJ.

Hewitt, R. (2006) *White Backlash and the Politics of Multiculturalism*, Cambridge University Press, Cambridge.

Hooks, B. (1992) *Black Looks: Race and Representation*, South End Press, Boston, MA.

Ignatiev, N. and Garvey, J. (1996) (eds) *Race Traitor*, Routledge, New York and London.

Isal, S. (2005) *Preventing Racist Violence*, The Runnymede Trust, London.

Jeffrey, N. (1999) The sharp end of Stephen's city. *Soundings*, **12**, 26–42.

Lawrence, D. (2006) *And Still I Rise: Seeking Justice for Stephen*, Faber and Faber, London.

McLaughlin, E. and Murji, K. (1999) After the Stephen Lawrence report. *Critical Social Policy*, **60**, 371–83.

Norton-Taylor, R. (1999) *The Colour of Justice*, Oberon Books, London.

The Stephen Lawrence Inquiry (1999a) *Report of an Inquiry by Sir William Macpherson of Cluny, Volume 1*, The Stationery Office, London.

The Stephen Lawrence Inquiry (1999b) *Report of an Inquiry by Sir William Macpherson of Cluny, Volume 2, Appendices*, The Stationery Office, London.

Ware, V. and Back, L. (2002) *Out of Whiteness: Color, Politics, and Culture*, University of Chicago Press, Chicago.

8 A Thoroughly Gendered Affair: Teenage Partner Violence and Exploitation

CHRISTINE BARTER

INTRODUCTION

This chapter addresses one of the least recognised forms of peer violence in the UK: teenage partner violence. In comparison, a significant body of US research has emerged on 'dating' violence over the past two decades, which testifies to its prevalence in teenage relationships. However, this interest has not been reflected in UK research or practice. It is unclear how applicable findings based on the US are to the UK context.

In response to this gap in our knowledge the current author, alongside colleagues, undertook a 3-year research project to explore young people's experiences of physical, emotional and sexual partner violence across eight schools in England, Scotland and Wales (see Barter *et al.*, 2009). The research findings clearly show that violence in young people's intimate relationships should be viewed as a significant child welfare problem.

The research findings were widely reported in the national media and have generated considerable policy and practice attention. The Home Office, in response to the research findings, launched a major public awareness campaign on the issue of abuse in teenage relationships (Home Office, 2010), which is to be underpinned by a school-based intervention. While the authors, who acted as consultants in the Home Office campaign, welcome this initiative, it is imperative that it is repeated and that sustained policy and practice attention is accorded to this form of intimate violence. The government's review on the sexualisation of young people by Papodoplous (2010) also drew on the research and its recommendations, and called for a longitudinal study to be undertaken on teenage partner violence. In response, the government set up the Violence Against Women and Girls (VAWG) Advisory Group whose recommendations and strategy (Department for Children, Schools and Families, 2010a) also clearly identify teenage relationship violence as a priority and call for the

Children Behaving Badly? Peer Violence Between Children and Young People
Edited by Christine Barter and David Berridge
© 2011 John Wiley & Sons Ltd.

Home Office campaign to be an annual event. Their recommendations also state that a pack for primary and secondary schools should be developed, which will build and develop the issues arising from the national campaign. The Department's response to the Advisory Group's recommendations (2010b), although supportive of many of its recommendations on gender equality and related issues, states they cannot commit to making the teenage partner abuse campaign an annual event although they will consider conducting further research in this area to underpin best practice.

This chapter will now explore the research findings that have so strongly influenced policy and practice in this area. Initially, incidence rates for the physical, sexual and emotional forms of teenage partner violence will be documented and the associated factors that may increase a young person's susceptibility to partner violence, as a recipient or assailant, will be addressed. The dynamics of teenage partner violence, including frequency, change over time and help-seeking will then be explored. In conclusion, key messages for enhancing safeguards for young people in this neglected area of child welfare will be presented.

TERMINOLOGY

Most of the US, and indeed wider international, literature has adopted the term 'dating violence' to describe this area of work. However, this terminology does not transfer well to the UK context, because young people do not use, or indeed recognise, this term. In addition, 'dating' seems to imply a degree of formality that does not necessarily reflect the diverse range of young people's intimate encounters and relationships. Similarly, Brown et al. (2007) argue that the term is outdated and restrictive. Furthermore, young people perceive the term 'domestic violence' to be something that relates to their parents rather than to themselves. Instead, the term 'partner exploitation and violence' seems more appropriate (we acknowledge this also has some limitations); to aid brevity 'partner violence' will be used in this chapter. A 'partner' was defined in the research as any young person with whom an individual had been intimate, ranging from a serious long-term boyfriend or girlfriend to a more casual partner or a one-off encounter. Importantly, terminology is not simply an interesting academic exercise because, unless appropriate definitions are used by professionals, young people may not perceive intervention as being relevant to them or their specific circumstances (Barter, 2009).

BACKGROUND

The majority of US and other international studies have used large-scale surveys to investigate the incidence rates for teenage partner violence, often across different sample communities. This body of research has testified both to its high prevalence within teenage relationships and its serious consequences for the well-being of victims and their future life prospects (Tangney et al., 1992; Harway and Liss, 1999; Smith, White and Holland, 2003). US research has also identified that teenage partner violence is associated with a range of adverse outcomes for young people, including mental health, depression and suicide (Silverman et al., 2001; Collin-Vézina, 2006). In addition, some studies indicate that adolescent partner violence is strongly associated with experiencing domestic violence in adulthood (O'Leary et al., 1989; Cleveland, Herrera and Stuewig, 2003). However, this survey-dominated approach has, with a few noticeable exceptions (see Jackson, 1999; Banister, Jakubec and Stein, 2003; Chung, 2005; Próspero, 2006; Sears et al., 2006; Silverman et al., 2006), meant that young people's own experiences, views and agency have been neglected (James, Jenks and Prout, 1998; Mullender et al., 2002). In addition, US research has largely focused on physical or sexual violence, although psychological and coercive control mechanisms have now begun to be explored.

The small number of UK studies has confirmed the impact and seriousness of teenage partner violence for young people's welfare (Hird, 2000). It is surprising that, given the critical nature of adolescence as a developmental period, so little attention has been given to this social problem (O'Keefe et al., 1986; Williams and Martinez, 1999).

PROFESSIONAL RESPONSE TO TEENAGE PARTNER VIOLENCE

Only a minority of US studies (Brown et al., 2007), and it appears none within the UK, have addressed multi-agency professional practice within this area of child welfare. Intervention work on teenage partner violence has been developed in some schools (see Chapter 15 for an evaluation of school initiatives in this area). This general disregard of peer violence may be due to the emphasis in child welfare research and practice on *adult–child* interactions, be they neglectful/abusive or in a professional context (Barter, 2009). However, recent UK governmental guidance in *Working Together to Safeguard Children* (HM Government, 2006) has, for the first time, officially recognised the need for professionals to safeguard children from harm arising from abuse or violence in their own relationships.

Concerning intimate violence, the guidance states that in cases involving sexually active children under the age of 13 there is a *presumption* that the case will be reported to social work services (HM Government, 2006, para. 5.25). For young people under 16, *consideration* must be given as to whether there should be a discussion with other agencies regarding the need for a referral, including where both parties are below this age and the relationship is consensual (para. 5.26). To assist with this assessment a risk-checklist is provided, which includes the child's living circumstances and background, age imbalance, overt aggression or power imbalances, evidence of coercion, attempts at secrecy by the partner, denial and minimisation or acceptance of the violence by the victim (para. 5.27). However, we have no information regarding practitioners' awareness of this guidance, how it is being interpreted and put into practice, either nationally or locally, and what multi-agency decision-making models and protocols are in place.

RESEARCH AIMS

Our research explored with young people their experiences of physical, emotional and sexual forms of violence in partner relationships, including their coping strategies and views on intervention. The more specific aims included exploring:

- the nature, frequency and dynamics of different forms of partner violence;
- whether any groups were particularly vulnerable to becoming victims and/ or assailants;
- the wider social processes and structures that underpin such violence.

Careful consideration was paid to ethics and consent throughout the project. A young people's and an adult advisory group provided advice and consultation throughout the 3-year project.

METHODOLOGY

The study used a multi-method approach. A confidential survey was completed by 1,353 young people, roughly the same number of girls and boys, aged between 13 and 17 years old, from eight schools in England, Scotland and Wales. A total of 91 in-depth interviews were undertaken with 62 girls and 29 boys (further details are provided in the main research report – see Barter *et al.*, 2009).

FINDINGS ON TEENAGE RELATIONSHIPS

Before we look at violence in teenage relationships, it is important to understand more about the relationships themselves and the wider factors that influenced young people's experiences in this area of their lives. Overall, 88 per cent of the young people responding to the survey reported some form of intimate relationship. A lower percentage of South Asian participants reported a relationship experience compared to all other groups. Girls' partners were generally older, and a minority had a 'much older' partner. Although we did not ask in the survey what 'much older' constituted, within the interviews girls spoke about an age-gap of around two or more years as constituting a 'much older' partner. Boys' partners had been either the same age or slightly younger.

We asked young people if they had experienced any family violence: overall, nearly a third of girls and 16 per cent of boys reported some form of violence towards themselves or another adult in their family. Comparing family violence to relationship experiences, we found that young people who reported family violence were more likely to have experienced an intimate relationship, and more likely to have experienced one at an earlier age than young people with no history of family violence. This may be as a result of young people seeking to compensate for their negative family experiences through forming external intimate relationships or, more pragmatically, it may result from young people wanting to remove themselves physically from their family situation by entering a relationship at an early age. Additionally, girls with a history of family violence had an increased likelihood of having a much older partner; the serious implications of this for their safety will be addressed later in the chapter.

INCIDENCE RATES FOR EXPERIENCING TEENAGE PARTNER VIOLENCE

PHYSICAL PARTNER VIOLENCE

The survey found that a quarter of girls and 18 per cent of boys who reported a relationship experienced some form of physical partner violence. Disconcertingly, 1 in 9 girls (but only 4% of boys) reported *severe* physical violence. However, it is only when incidence rates are looked at alongside impact that a comprehensive understanding of partner violence can emerge. Three-quarters of girls compared to 14 per cent of boys stated that the physical violence had negatively impacted on their welfare. Girls more often stated that the violence made them feel scared /frightened and upset/unhappy. This is illustrated by the following interview abstract (all names have been anonymised).

Interviewer:	Did you think that Joel loved you?
Amy:	At one point.
Int:	At one point, did it stop feeling like love at some point?
Amy:	Yeah.
Int:	Yeah what point did it stop feeling like love do you think?
Amy:	When he started hitting me and beating me up.
Int:	Did he hurt you?
Amy:	Yeah.

However, boys' evaluations concerning the impact of physical partner violence, both in the survey and interviews, were very different. In all sources of
data, boys strongly argued that they viewed girls' use of violence against them
as amusing, sometimes annoying, but none reported a negative emotional
effect:

> Callum: She tried to batter me but I'm too strong ... it's nothing ... just a laugh.

Callum's response was typical of the boys' reaction to their girlfriends' attempts
at violence. It could be argued that due to pressures to portray a 'hard', non-
emotional form of masculinity (Frosh, Phoenix and Pattman, 2002), boys found
it especially difficult to acknowledge their vulnerability to victimisation and
the negative impact this may entail. However, if this were true, it would seem
inconsistent to admit to being a victim of physical violence but then deny any
impact. The interview data showed little evidence to support a 'hidden impact'
theory. Indeed, in instances where boys reported the violence as mutual, they
had often used disproportionate force compared to their female partners:

> Int: Did she hit you first?
> Hardeep: Yes.
> Int: And were you shocked when it happened, or did you think she was
>   going to do it.
> Hardeep: I was a bit shocked ...'cos she didn't stop did she and you can't not
>   hit a girl if she's attacking you ... I think I let it happen again a few
>   more times and then I hit her forehead and she got knocked out and
>   we broke up.

In Hardeep's account, he justified his violence as a response to his girlfriend's
initial attack, although his reaction was disproportionate. Indeed, Hardeep
described a number of relationships in which his use of violence was justified
due to his partners' actions. As the interview progressed, Hardeep often
changed the context of incidents, making the researcher question the authen-
ticity of the partner's role. Thus, 'saving face' may be a more accurate explanation for his violence than self-defence. Consequently, we need to be cautious
in accepting descriptions of teenage partner violence as mutual or reciprocal
because these imply a degree of equality in relation to physical force and
impact. Our research clearly shows this is rarely the case.

The incidence rates for physical violence found in our research are comparable to those identified in US studies, where between a third and a half, both
of female and male teenage respondents, report physical aggression (O'Keefe
et al., 1986; Foshee *et al.*, 1996; Williams and Martinez, 1999; Halpern *et al.*,
2001; Hickman, Jaycox and Aronoff, 2004). Our reported incidence rates for
boys are somewhat lower than those found in some US studies. However, our
findings reflect previous research, which has clearly demonstrated that girls
generally suffer more severe forms of physical violence than do boys (Foshee,
1996; Jackson, Cram and Seymour, 2000; Silverman *et al.*, 2001; Ackard
Neumark-Sztainer and Hannan, 2003; Arriaga and Foshee, 2004).

Some commentators, primarily using US survey-based findings, have argued that boys and girls experience similar levels of physical violence from their partners (Foshee, 1996; Arriaga and Foshee, 2004; Roberts, Auinger and Klein, 2005). This has led to propositions that teenage partner violence demonstrates a greater degree of gender symmetry compared to adult domestic violence, where women are predominantly the victims. As demonstrated in both our survey and in-depth interview findings, once *impact* is acknowledged, the gender-symmetry contention becomes less plausible. Thus, when incidence rates for physical violence are contextualised by impact, it is clear that for girls physical violence from a partner represents a significant social problem that negatively affects their well-being. This is not the case for boys. In addition, the interview findings show how, for girls, physical and sexual violence are intrinsically linked. In many accounts, girls' first experience of physical violence often occurred due to their refusal to undertake certain sexual acts:

> Sian: I only went out with him for a week. And then ...' cos I didn't want to do what he wanted to [have sexual intercourse] he just started ... picking on me and hitting me.

We now consider young people's experiences of sexual violence before focusing on emotional forms of exploitation and control.

SEXUAL PARTNER VIOLENCE

Previous findings concerning sexual coercion and violence in teenage relationships have found disparate incidence rates, ranging from 4 per cent to as high as 78 per cent. This wide variation reflects, in part, a definitional problem of what constitutes sexually aggressive acts. For example, Muehlenhard and Linton (1987) found that 15 per cent of their sample had been rape victims, although as many as 80 per cent had experienced some form of unwanted sexual activity from their boyfriends, mostly forced kissing and touching. Others report levels more consistent with our own findings – for example, Ackard *et al.* (2003) found that 4 per cent of adolescent girls reported being physically forced into sexual contact against their will in a relationship or during a date. However, what nearly all studies consistently show, as does ours, is that girls are most likely to be victims and males perpetrators (Lane and Gwartney-Gibbs, 1985; Roscoe and Callahan, 1985; Muehlenhard and Linton, 1987; Gamache, 1991; Silverman *et al.*, 2001; Ackard *et al.*, 2003.)

Our research sought to overcome this methodological dilemma by including in the survey a range of specific aspects of sexual violence, and analysing responses both on an individual basis and as a combined category of sexual violence. Four questions were used in the survey to gauge the level of sexual violence in young people's relationships. The questions were designed to reflect the role that both 'pressure' and physical force can play in perpetrating sexual violence. In addition, two levels of sexual exploitation were investigated. First, a wide definition of sexual violence was utilised, which asked if respondents had ever been 'pressured' or physically forced 'to do something sexual, such as kissing, touching or something else'. This was followed by a more restricted definition that focused on ever being pressured or forced into 'having sexual intercourse'.

As anticipated, girls were significantly more likely than boys to experience sexual violence. Combining all reported incidents, no fewer than *1 in 3* girls and 16 per cent of boys reported some form of sexual partner violence. Breaking this down into the specific questions asked, for both genders 'pressure' was used much more frequently by partners than physical force. Concentrating on girls' experiences first, just over a quarter of girls stated that they felt pressured into doing something sexual against their wishes. Worryingly, more than one girl in eight had been physically forced into doing something sexual. In relation to sexual intercourse, 16 per cent of girls reported that they had been pressured into intercourse and as many as 6 per cent stated they had been physically forced – in other words, raped:

> Louise: Um ... well yeah, he was pressuring me a lot. But there'd be a few times where he was like really trying to force me ... yeah it was a few times he did yeah.

It was striking that girls as young as 13 were as likely as those aged 16 to experience sexual violence. However, older girls were more likely to report being physically forced. It may be that, as girls get older, they are more able to resist sexual pressure and therefore some boys resort to physical force. However, we should not assume that sexual coercion involving persistent pressure is less harmful to girls' well-being than the use of physical force. Our survey findings did not show any significant difference between impact ratings for pressure compared to the use of force. This is further elaborated within the interview data. For girls, issues of self-blame were very prominent, especially in relation to sexual coercion, where girls felt they had 'given in' to sexual pressure from their partners. Often it was this aspect of the sexual violence, rather than the act itself, that girls said affected them in the long term. For example:

> Rebecca: He tried making me, he like, he was like oh, he kept trying to make me have sex with him and I was like, and first of all I was like 'no no no' and then he was like trying kissing my neck and stuff like that to try and make me do it ... I was like 'no no no' because I hadn't done it before he was like 'go on, go on, go on' and I was like 'no' and then I finally like give in to him and we went off to go and do it ... I was like 'no I can't I can't' and he, oh my god, and he made me ... and then I done it and it was proper horrible and I'm never doing it again but it was horrible and I can't believe I done it.

Boys reported lower levels of sexual violence, although some anomalies exist that call into question the validity of their responses; this will be addressed shortly. Overall, 15 per cent of boys reported being pressured to undertake something sexual against their wishes, with six per cent stating that physical force had been used. The same proportion of males (6%) stated that their partner had pressured them into sexual intercourse and 3 per cent reported physical force in relation to sexual intercourse. When we looked more closely at boys' sexual victimisation, we found that a group of boys, each aged 14, from the same school had reported high levels of sexual violence from female partners. It may be that this school had a specific problem with female perpetrators of violence towards 14-year-old boys or, and perhaps more realistically, these youths were untruthful in their answers. None of the boys who were interviewed stated that they had experienced sexual violence or used physical force themselves for sexual advantage. However, boys did reveal a range of coercive 'tactics' they used to pressure girls into sexual contact. In the one group interview undertaken with boys, the participants responded to descriptions of each others' coercive tactics with admiration, illustrating how male peers reinforce the use and acceptability of sexual coercion.

EMOTIONAL PARTNER VIOLENCE

Emotional forms of violence are possibly the most difficult to recognise and quantify, due to the wide range of behaviours that may constitute victimisation. Stark (2009), based on his research with adults, argues that what he terms 'coercive control' is the most prevalent form of domestic violence, because it underpins both physical and sexual forms of intimate violence, but is often the most hidden form of abuse. Stark argues that this is due to the individualised form this abuse takes, with perpetrators targeting specific behaviour at their victims, which becomes meaningful only when placed within the wider context of an abusive history. Consequently, the complexity of emotional violence, and the wide range of behaviours it can comprise, makes it difficult to capture in a self-completion survey. Eight questions were used in our survey to ascertain the incidence of this form of violence in young people's relationships. Each was designed to assess a particular aspect of emotional violence: from harming a young person's self-esteem through ridiculing them, making negative remarks, surveillance, to controlling behaviour including threats of violence. By examining responses to the questions individually, a gender divide became more apparent.

For each of the eight components of emotional violence, a higher proportion of girls than boys reported victimisation. However, looking at which types of emotional violence young people were most likely to experience, a similar pattern emerges for both girls and boys. The most commonly experienced form of emotional violence, irrespective of gender, was being made fun of; nearly half of girls and a third of boys reported this. The second most frequently reported behaviour was constantly being checked-up on by partners; again slightly more girls than boys reported this form of control. Analysis of overt forms of controlling behaviour, determined by asking young people if their partners ever told them whom they could see and where they could go, produced a much more distinct gender divide. One in three girls reported experiencing this, compared to just over one in eight boys. Similarly, more direct forms of emotional violence were also more prominent for girls. Just over a third of girls reported that their partners had shouted at them, screamed in their face or called them hurtful names. A similar proportion of girls also stated that their partners said negative things about their appearance, body, friends or family. In comparison, one in five boys reported being shouted at and only 15 per cent experienced negative comments about them or their families.

Overall, nearly three-quarters of girls and half of boys who had experienced a relationship reported emotional partner violence. The majority of these young people recorded more than one form of emotional violence. As with both physical and sexual forms of violence, more girls than boys added that it had had a negative effect on their welfare, although proportionally fewer participants reported a negative impact compared with other forms of violence. A third of girls and 6 per cent of boys stated that the emotional violence had negatively affected their well-being. Looking more closely at the findings, it is clear that participants who experienced an isolated form of emotional abuse, such as being shouted at or called a name, generally did not report a negative outcome. Indeed, it may be unrealistic to expect young people, or indeed adults, never to lose their temper. It is important to recognise that a minority of girls who experienced an isolated incident of emotional harm also reported a negative outcome.

This creates a dilemma for professionals. It seems reasonable to assume that these limited experiences do not always require a professional response. If professional responses seek to 'problematise' actions, which the vast majority of young people view as insignificant, this may result in young people viewing the intervention programme as inappropriate and unrealistic. However, professionals also need to assist young people to question if some aspects of emotional violence may hold unrecognised implications for their welfare. This is a difficult balance to achieve. Practitioners need to ensure that young people do not feel that their experiences and views are ignored, or invalidated, while at the same time challenging normative expectations around relationship behaviours. It was interesting that in interviews for the study, girls often began to question behaviours that they had previously viewed as acceptable, or at least an expected aspect of teenage relationships. Thus, it appears that the actual process of describing experiences, which may initially be viewed as normal, may enable girls to begin to question the acceptability of their partner's actions and intentions.

Yet, in a number of interviews, the level of coercive control in girls' relationships was highly worrying. Girls were subject to high levels of control over where they could go, whom they could see or what they could do. Some girls were under constant surveillance through the use of on-line technologies, mobile telephones and text messaging. Control could result in isolation from peer networks, as in the following situation:

Emma: Like when I'd be out with my friends and he'd drag me off and say he didn't want me out any longer, and I'd got to go in and it could be like half-past six.

In some cases, girls were unsure if their partner's behaviour was caring concern or coercive control. Many girls often stated that they were too scared of their partner's reaction to challenge their behaviour. Boys did not experience this fear; they mainly ignored their partner's attempts at control, or simply ended the relationship:

Int: How did you deal with it [constant checking up by phone]?
Josh: I turned my phone off.

Thus, and in keeping with previous research findings, while both boys and girls use verbal violence and control mechanisms, the impact of these on girls appears to be much greater than for boys (Lavoie, Robitaille and Hébert, 2000; Sears *et al.*, 2006).

IMPLICATIONS OF HOW PARTNER VIOLENCE IS VIEWED BY YOUNG PEOPLE

The above research findings on the impact of violence provide the wider context in which teenage partner exploitation needs to be viewed. If boys view the impact of their own victimisation as negligible, they may apply this under-standing to their actions. They may believe that their partners are also unaf-fected by their use of violence. These observations were upheld in the interviews with boys, who characterised their own use of violence as 'messing around'. In contrast, girls' narratives around their partners' explanations of their violence as 'messing around' were fundamentally different. There is a need for boys to be made aware of the negative consequences of their behaviour within rela-tionships. It may also be that boys are aware of their actions, as evidenced in some of the interviews, but are unrepentant.

This is not to imply that boys' experiences of victimisation should be ignored. It is important to recognise that, at least for a minority of boys, their experiences resulted in a negative impact. For these boys, the impact of the violence may be especially difficult to deal with due to the attitudes of their peers. Nevertheless, we must be cautious that attention to this small minority of male teenage victims does not detract from the much wider, and more significant, experiences of girls.

NATURE OF VIOLENCE

It is important to understand how violence changes, either in intensity or nature, over time. To explore this, we asked our participants if the violent behaviours stopped, stayed the same or worsened. With regards to the behaviour stopping, we do not know if this was due to the relationship ending or a discontinuation of the behaviour itself. Again, gender divisions emerged in the young people's responses. For the majority of boys, the violence stopped. Fewer girls reported this. For girls, the violence was much more likely to stay the same or escalate. We can extrapolate from these figures that the majority of girls remained in a relationship after the violence occurred, reinforcing previous US research findings (Sugarman and Hotaling, 1989; Bergman, 1992; Jackson et al., 2000). This has led commentators to conclude that, although violence is associated with emotional trauma and fear, in itself it is insufficient to terminate a relationship (Henton et al., 1983; Roscoe and Callahan, 1985). Many of the girls we spoke to remained in the violent relationship, often for some considerable time. It may be that fears around repercussions for leaving a violent partner inhibit leaving. Or perhaps girls' desire to have a boyfriend, and the social acceptance this brings, outweighs their desire to leave (Hird, 2000; Banister et al., 2003). Our interview data support both these contentions.

We should not presume that leaving a violent relationship will necessarily reduce a young person's risk of serious harm. Research findings on adult experiences of domestic violence clearly show that ending a violent relationship can be the most dangerous time for survivors (Abrahams, 2007). This was supported in our interview findings. Even when girls were able to leave a violent partner, the violence did not necessarily stop and in some cases it resulted in an escalation of violence from the ex-partner. They knew where the girls went to school, how they got there and where their friends lived. As most girls had not told any adults about their experiences, their ability to protect themselves from their ex-boyfriend's violence was severely limited.

HELP SEEKING

For all three forms of violence, young people either told no-one or, if they approached someone for assistance, this was most often a peer. Although in many cases friends provided a valuable source of support, the interviews also showed that some peers held inappropriate views regarding the acceptability of violence:

> Moira: Everybody does it [control], I thought he was weird and then I talked
>   to my friends and all their boyfriends are the same.

Only a minority of participants told an adult about the violence, including their parents. Professionals were even less likely to be approached for help. These worrying findings reflect previous research, which consistently highlights the reluctance of young people to approach adults for assistance in this area (Watson *et al.*, 2001; Western Australia Crime Research Centre and Donovan Research, 2001; Ocampo, Shelley and Jaycox, 2007). It is obviously of great concern that the vast majority of young people feel unable, or are unwilling, to talk with their parents or other adults about these very important issues. Our interviews showed that school learning mentors could be an exception to this rule:

Tanisha: She's [school mentor] really supportive, she understands and knows what our lives are like at home.

FACTORS ASSOCIATED WITH EXPERIENCING TEENAGE PARTNER VIOLENCE

FAMILY AND PEER VIOLENCE

US research has identified a range of risk factors that may increase a teenager's susceptibility to partner violence. These risk factors include previous experiences of parental domestic violence, physical and sexual abuse, and violent peer groups (Roscoe and Callahan, 1985; O'Keefe, Brockopp and Chew, 1986; Smith and Williams, 1992; O'Keefe, 1998; Wolfe *et al.*, 2001a; Simonelli *et al.*, 2002; Whitfield *et al.*, 2003). Our research also found that family and peer violence were associated with increased susceptibility to all forms of partner violence. However, having an aggressive peer group was identified as a greater risk than family violence for boys' instigation of partner violence.

OLDER MALE PARTNERS

Having an older partner, and especially a 'much older' partner, was a significant risk factor for girls. Overall, *three-quarters* of girls with a 'much older' partner experienced physical violence, *80 per cent* emotional violence and *75 per cent* sexual violence. All the girls interviewed who had a 'much older' partner, defined by girls as being at least two years older, experienced some form of violence. The interviews showed that all acts of severe physical and sexual violence were instigated by older partners, in some cases adult men.

SAME-SEX PARTNER

Having a same-sex partner was also associated with increased incidence rates for all forms of partner violence. However, participants with a same-sex partner also reported higher levels of family violence and were more likely to have an older partner, both of which were also significant risk factors, the relative weight of each being unknown.

CONCLUSION

These research findings have important child welfare implications for all professionals working with children and young people. They clearly highlight partner violence as a significant concern for young people's well-being, providing unequivocal evidence for the need to develop more effective safeguards in this area. Children and adolescents require protection from this form of violence. It seems that domestic violence starts at a much younger age than previously recognised. Given the incidence rates, it could be argued that partner violence is a greater problem for young people than bullying, and consequently deserves an equivalent degree of research, policy and practice attention.

The impact of partner violence is indisputably differentiated by gender: girls report much higher levels of negative impact than do boys. This is not to imply that boys' experiences of victimisation should be ignored. Nevertheless, interventions in this area of child welfare need to recognise the prominence of female vulnerability to partner violence. Boys require interventions that address their use of violence, irrespective of whether they are aware of its impact or not. Over 80 per cent of girls with a 'much older' partner experienced some form, and in many cases multiple forms, of partner violence. If a similar incidence rate for abuse were found for 'much older fathers', the development and implementation of safeguards would be guaranteed. Why should girls not expect the same level of response when they are suffering violence at the hands of their boyfriends?

The serious implications of partner violence for young people's welfare are unquestionable, but how best to respond remains disputed. Ultimately, in order to protect young people from this form of intimate violence, a greater degree of professional recognition and concern, as adult domestic violence currently receives, is now required to respond to the experiences of children and teenagers. Young people should not have to wait any longer for their relationships, and the problems they encounter in them, to be taken seriously.

MESSAGES FOR PRACTICE

RECOGNISING DIFFERENT FORMS OF TEENAGE PARTNER VIOLENCE

Teenage partner violence requires an integrated approach to prevention that recognises specific forms of violence, both individually and as they co-exist.

THE ROLE OF NEW TECHNOLOGIES

The use of new technologies, such as text messaging, instant messaging and social networking sites, to control partners needs to be challenged through safeguarding initiatives for young people.

FAMILY AND PEER VIOLENCE

Histories of family and peer violence were significantly associated with greater susceptibility to partner violence. Child welfare professionals working with adolescents need to routinely include this area in their overall assessments of young people's needs.

OLDER BOYFRIENDS

Perhaps one of the most alarming findings from the study concerned violence from older partners, and especially 'much older' partners. The level of exploitation and violence in these relationships is so pronounced that it may be appropriate to consider any girl with a 'much older' partner *per se* as a 'child in need'.

ENHANCING HELP SEEKING

Young people's help-seeking strategies, which favour peers, need to be acknowledged in intervention programmes. Peer support schemes in schools and other services should be expanded to include this important area of peer violence. Young people's acceptance of the accessibility of learning mentor schemes provides a valuable message for professionals working with adolescents in this area of child welfare.

STATUTORY RESPONSE

Local Safeguarding Children Boards (LSCBs) will need to develop strategies to address this form of intimate partner violence. Schools will require specific guidance on how teenage partner violence can be addressed through the personal, social, health and economic education (PSHE) curriculum.

REFERENCES

Abrahams, H. (2007) *Supporting Women After Domestic Violence: Loss, Trauma and Recovery*, Jessica Kingsley Publishers, London.

Ackard, D.M., Neumark-Sztainer, D. and Hannan, P. (2003) Dating violence among a nationally representative sample of adolescent girls and boys: associations with behavioural and mental health. *Journal of Gender Specific Medicine*, **6**, (3), 39–48.

Arriaga, X.B. and Foshee, V.A. (2004) Adolescent dating violence: do adolescents follow in their friends', or their parents', footsteps? *Journal of Interpersonal Violence*, **19** (2), 162–84.

Banister, E.M., Jakubec, S.L. and Stein, J.A. (2003) 'Like, what am I supposed to do?' Adolescent girls' health concerns in their dating relationships. *Canadian Journal of Nursing Research*, **35** (2), 16–33.

Barter, C. (2009) In the name of love: exploitation and violence in teenage dating relationships. *British Journal of Social Work*, **39**, 211–33.

Barter, C., McCarry, M., Berrdige, D. and Evans, K. (2009) *Partner Exploitation and Violence in Teenage Intimate Relationships*, NSPCC, London.

Bergman, L. (1992) Dating violence among high school students. *Social Work*, **31** (1), 21–7.

Brown, L.K., Puster, K.L., Vasquez, E.V., Hunter, H.L. and Lescano, C.M (2007) Screening practices for adolescent dating violence. *Journal of Interpersonal Violence*, **22** (4), 456–64.

Chung, D. (2005) Violence, control, romance and gender inequality: young women and heterosexual relationships. *Women's Studies International Forum*, **28**, 445–55.

Cleveland, H., Herrera, V. and Stuewig, J. (2003) Abusive males and abused females in adolescent relationships: risk factor similarity and dissimilarity and the role of relationship seriousness. *Journal of Family Violence*, **18** (6), 325–39.

Collin-Vézina, D., Hébert, M., Manseau, H., Blais, M. and Fernet, M. (2006) Self-concept and dating violence in 220 adolescent girls in the child protection system. *Child Youth Care Forum*, **35**, 319–26.

Department for Children, Schools and Families (DCSF) (2010a) *Violence Against Women and Girls (VAWG) Advisory Group Final Report and Recommendations*, DCSF, London.

Department for Children, Schools and Families (2010b) *Response to the Violence Against Women and Girls Advisory Group's Recommendations*, DCSF, London.

Foshee, V.A. (1996) Gender differences in adolescent dating abuse prevalence, types and injuries. *Health Education Research*, **11**, 275–86.

Frosh, S., Phoenix, A. and Pattman, R. (2002) *Young Masculinities: Understanding Boys in Contemporary Society*, Palgrave, Basingstoke.

Gamache, D. (1991) Domination and control; the social context of dating violence, in *Dating Violence: Young Women in Danger* (ed. B. Levy), Seal Press, Seattle.

Halpern, T.C., Oslak, S.G., Young, M.L., Martin, S.L. and Kupper, L.L. (2001) Partner violence among adolescents in opposite-sex romantic relationships: findings from the national longitudinal study of adolescent health. *American Journal of Public Health*, **91** (10), 1679–86.

Harway, M. and Liss, M. (1999) Dating violence and teen prostitution: adolescent girls in the justice system, in *Beyond Appearance: A New Look at Adolescent Girls* (eds N.G. Johnson, M.C. Roberts and J. Worell), American Psychological Association, Washington.

Henton, J., Cate, R., Koval, J., Lloyd, S. and Christopher, S. (1983) Romance and violence in dating relationships. *Journal of Family Issues*, **4**, 467–81.

Hickman, L., Jaycox, L. and Aronoff, J. (2004) Dating violence among adolescents: prevalence, gender distribution and prevention program effectiveness. *Trauma, Violence and Abuse*, **5** (2), 123–42.

Hird, M.J. (2000) An empirical study of adolescent dating aggression. *Journal of Adolescence*, **23**, 69–78.

Hird, M.J. and Jackson, S. (2001) Where angels and wusses fear to tread: sexual coercion in adolescent dating relationships. *Journal of Sociology*, **37** (1), 27–43.

HM Government (2006) *Working Together to Safeguard Children*, Stationery Office, London.

Home Office (2010) New campaign focuses on abuse in teenage relationships, www.homeoffice.gov.uk/about-us/news/teenage-relationship-abuse.html (accessed on 12 February 2010).

Jackson, S.M. (1999) Issues in the dating violence research: a review of the literature. *Aggression and Violent Behavior*, **4** (2), 233–47.

Jackson, S.M., Cram, F. and Seymour, F.W. (2000) Violence and sexual coercion in high school students' dating relationships. *Journal of Family Violence*, **15**, 23–36.

James, A., Jenks, C. and Prout, A. (1998) *Theorizing Childhood*, Polity, Cambridge.

Lane, K.E. and Gwartney-Gibbs, P.A. (1985) Violence in the context of dating and sex. *Journal of Family Issues*, **6** (1), 45–59.

Lavoie, F., Robitaille, L. and Hébert, M. (2000) Teen dating relationships and aggression: an exploratory study. *Violence Against Women*, **6** (1), 6–36.

Muehlenhard, C. and Linton, M. (1987) Date rape and sexual aggression in dating situations: incidence and risk factors. *Journal of Counselling Psychology*, **34** (2), 186–96.

Mullender, A., Hague, G.M., Imam, I., Kelly, L., Malos, E.M. and Regan, L. (2002) *Children's Perspectives on Domestic Violence*, Sage, London.

Ocampo, B.W., Shelley, G.A. and Jaycox, L.H. (2007) Latino teens talk about help seeking and help giving in relation to dating violence. *Violence Against Women*, **13** (2), 172–89.

O'Keefe, M. (1998) Factors mediating the link between witnessing inter-parental violence and dating violence. *Journal of Family Violence*, **13** (1), 39–57.

O'Keefe, M.K., Brockopp, K. and Chew, E. (1986) Teen dating violence. *Social Work*, **31** (6), 465–8.

O'Leary, D.A., Barling, J., Arias, I., Rosenbaum, A., Malonne, J. and Tyree, A. (1989) Prevalence and stability of physical aggression between spouses: a longitudinal analysis. *Journal of Consultant Clinical Psychology*, **57**, 263–8.

Papadopoulos, L. (2010) *Sexualisation Review of Young People*, www.homeoffice.gov.uk/documents/Sexualisation-young-people.pdf, Home Office, London.

Próspero, M. (2006) The role of perceptions in dating violence among young adolescents. *Journal of Interpersonal Violence*, **2** (4), 470–84.

Roberts, T.A., Auinger, P. and Klein, J.D. (2005) Intimate partner abuse and the reproductive health of sexually active female adolescents. *Journal of Adolescent Health*, **36** (5), 380–5.

Roscoe, B. and Callahan, J.E. (1985) Adolescents' self-reporting of violence in families and dating relations. *Adolescence*, **20**, 546–53.

Sears, H., Byers, S., Whelan, J., Saint-Pierre G. and The Dating Violence Research Team (2006) 'If it hurts you, then it is not a joke.' Adolescents' ideas and experiences of abusive behaviour in dating relationships. *Journal of Interpersonal Violence*, **21** (9), 1191–207.

Silverman, J.G., Raj, A., Mucci, L.A. and Hathaway, J.E. (2001) Dating violence against adolescent girls and associated substance use, unhealthy weight control, sexual risk behaviour, pregnancy, and suicidality. *Journal of the American Medical Association*, **286** (5), 572–9.

Silverman, J.G., Decker, M.R., Reed, E. *et al.* (2006) Social norms and beliefs regarding sexual risk and pregnancy among adolescent males treated for dating violence perpetration. *Journal of Urban Health*, **83** (4), 723–35.

Simonelli, C.J., Mullis, T., Elliot, A.N. and Pierce, T.H. (2002) Abuse by siblings and subsequent experiences of violence within the dating relationship. *Journal of Interpersonal Violence*, **17**, 103–21.

Smith, J.P. and Williams, J.G. (1992) From abusive household to dating violence. *Journal of Family Violence*, **2**, 153–65.

Smith, P.H., White, J.W. and Holland, L.J. (2003) A longitudinal perspective on dating violence among adolescent and college-age women. *American Journal of Public Health*, **93**, 1104–9.

Stark, E. (2009) *Coercive Control: How Men Entrap Women in Personal Life*, Oxford University Press, Oxford.

Sugarman, D. and Hotaling, G.T. (1989) A review of contextual and risk factors, in *Dating Violence: Young Women in Danger* (ed. B. Levy), Seal Press, Seattle, WA.

Tangney, J.P., Wagner, P., Fletcher, C. and Gramzow, R. (1992) Shamed into anger? The relation of shame and guilt to anger and self-reported aggression. *Journal of Personality and Social Psychology*, **62** (4), 669–75.

Watson, J.M., Cascardi, M., Avery-Leaf, S. and O'Leary, K.D. (2001) High school students responses to dating aggression. *Violence and Victims*, **16** (3), 339–48.

Western Australia Crime Research Centre and Donovan Research (2001) *Young People and Domestic Violence: National Research on Young People's Attitudes and Experiences of Domestic Violence*, National Community Crime Prevention Programme, Canberra.

Whitfield, C.L., Anda, R.F., Dube, S.R. and Felitti, V.J. (2003) Violent childhood experiences and the risk of intimate partner violence in adults: assessment in a large health maintenance organization. *Journal of Interpersonal Violence*, **18**, 166–85.

Williams. S.E. and Martinez, E. (1999) Psychiatric assessment of victims of adolescent dating violence in a primary care clinic. *Clinical Child Psychology and Psychiatry*, **4** (3), 427–39.

Wolfe, D.A., Scott, K., Reitzel-Jaffe, D., Wekerle, C., Grasley, C. and Stratman, A.L. (2001a) Development and validation of the conflict in adolescent dating relationships inventory. *Psychological Assessment*, **13** (2), 277–93.

9 Children and Young People with Harmful Sexual Behaviours

SIMON HACKETT

INTRODUCTION

This chapter is concerned with problematic, abusive and harmful sexual behaviours perpetrated by children and young people. Under-reporting, the hidden nature of child sexual abuse and hostility towards sex offenders in society make it difficult to accurately measure the scale of the problem (H. Masson, unpublished report). However, official statistics suggest that children and young people account for somewhere between a quarter and a third of all sexual abuse coming to the attention of the professional system in the UK (Erooga and Masson, 2006). The aim of this chapter is to provide a clear and concise analysis of the existing research base and to suggest some key pointers for professionals in developing an approach that balances risk and helps meet the needs of young people.

WHAT ARE 'PROBLEMATIC', 'ABUSIVE' AND 'HARMFUL' SEXUAL BEHAVIOURS IN CHILDREN AND YOUNG PEOPLE?

The use of these three distinct adjectives to introduce the focus of the chapter is evidence of the definitional problems that face professionals when deciding how to respond to sexual behaviours presented by children and young people. Such behaviours exist on a continuum that ranges, on the one hand, from normal and developmentally appropriate to highly abnormal and violent on the other (see Figure 9.1).

Making distinctions in individual cases about where on this continuum any given behaviour fits is a complex process, not least because the perceived appropriateness of sexual behaviours is culturally influenced and varies substantially across time both between and within societies. Additionally, it

Children Behaving Badly? Peer Violence Between Children and Young People
Edited by Christine Barter and David Berridge
© 2011 John Wiley & Sons Ltd.

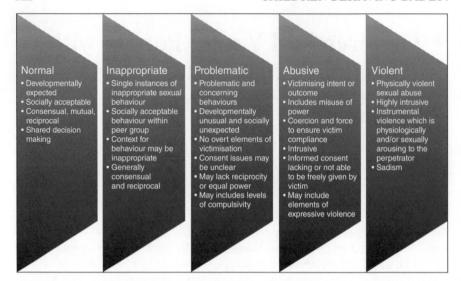

Figure 9.1   A continuum of children and young people's sexual behaviours

is important to place any assessment of a child's sexual behaviour within a developmental context, not only because of the differing status of pre-adolescents and adolescents within the criminal justice system, but also because sexual behaviour has very different meanings and motivations across these two developmental stages. As Ryan (2000) points out, some behaviours are normal if they are demonstrated in pre-adolescent children, but concerning if they continue into adolescence. Others, by contrast, are considered a normal part of the development of adolescents, but would be highly unusual in pre-adolescent children, thereby warranting referral for specialist help.

One helpful definitional distinction can be drawn between sexual behaviours that are 'abusive' and those that are 'problematic'. The term 'sexually *abusive* behaviour' is mainly used to indicate sexual behaviours that are initiated by a child or young person where there is an element of manipulation or coercion (Burton *et al.*, 1998), or where the subject of the behaviour is unable to give informed consent. By contrast, the term 'sexually *problematic* behaviour' refers to activities that do not include an element of victimisation, but that may interfere with the development of the child demonstrating the behaviour, or that might provoke rejection, cause distress or increase the risk of victimisation of the child. The important distinction here is that, while abusive behaviour is, by association, also problematic, problematic behaviours may not be abusive. As both 'abusive' and 'problematic' sexual behaviours are developmentally inappropriate and may cause developmental damage, a useful umbrella term is 'harmful sexual behaviours'.

WHO ARE PRE-ADOLESCENT CHILDREN WITH SEXUAL BEHAVIOUR PROBLEMS?

Pre-adolescent children with sexual behaviour problems are a diverse group with differing levels of need. These children also display a wide range of problematic sexual behaviours that are beyond what might be considered normal for their developmental stage. However, such children constitute a fundamentally different population to adolescents with sexually abusive behaviours, given the aetiology and nature of the behaviours, their developmental histories and legal status.

Gray and colleagues (1999) reported data on the demographics, psychological adjustment, victimisation and perpetration histories of 127 children aged 6–12 years (65% boys, 35% girls) who had engaged in what they termed 'developmentally unexpected' sexual behaviours. The average age of children in the sample was just over eight and a half years old. Most of the children (78%) were living at home with their biological parents at the time of the sexualised behaviour, and more than half had directed their sexual behaviour towards a sibling. Many of the children had a conduct disorder (76% overall), with boys more frequently diagnosed (83%) than girls (62%). Attention deficit hyperactivity disorder (ADHD) was also common. The overwhelming majority of the children had extensive abuse histories. Eighty-four per cent were known to have been sexually abused and 48 per cent had experienced physical abuse. In common with other descriptions of children with sexual behaviour problems, findings from this study suggest that this group of children experienced what Gray and colleagues conclude are 'catastrophic levels of maltreatment' (1999, p. 616) from early in their childhoods, combined with high levels of family violence, family poverty and poor parenting. Problematic sexual behaviours may emerge as a direct consequence of children's own experience of being sexualised through abuse, or may represent a more complex and indirect response to trauma and neglect. Given this, the welfare of these children must be the primary concern of intervention, and cases involving younger children should be dealt with in qualitatively different ways to those involving adolescent sex offenders (Chaffin, Letourneau and Silovsky, 2002).

THE RISK OF CONTINUING INAPPROPRIATE SEXUAL BEHAVIOUR IN PRE-ADOLESCENT CHILDREN

There has been little research into the likelihood that younger children's problematic sexual behaviours will persist and escalate through childhood and into adolescence. However, two randomised control studies (Pithers and Gray, 1993; Bonner, Walker and Berliner, 1999) have found that short-term therapeutic intervention with children and their parents can greatly reduce, if not eliminate, inappropriate sexual behaviours in most pre-adolescent children. In these studies, about 15 per cent of the children continued to demonstrate inappropriate sexual behaviours after 12 weeks of group sessions. When followed up one and two years after the groupwork intervention, change had been sustained in most cases. The key message here is that, with short-term intervention and ongoing support, it is unlikely that such behaviours will continue. Indeed, because young children demonstrating sexual behaviour problems are generally trying to resolve feelings of confusion, anxiety, shame or anger about sex and sexuality through behaviours, they need responses that are supportive, understanding and promote their integration into their peer group, rather than more punitive responses that simply serve to add to their problems (Johnson and Doonan, 2005).

WHO ARE YOUNG PEOPLE WITH HARMFUL SEXUAL BEHAVIOURS?

The vast majority of adolescents with harmful sexual behaviours are male. For example, in a UK study of all 227 young people referred for sexually abusive behaviours in one city over a 6-year period, 92 per cent of the young people referred were male (Taylor, 2003). Although it is sometimes assumed that young people's harmful sexual behaviours are experimental or of a minor nature, this is not borne out in the literature. In Taylor's (2003) study, 93 per cent of the sample were referred for behaviours involving physical contact with the victim's genitals, 31 per cent of the young people had actually penetrated their victims and a further 15 per cent had attempted penetration. It was previously thought that the 'typical' young person with sexual behaviour problems was a male in his mid- to late adolescent years. However, the onset of puberty is now acknowledged as a peak time for the development of such behaviours. In Taylor's (2003) study, the average age when a child was first reported for harmful sexual behaviours was 11 years 6 months.

Most young people victimise children known to them within the family or community. In Taylor's (2003) study, out of a total of 402 alleged incidents, only 3 per cent involved strangers. The average age of the victims was just over 8 years, but Taylor found two peak ages for victims of 5 and 12 years. Sixty-four per cent of victims were female and just over half were younger than the perpetrator by at least two years, with 36 per cent being peers (within two years of the perpetrator's age) and a further 9 per cent being older by at least two years.

While it is possible to identify some characteristics that appear to be particularly common in the backgrounds and presentation of young people with harmful sexual behaviours, there is also considerable diversity between such young people. This diversity applies not only to the sexually abusive behaviour displayed (such as the nature of the behaviours, the degree of physical force used in their commission, the accompanying levels of sexual arousal, the age and gender of victims), but also to broader developmental issues relating to the age of young people perpetrating the abuse, their family and educational backgrounds, and their intellectual capacities, experiences and motivations. It is likely that there are a number of sub-groups within the total population of young people presenting with harmful sexual behaviours, each of which has distinct needs.

Several attempts have been made to describe typologies or sub-groups of young sexual abusers (O'Brien and Bera, 1986; Langstrom, Grann and Linblad, 2000; Worling, 2001). As Worling (2001) noted, most researchers have taken their lead from the adult field and compared adolescents who offend against children with those who target peers or adults – the classic 'child abuser' versus 'rapist' distinction. So, a common picture is that of the adolescent child abuser who has poor social skills and low self-esteem, is frequently rejected by peers and has problems with intimacy, which means that he seeks sexual gratification through younger children. By contrast, adolescent 'rapists' have been seen to have higher levels of non-sexual criminality and conduct disorder, and to display higher levels of general delinquency. The assumption of higher levels of violence and aggression among juvenile offenders against peers or adults, including the use of weapons, has consistent empirical support (Parks, 2007, p. 154), as does their higher rate of general anti-social behaviour and criminality over and above young people who abuse younger children. Although this broad categorisation is somewhat crude, and of course some adolescents demonstrate features of both categories, it is helpful in showing that not all adolescents who demonstrate harmful sexual behaviours are the same, and that intervention responses need to be tailored to an individual's specific needs.

One of the more controversial debates in the field has been the extent to which young men presenting with abusive sexual behaviours have themselves been sexually abused. While younger children with sexual behaviour problems and young women with harmful sexual behaviours typically have chronic sexual victimisation histories (Burton, 2000), there is significant variance in relation to the reported rate of sexual victimisation in populations of adolescent male sexual abusers. For example, Dolan et al. (1996) found 26 per cent of young people had either a documented history or self-reported sexual abuse; in Manocha and Mezey (1998) the figure was 29 per cent; and in Taylor (2003) the overall figure was 32 per cent. Other studies report sexual victimisation of between 40 and 65 per cent (Becker, Cunningham-Rathner, 1986; Davis and Leitenberg, 1987; Vizard et al., 1995; Worling, 1995).

Such variance is likely to be due to a range of factors, including the chosen definition of sexual abuse, the methods used to determine abuse histories and the nature of different clinical samples. It is also possible that there are differences in rates of sexual abuse within sub-populations of young men who have sexually abused. For example, Taylor (2003) found that males who chose male victims were more likely to have experienced sexual abuse themselves than males with female victims (38% as opposed to 23%); and that, of the total sample, those young people whose harmful sexual behaviours began before the age of 12 were more than twice as likely to have experienced sexual abuse as those whose harmful sexual behaviours began after 12.

YOUNG WOMEN WITH HARMFUL SEXUAL BEHAVIOURS

Although there is increasing recognition of the small proportion of young women who sexually abuse others, little empirical research has been undertaken into this. Of 227 young people in Taylor's (2003) sample, only 19 were female. None of these young women had been cautioned or convicted as a result of their behaviours. The vast majority (74%) were the subject of one complaint only. All victims were known to the young women concerned and the overwhelming majority (80%) were younger children. Fifty-eight per cent of the young women had victimised males only, as opposed to 32 per cent whose victims were exclusively female.

Matthews and colleagues (1997) compared a sample of 67 young females and 70 young males who had displayed sexually abusive behaviours, taking into account their developmental and victimisation histories, as well as their abusive behaviours. When compared to the young men with harmful sexual behaviours, the young women in the sample had typically experienced more chronic and extensive maltreatment in their childhoods, had been sexually abused at an earlier age and were more likely to have been abused by more than one abuser.

Although necessarily tentative, Matthews and colleagues suggest that their findings indicate a number of preliminary sub-groups of young women with sexually abusive behaviour. First, they suggest that a distinct group of young women is identifiable whose sexually abusive behaviour is primarily exploratory in nature and curiosity-driven. The behaviour is usually comprised of either an isolated incident or a few instances of largely touching or oral sex, generally within the context of babysitting. The authors found that young women in this group were least likely to report past histories of victimisation or extensive family problems.

By contrast, a second group of young women was in evidence for whom the sexually abusive behaviours appeared to emerge very shortly after, and were triggered by, their own victimisation experiences. Many of these young women replicated their own sexual abuse very directly in the behaviours they directed towards others.

A third group of young women had experienced very high levels of abuse and neglect, including intrafamilial sexual abuse, when they were very young and demonstrated high levels of individual and family psychopathology. The authors suggest that many of these young women had attempted to cope with their abuse by developing a sexualised presentation, which for some had included deviant patterns of sexual arousal. Many of these young women had high levels of depression, anxiety and symptoms of post-traumatic stress.

Overall then, it appears that a small proportion of all adolescent sexual abusers are young women and that these young women may have backgrounds that differentiate them from their male adolescent abuser counterparts. This highlights the need for an intervention approach that acknowledges their difference and, in particular, works to directly address young women's unresolved victimisation histories, because these seem to be so significant in the presentation of such young women.

YOUNG PEOPLE WITH LEARNING DISABILITIES WITH HARMFUL SEXUAL BEHAVIOURS

Recent evidence suggests that a significant minority of young people being referred to sexual aggression service providers in the UK have learning disabilities (Masson and Hackett, 2003). In a review of the available literature on adolescents with learning disabilities, O'Callaghan (1998) warns against concluding that learning disabled young people have a greater propensity to sexually abuse that non-learning disabled young people. He points out that learning disabled young people are much more 'visible' than other young people to professionals and thereby are subject to a higher level of scrutiny in terms of their sexual behaviour. At the same time, young people with learning disabilities are often afforded fewer opportunities to develop intimate relationships with their peers and may be given limited sex education. Timms and Goreczny (2002) suggest that young people with learning disabilities are often indifferent to social taboos existing around sexual behaviours. As a result, it is important that we do not portray exploratory behaviours as 'abusive' or pathologise young people with learning disabilities as 'abusers' when the behaviours being demonstrated would be seen as normal in non-disabled teenagers.

There is also some evidence that the sexually abusive behaviours of young people with learning disabilities are often less sophisticated, use fewer grooming strategies and are more opportunistic when compared to non-learning disabled groups (Timms and Goreczny, 2002). O'Callaghan (1998) suggests that some young people with learning disabilities may relate on a psychosocial level to children whose chronological age is much lower, but whose functional age is similar to theirs. He suggests the concept of 'abuse without abuser' to describe sexual behaviours in which the person initiating the sexually abusive interaction does not understand the nature of consent or the impact of the behaviour on others. O'Callaghan (1998) stresses that responses to young people demonstrating abusive sexual behaviours should not be the same as for non-disabled young people. He advocates a balanced approach, which both understands their differential life opportunities and developmental processes, but also takes the abusive behaviours seriously.

RISK FACTORS AND THE LIKELIHOOD THAT ADOLESCENTS WITH HARMFUL SEXUAL BEHAVIOURS WILL REOFFEND

Although it is commonly assumed that young people demonstrating sexually abusive behaviours are highly likely to reoffend and also to develop into adult sex offenders, this is not supported in the research. The average sexual recidivism rates for young people who have sexually abused are between 3 and 14 per cent, according to Prentky *et al.* (2000). There is a suggestion that practitioners persistently over-estimate the level of risk presented by young people (Chaffin *et al.*, 2002). Worling and Curwen (2000) collected recidivism data on 148 adolescent sex offenders assessed at a specialised community programme in Canada. The follow-up period averaged 6 years and the mean age of the young people at follow-up was just over 21 years. The authors compared young people who had been offered 'treatment' as a result of their sexual behaviours as against those who had not, and they found that 5 per cent of treatment completers and 18 per cent of the comparison group were reconvicted of a sexual offence, although the figures for non-sexual recidivism were higher for both groups. Importantly, Worling and Curwen also looked at what was different about those young people who reoffended sexually as opposed to those who did not. They found that the two factors that best characterised sexual recidivists were reports of past and present sexual fantasies about children and more ongoing child–victim grooming behaviours.

Even taking into account under-reporting and the difficulties associated with conviction rates, recidivism studies do indeed suggest that a significant number of young people committing sexual abuse do not continue to sexually offend into adulthood. Indeed, the risk for non-sexual offending appears to be higher than that for future sex offences. At the same time, there appears to be a sub-group of young sexual offenders who are at higher risk of recidivism. While we need more research on this issue, factors such as general delinquency and anti-social behaviours, use of violence, psychopathy, impulsivity and conduct disorder appear to be the most significant risk markers for this group (Rasmussen, 1999; Prentky *et al.*, 2000) and should therefore serve as the key high risk factors for professionals when assessing the risk of sexual reoffence.

FAMILIES OF CHILDREN AND YOUNG PEOPLE WITH HARMFUL SEXUAL BEHAVIOURS

Families of young people with harmful sexual behaviours are widely described in the literature as multiply troubled and dysfunctional, with children and young people often experiencing changes of primary carer including periods of being 'looked after' in public care. Manocha and Mezey (1998) found that discordant and problematic family relationships were reported as features of a third of all the families in their study. Domestic violence, parental criminality and substance misuse, a lack of sexual boundaries and a history of sexual abuse in the family added, in a substantial minority of families, to the catalogue of family problems.

While they are often described very negatively, it is important to recognise that parents whose children have sexually abused need support and assistance in coming to terms with their children's behaviours. Being the parent of a child with sexual behaviour problems can be a hugely stigmatising and isolating experience for many parents. It is hard to imagine many other childhood disorders or behavioural problems that afford a lesser degree of community sympathy than the discovery that one's child has abused other children. The need to engage with parents of children and young people who have displayed abusive and problematic sexual behaviours is indicated strongly by the few studies that currently exist (Pithers *et al.*, 1998). However, as well as having much to offer in the management of, and response to, their children's problems, parents of this group of children and young people are likely to have extensive needs of their own. Parents often have unresolved abuse in their own histories, and other needs that warrant a helpful response in their own right (New, 1999). Supporting parents in meeting their own needs is often a necessary precursor to their facing up to the impact of sexual abuse in their families (Hackett, 2001).

HOW SHOULD PROFESSIONALS RESPOND?

Early practice responses to young people with sexually abusive behaviours were largely based on adult models of assessment and treatment derived from adult sex offender work, with adaptations for use in work with young people. More recently, it has become clear that the confrontational methods that were originally proposed are counter-productive with children and young people. There is now consensus in the field about the necessity of focused and holistic work (Hackett, Masson and Phillips, 2006), which targets both the harmful sexual behaviour and addresses more general areas of unmet need.

ASSESSMENT

In all cases it is important to have as clear a view as possible about a child's or young person's sexual behaviours and the degree to which they should be considered appropriate, concerning or harmful for a child of that age. As such, according to Chaffin and colleagues (2002), assessments should include:

- a thorough analysis of the problematic sexual behaviours, including their onset, motivating factors, types of behaviour exhibited, changes in the behaviours over time and the child's responses to attempts by caregivers to correct such behaviours;

- a detailed social history both of the child and the family, with specific attention given to significant family losses or other traumatic events, child moves and episodes in substitute care;
- a detailed exploration of the child's prior experiences of victimisation (this should not be limited to the question of whether a child has been abused, but should include as much information as can be gathered about the dynamics of any abuse and, especially if the abuse was sexual in nature, the abusive behaviours that the child was involved in, because these can cast light upon the child's subsequent sexualised behaviours);
- an analysis of the child's wider social functioning, relationships and interactions, including both strengths and competencies as well as risks and deficits;
- other behavioural issues which may be related to the problematic sexual behaviours, such as conduct problems, ADHD or post-traumatic responses exhibited by the child;
- the family environment, including how sex and sexuality are viewed and expressed in the home, family disciplinary practices and parenting styles, the level of supervision afforded to children, and the carers' previous attempts to manage and respond to the child's sexual behaviours.

One of the major advances in recent years in the assessment of adult sex offenders has been the widespread discussion about the relative merits of actuarial models of risk assessment on the one hand, and clinically based assessment on the other (Craig, Browne and Stringer, 2003). At present, while a number of promising actuarial-based models have emerged in the adult field, for example Static 99 (Hanson and Thornton, 1999), such models are uncommon in the adolescent field. In the US, Prentky and Righthand (2003) have proposed a model of assessment for adolescents aged 12–18 years including both static and dynamic risk factors; they have named this the J-SOAP-II. Perhaps the most widely used assessment protocol in the UK currently is the AIM model (Print *et al.*, 2001). This provides a helpful conceptual framework and practice model for the initial assessment of young people based on four key domains of:

- **offence-specific factors** – including the young person's offending history, the nature of the offence behaviours, previous offence history;
- **developmental issues** – including the young person's own experiences of abuse and trauma, the quality of early life experiences and wider behavioural issues;
- **family** – including the functioning within the family, family attitudes and beliefs, sexual boundaries and parental competence;
- **environment** – including opportunities for further offending and the degree of community support.

One of the strengths of this model is that it not only highlights risks and deficits but it also encourages practitioners to assess and promote protective factors in each of the four domains. Additionally, the model recommends a range of responses commensurate with risk and need in individual cases, and proposes a tiered response to ensure that children presenting with low-risk inappropriate sexual behaviours receive a level of support and information that is commensurate with their needs, but are not subjected to long-term, highly intrusive and potentially damaging programmes of intervention. Conversely, the approach emphasises that young people with more extensive and chronic problems receive intensive and specialist support.

EFFECTIVE THERAPEUTIC INTERVENTIONS

Chaffin and colleagues (2002) highlight the absence of any published studies comparing outcomes for young people randomly assigned to treatment versus no-treatment conditions, and suggest that, strictly speaking, it is therefore not possible to empirically demonstrate whether such 'treatment' is beneficial, harmful or of no benefit at all. However, the current preference for the majority of services in both North America and the UK is for interventions loosely based on a cognitive behavioural model (Hackett, Masson and Phillips, 2005). This approach has traditionally emphasised a number of discrete elements to 'sex-offence'-specific areas of work with young people, such as:

- detailed behavioural analysis of sexual abuse behaviours, including their triggers (antecedents) and consequences;
- identifying and changing cognitive distortions (e.g. that sex with a child is not harmful);
- developing young people's level of empathic concern, both global and specific to victims;
- educative work on sexual values, attitudes, the nature of sexual abuse and issues of informed consent;
- anger management;
- social skills training;
- addressing deviant sexual arousal;
- relapse prevention – in particular, the teaching of self-control skills, rehearsal and the management of risk situations.

However, it is increasingly recognised that programmes of work designed to focus *exclusively* on sexually abusive behaviours in young people are limited in value and should be supported by attention to enhancing the young person's broader life skills, addressing social isolation, opening up access to appropriate opportunities in the education system, addressing family problems and improving the young person's relationships with parents or carers (Righthand and Welch, 2001). One such approach which is gaining increasing support is multi-systemic therapy (MST), which draws upon systems theory and the theory of social ecology (Bronfenbrenner, 1979) and has as its primary purpose an understanding of the fit between identified problems and their broader systemic context. It is an intensive community- and home-based approach that has generated a good level of empirical support in response to a broad set of adolescent problem behaviours, including sexually abusive behaviour (Borduin *et al.*, 1990; Swenson *et al.*, 1998).

Little specific research has been conducted into the most effective ways of intervening with families of children and young people with sexual behaviour problems, although there is now widespread agreement that family intervention is important. While much of the literature is focused on family deficits and dysfunction, recent clinical accounts of work with families support a strengths-based approach to parents and carers (Hackett *et al.*, 2005). Parental support groups may be particularly useful for parents who are socially isolated (Hackett, Telford and Slack, 2002). However, regardless of the modality of family work, the process of opening up opportunities for parents to shape their own futures and contribute to the 'solution' of family problems mirrors the process of working with children and young people to face their abusive behaviours.

CONCLUSIONS AND KEY MESSAGES

The characteristics of children and young people with harmful sexual behaviours point to the need for a holistic approach, which considers all areas of a child's life. Younger children presenting with problematic sexual behaviours are often extremely vulnerable and have frequently been extensively sexually abused themselves. In such cases, children's problematic behaviours may be a direct consequence of their own experience of being sexualised through abuse. Given this, the best response to these children may be similar to that offered to child victims of abuse. Adolescents who display harmful sexual behaviours share many characteristics with other young people who have a wide range of difficulties. It is important to address their broader problems, as well as dealing with their sexually abusive behaviours; and to remember that they are young people first, and 'sex offenders' second. Key messages for practice therefore include the following:

- Interventions with young people who have sexually abused should respond to the young person *holistically* and be sensitive to his or her developmental status. It is unhelpful to single out and target sexually abusive behaviour in isolation from other key developmental areas. At the same time, it is counter-productive to leave the sexually abusive behaviour unchallenged.
- Working with the carers and parents of children and young people who have sexually abused should be a central aspect of service provision. A multi-modal approach is warranted to help a young person and his or her family

address the wide-ranging issues underpinning, and emanating from, adolescent sexual aggression. Such an approach should involve young people, families, carers and other systems involved with young people.

- Interventions of a cognitive behavioural nature, which target offence-specific factors such as sexual fantasy, and which help a young person to manage risk and developmental strategies to prevent relapse, are indicated for work with this population of young people.
- Attention should be given to *how* any intervention programme is delivered, with an emphasis on supportive and empathic interactions. Inflexible or aggressive approaches are counter-productive. Consideration should be given to strengths-based and resilience-promoting approaches, rather than an exclusive focus on risks and deficits.
- Effective intervention with this group of young people should be underpinned by efforts to evaluate and monitor change, while actively involving young people and their families in this process.

REFERENCES

Becker, J.V., Cunningham-Rathner, J. and Kaplan, M.S. (1986) Adolescent sexual offenders: demographics, criminal and sexual histories, and recommendations for reducing future offenses. *Journal of Interpersonal Violence*, **1**, 431–45.

Bonner, B.L., Walker, C.E. and Berliner, L. (1999) *Children with Sexual Behavior Problems: Assessment and Treatment. Final Report*, Department of Health and Human Services, Washington.

Borduin, C., Hengeller, S., Blaske, D. and Stein, R. (1990) Multisystemic treatment of adolescent sexual offenders. *International Journal of Offender Therapy and Comparative Criminology*, **34**, 105–13.

Bronfenbrenner, U. (1979) *The Ecology of Human Development: Experiments by Nature and Design*, Harvard University Press, Cambridge.

Burton, D.L. (2000) Were adolescent sexual offenders children with sexual behaviour problems? *Sexual Abuse*, **12** (1), 37–48.

Burton, D.L., Rasmussen, L.A., Bradshaw, J., Christopherson, B.J. and Huke, S.C. (1998) *Treating Children with Sexually Abusive Behaviour Problems: Guidelines for Child and Parent Intervention*, Haworth Press, New York.

Chaffin, M., Letourneau, E. and Silovsky, J.F. (2002) Adults, adolescents and children who sexually abuse children: a developmental perspective, in *The APSAC Handbook on Child Maltreatment*, 2nd edition (eds J. Myers, L. Berliner, J. Briere, C.T. Hendrix, C. Jenny, and T. Reid), Sage, Thousand Oaks.

Craig, L., Browne, K. and Stringer, I. (2003) Risk scales and factors predictive of sexual offence recidivism. *Trauma, Violence and Abuse*, **4** (1), 45–69.

Davis, G. and Leitenberg, H. (1987) Adolescent sex offenders. *Psychological Bulletin*, **101**, 417–27.

Dolan, M., Holloway, J., Bailey, S. and Kroll, L. (1996) The psychosocial characteristics of juvenile sexual offenders referred to an adolescent forensic service in the UK. *Medical Science Law*, **36** (4), 342–52.

Erooga, M. and Masson, H. (2006) Children and young people with sexually harmful or abusive behaviours: underpinning knowledge, principles, approaches and service provision, in *Children and Young People who Sexually Abuse Others. Current Developments and Practice Responses* (eds M. Erooga and H. Masson), Routledge, London.

Gray, A., Pithers, W.D., Busconi, A. and Houchens, P. (1999) Developmental and etiological characteristics of children with sexual behavior problems: treatment implications. *Child Abuse and Neglect*, **23** (6), 601–21.

Hackett, S. (2001) *Facing the Future. A Guide for Parents of Young People Who Have Sexually Abused*, Russell House Publishing, Lyme Regis.

Hackett, S., Masson, H. and Phillips, S. (2005) *Services for Young People who Sexually Abuse*, Youth Justice Board, London.

Hackett, S., Masson, H. and Phillips, S. (2006) Exploring consensus in practice with youth who are sexually abusive: findings from a Delphi study of practitioner views in the United Kingdom and the Republic of Ireland. *Child Maltreatment*, **11** (2), 146–56.

Hackett, S., Telford, P. and Slack, K. (2002) Groupwork with parents of children who sexually harm, in *Young People who Sexually Abuse. Building the Evidence Base for Your Practice* (ed. M.C. Calder), Russell House Publishing, Lyme Regis.

Hanson, R.K. and Thornton, D. (1999) *Static-99: Improving Actuarial Risk Assessments for Sex Offenders*, Department of the Solicitor General of Canada, Ottawa.

Johnson, T.C. and Doonan, R. (2005) Children with sexual behavior problems: what we have learned in the last two decades, in *Children and Young People who Sexually Abuse: New Theory, Research and Practice Developments* (ed. M.C. Calder), Russell House Publishing, Lyme Regis.

Langstrom, N., Grann, M. and Linblad, F. (2000) A preliminary typology of young sex offenders. *Journal of Adolescence*, **23**, 319–29.

Manocha, K.F. and Mezey, G. (1998) British adolescents who sexually abuse: a descriptive study. *Journal of Forensic Psychiatry*, **9** (3), 588–608.

Masson, H. and Hackett, S. (2003) A decade on from the NCH Report (1992): adolescent sexual aggression policy, practice and service delivery across the UK and Republic of Ireland. *Journal of Sexual Aggression*, **9** (2), 109–24.

Matthews, R., Hunter, J.A. and Vuz, J. (1997) Juvenile female sexual offenders: clinical characteristics and treatment issues. *Sexual Abuse: A Journal of Research and Treatment*, **9**, 187–99.

New, M., Stevenson, J. and Skuse, D. (1999) Characteristics of mothers of boys who sexually abuse. *Child Maltreatment*, **4** (1), 21–31.

O'Brien, M.J. and Bera, W. (1986) Adolescent sex offenders: descriptive typology. *Newsletter of the National Family Life Education Network*, **1**, 1–5.

O'Callaghan, D. (1998) Practice issues in working with young abusers who have learning difficulties. *Child Abuse Review*, **7**, 435–48.

Parks, G. (2007) Emerging data for risk prediction and identification of offender subgroups: implications for specialised treatment and risk management, in *Working with Children and Young People who Sexually Abuse: Taking the Field Forward* (ed. M. Calder), Russell House Publishing, Lyme Regis.

Pithers, W.D. and Gray, A. (1993) *Pre-adolescent Sexual Abuse Research Project*, National Center on Child Abuse and Neglect, Washington, DC.

Pithers, W.D., Gray, A., Busconi, A. and Houchens, P. (1998) Caregivers of children with sexual behavior problems: psychological and familial functioning. *Child Abuse and Neglect*, **22** (2), 129–41.

Prentky, R. and Righthand, S. (2003) *Juvenile Sex Offender Assessment Protocol-II (J-SOAP-II) Manual*, Office of Juvenile Justice and Delinquency Prevention, Washington, DC.

Prentky, R., Harris, B., Frizzell, K. and Righthand, S. (2000) An actuarial procedure for assessing risk with juvenile sex offenders. *Sexual Abuse*, **12** (4), 71–89.

Print, B., Morrison, T. and Henniker, J. (2001) An inter-agency assessment framework for young people who sexually abuse: principles, processes and practicalities, in *Juveniles and Children who Sexually Abuse: Frameworks for Assessment*, 2nd edition (ed. M.C. Calder), Russell House Publishing, Lyme Regis.

Rassmussen, L. (1999) Factors related to recidivism among juvenile sexual offenders. *Sexual Abuse: A Journal of Research and Treatment*, **11** (1), 69–85.

Righthand, S. and Welch, C. (2001) *Juveniles Who Have Sexually Offended. A Review of the Professional Literature*, Office of Juvenile Justice and Delinquency Prevention, Washington, DC.

Ryan, G. (2000) Childhood sexuality: a decade of study. Part 1– Research and curriculum development. *Child Abuse and Neglect*, **24** (1), 33–48.

Swenson, C., Henggeler, S., Schoenwald, S., Kaufman, K. and Randall, J. (1998) Changing the social ecologies of adolescent sexual offenders: implications of the success of multi-systemic therapy in treating serious antisocial behaviour in adolescents. *Child Maltreatment*, **3** (4), 330–8.

Taylor, J.F. (2003) Children and young people accused of child sexual abuse: a study within a community. *Journal of Sexual Aggression*, **9** (1), 57–70.

Timms, S. and Goreczny, A.J. (2002) Adolescent sex offenders with mental retardation. Literature review and assessment considerations. *Aggression and Violent Behavior*, **7**, 1–9.

Vizard, E., Monck, E. and Misch, P. (1995) Child and adolescent sex abuse perpetrators: a review of the research literature. *Journal of Child Psychology and Psychiatry*, **36** (5), 731– 56.

Worling, J. (1995) Sexual abuse histories of adolescent male sex offenders: differences on the basis of the age and gender of the victims. *Journal of Abnormal Psychology*, **104** (4), 610–13.

Worling, J. (2001) Personality based typology of adolescent male sexual offenders: differences in recidivism rates, victim-selection characteristics, and personal victimisation histories. *Sexual Abuse: A Journal of Research and Treatment*, **13** (3), 149–66.

Worling, J. and Curwen, T. (2000) Adolescent sexual offender recidivism: success of specialized treatment and implications for risk prediction. *Child Abuse and Neglect*, **24**, 965–82.

10 Homophobia and Peer Violence

IAN RIVERS

Within the context of peer violence, homophobia can be defined as any form of physical (e.g. hitting or kicking), verbal (e.g. name-calling, labelling), or social (e.g. being ignored or excluded) aggression perpetrated against an individual because of her or his actual or perceived sexual orientation or, alternatively, because that individual's behaviour is not typical of her or his sex (Rivers, Poteat and Noret, 2007). Homophobia can also be characterised as an attitude or belief that not only promotes or sustains discrimination against lesbians and gay men, but also politically those who identify as bisexual or transgender.

Among adolescents, homophobia has a number of signature characteristics that separate it from other forms of peer aggression, particularly at school. For example, homophobia tends to be perpetrated by groups of peers (both male and female) rather than individuals. It is often class- or cohort-based and thus, unlike other forms of victimisation, it is rarely perpetrated by older adolescents (Rivers, 1999). Male victims of homophobia tend to report being called names or being ridiculed in front of others, particularly in venues such as school classrooms and corridors. Physical violence is often present too and tends to be perpetrated by other young men, encouraged by their classmates – both boys and girls. Among girls, homophobia is often social in nature, involving rumour mongering and social isolation. Because of this, it is much more difficult to spot, or report, and therefore often goes unnoticed (Rivers and Cowie, 2006).

Much of the research that has been conducted on homophobia within the context of peer aggression has, until recently, either been gathered using retrospective reports wherein lesbian, gay, bisexual and transgender (LGBT) adults have been asked to recount their experiences of homophobia at school, or it has involved anonymous or confidential surveys of young people attending youth and community groups, or who have accessed information on the internet. To date, the largest survey conducted in the UK has been that sponsored by Stonewall, where 1,145 youth enrolled in secondary schools and further education colleges participated (Hunt and Jensen, 2007). The survey

Children Behaving Badly? Peer Violence Between Children and Young People
Edited by Christine Barter and David Berridge
© 2011 John Wiley & Sons Ltd.

revealed that 65 per cent of those youth who completed questionnaires had been bullied because of their sexual orientation at school, with the figure rising to 75 per cent among those attending faith schools. Despite the fact that the government recommended that all schools include homophobia in their anti-bullying policies, across England and Wales, only one-quarter of them were reported to have policies that explicitly stated that homophobic bullying was wrong.

In their replication of the very first survey of homophobia in UK schools conducted by the Inner London Education Authority in the early 1980s (see Warren, 1984), Ellis and High (2004) suggested that there had been a substantial increase in bullying behaviour perpetrated against LGB youth. They compared their sample of 384 LGB young people surveyed in 2001 to the data collected two decades earlier by Warren. They found that LGB young people in the 2001 study were nearly four times more likely to report feeling isolated at school than those in the 1984 report. They were almost five times more likely to be victims of verbal abuse, seven times more likely to be report being teased, three times more likely to be the victim of a physical assault, five times more likely to be excluded from their group by peers, and almost nine times more likely to feel 'pressured to conform'. Ellis and High's research suggested that, in the intervening two decades, the introduction of legislation such as Section 28 of the 1988 Local Government Act, which prohibited the teaching of homosexuality as a pretended family relationship, had a significant impact upon the willingness to schools to combat homophobia effectively.

In the US, researchers based at the University of California (California Safe Schools Coalition [2004]) surveyed 237,544 students attending schools state-wide (grades 7–11), who were asked about their experiences of bullying, including homophobic bullying. The results illustrated that 8 per cent of the population had been victims of homophobia, with two out of every three students who identified as LGBT reporting having been victimised on the grounds of actual or perceived sexual orientation. In this study, the researchers defined bullying as 'being repeatedly shoved, hit, threatened, called mean names, teased in a way you didn't like, or had other things done to you' (p. 6).

The data showed that those students who were bullied because of their actual or perceived sexual orientation were more likely to report receiving lower grades for academic work (grade 'C' or below) when compared to non-bullied students (24% versus 17%). They were more likely to report that they had missed school 'in the last 30 days' because they felt unsafe (27% versus 7%). In addition, they were almost twice as likely to report participating in health risk behaviours, such as substance abuse, driving under the influence of alcohol, or being a passenger in a car where the driver had consumed alcohol. They were nearly six times more likely to report being threatened or hurt by someone wielding a weapon (28% versus 5%), and four times more likely to report carrying a weapon to school (19% versus 5%).

One important finding from the Californian study was undoubtedly the fact that young people who experience homophobia are not always LGBT. In some cases students are bullied or harassed because they are perceived to be in some way different from their peers. It is a facet of much of the research to date that we have rarely looked at homophobia through any lens other than that of an LGBT person. We have not always questioned why young people use sexuality above any other mark of individuality to determine who is 'in' and who is 'out' of favour. Nor, by the same token, have we considered fully how homophobia differs from other forms of discrimination at school.

Between 2002 and 2007, two large-scale studies were undertaken by a research team in the north of England based at York St John University, addressing bullying and discrimination in secondary schools. Comparing data drawn from one survey conducted in 2003 ($n = 1,896$; 1,026 boys and 870 girls) and another in 2006 ($n = 2,949$; 1,459 boys and 1,490 girls), Rivers and Noret (2007) found that rates of homophobic bullying had increased from 3.2 per cent to 4.3 per cent for boys, and from 0.8 per cent to 3.0 per cent for girls. Reports of perpetration had dropped from 4.0 per cent to 1.7 for boys, and from 2.6 per cent to 1.0 per cent for girls. Of those boys who were exposed to homophobic bullying (either as a victim, perpetrator or bystander), the most frequently cited form of aggression to take place was physical violence, followed by name-calling and rumour mongering. Among girls, rumour mongering was the most prevalent form of aggression, followed by name-calling and social isolation.

Of those pupils who were victims of homophobic bullying, Rivers and Noret also found that 48 per cent identified as being attracted to members of the opposite sex and only 25 per cent reported a same-sex attraction (the remaining pupils reported that they had not thought about it or were unsure). Data were also analysed according to the severity of bullying reported. Using a composite measure that combines the number of the different types of bullying or victimisation experienced (e.g. physical, verbal and social), its frequency across the week, and the number of locations within and outside the school grounds where incidents occurred (e.g. school yard, classrooms, corridors, on the way home), the authors were able to compare the experiences of pupils who had been victimised because of their actual or perceived sexual orientation with those who reported being victimised for other reasons.

As Table 10.1 demonstrates, pupils were provided with 15 alternatives relating to why they had been bullied at school, or travelling to and from school. Among boys, the most severe bullying was reported by those who were members of the traveller community, followed by those with special needs and/ or a disability – being called 'gay' ranked fourth in the list. Among girls, the most severe bullying was reported by those who indicated that they were victimised 'because of the brand of clothes I wear'. Being called 'lesbian' was ranked sixth in terms of severity – following poor school work, being good at sports, being not so good at sports and having a disability.

Table 10.1 Reasons for being bullied or harassed in school according to severity[a]

Item	N	Mean score	Ranking[b]
Because of my weight, size or body shape			
– boys	105	6.36	14
– girls	112	6.61	8
Because of my appearance (general)			
– boys	85	6.84	12
– girls	109	6.41	10
Because of my ethnicity/colour			
– boys	22	6.72	13
– girls	20	6.20	12
Because I am a traveller			
– boys	3	9.33	1
– girls	2	5.50	15
Because I am called 'gay' or 'lesbian'			
– boys	61	8.16	4
– girls	44	7.23	6
Because my school work is good			
– boys	73	6.93	11
– girls	82	6.65	7
Because my school work is not so good			
– boys	14	7.21	10
– girls	11	8.36	2
Because I have special needs			
– boys	19	9.00[c]	2
– girls	10	5.90	14
Because I have a disability			
– boys	6	9.00[c]	3
– girls	6	7.33	5
Because of my friends			
– boys	53	8.13	5
– girls	106	6.54	9
Because I am good at sports			
– boys	12	7.45	8
– girls	10	8.10	3
Because I am not so good at sports			
– boys	34	8.03	6
– girls	19	7.42	4
Because of my possessions			
– boys	12	7.33	9
– girls	7	6.26	11
Because of the brand of clothes I wear			
– boys	22	7.86	7
– girls	16	8.88	1
Other reasons			
– boys	94	6.15	15
– girls	142	5.96	13

Notes:
[a] Severity score $\alpha = 86.6$.
[b] Ranks are by sex.
[c] Rank order determined by standard deviation in scores.

CHILDREN RAISED BY GAY AND LESBIAN PARENTS OR CARERS

It might be expected that as LGBT youth are often victims of homophobia at school, so too might those young people raised by lesbian and gay parents or carers. However, various studies have shown that this is not the case. For example, studies that have focused upon the psychological functioning of children raised by parents who are lesbians and gay men have shown elements of resiliency, and few signs of psychological disturbance when compared to children raised by heterosexuals (Flaks *et al.*, 1995; Chan, Raboy and Patterson, 1998; Wainright, Russell and Patterson, 2004). In the UK, in a longitudinal study conducted by Tasker and Golombok (1997), the researchers found that children raised by lesbian couples did not differ significantly in terms of exposure to bullying at school when compared with the children of heterosexual couples. Nor did the quality of their peer relationships differ as a function of years raised by lesbian parents. However, interviews conducted with 10-year-olds identified through the National Lesbian Family Study (NLFS) suggest that just under half had experienced homophobia (see Gartrell *et al.*, 2005). It seems likely that those young people who perceive others' attitudes towards having a lesbian mother as negative can experience lower self-esteem, which ultimately has an impact upon social acceptance, self-worth, behavioural conduct, concerns about physical appearance and the development of friendships (Gershon, Tschann and Jemerin, 1999).

WHY DOES HOMOPHOBIA EXIST IN PEER CULTURE?

In his book *Sexual Bullying*, Duncan (1999) argues that teachers often assume that their pupils will mature into sexually responsible heterosexual adults who go on to form at least one lasting intimate relationship with a member of the opposite sex, find a family and live a life of respectable obscurity. He argues that, for many years, schools have adopted a 'minimal impact' approach when dealing with issues of sexuality: they regard procreation and, if absolutely necessary, AIDS prevention as the totality of personal, social, and/or health and economic education (PSE/PSHE). If homosexuality is discussed, then it is in the context of HIV/AIDS. LGBT sexual health is never addressed and, should a class discussion extend to different types of families and different types of relationships, lesbians and gay men may warrant an uneasy mention, but no more than that.

Duncan characterised the silence that surrounds an acknowledgement that same-sex attraction exists among members of a school's population as 'deathly'. Teachers and governors have few resources to call upon when a pupil decides to 'come out' at school, and they have even less training on how to deal with the aftermath when a young person's LGBT status becomes known to the wider school community. In effect, many schools become vacuums, drawing in daily the hostile and negative attitudes and beliefs about homosexuality that exist within families, local communities, on the television and, of course, on the internet. These educational vacuums then push their inhabitants, at 16 years of age, out into the world of work, often with their prejudices and intolerances left unchallenged. But why is it that these prejudices exist at all?

In their study of the gender stereotyping, homophobia and sexual coercion among 1,045 Canadian adolescents, Morrison *et al.* (1997) found that young people's negative attitudes towards homosexuality were related not only to their beliefs about gender stereotypes and the perceived social desirability of heterosexuality, they were also related to popular misconceptions about the sexually coercive nature of lesbian and gay relationships. Similar to Duncan's (1999) observations, Morrison and colleagues argued that the failure to challenge these stereotypes and misconceptions is a result of the socio-cultural pressures placed upon teachers to adhere to an 'idealised' standard, promoting a culture of 'silence' where the individual is unable to speak with authority about what she or he 'knows, sees, or feels' (p. 367). Thus, in the absence of any opportunity to challenge the myths created and promoted within adolescent groups, those myths continue unabated and young LGBTs are victimised.

Gallup (1995) posited a similar argument to that of Morrison *et al.* (1997) but using an ethological paradigm. He suggested that homophobia evolved as 'a means of minimising the likelihood that offspring would become homosexual' (p. 54). His research was based upon three basic assumptions:

- Homosexuality has been a feature of human evolution for a substantial period.
- An individual's sexual orientation can be affected by modelling or seduction.
- There is a foundation to heterosexual concerns about the seduction of children by lesbians and gay men.

He undertook four surveys that were designed to explore the overarching hypothesis that anti-homosexual attitudes may vary as a function of the contact a lesbian or gay man has with children. His results showed that heterosexuals were more likely to express discomfort with lesbian or gay teachers, doctors or school bus drivers than with any other professionals (e.g. lawyer, sales staff or car mechanic). Greater discomfort was expressed by participants if they believed a paediatrician or child psychiatrist was gay (such discomfort was primarily situated around concerns relating to HIV/AIDS transmission). In terms of fears of sexual coercion, Gallup's third survey showed that participants' concerns were heightened if they knew their child was staying at a friend's house where the same-sex parent was lesbian or gay. Finally, in his fourth survey, he found that men were more homophobic than women, and that those who reported being more religious, or reported being parents already, were more likely to express anti-homosexual attitudes than their counterparts.

Gallup (1995) argued that his data provided tentative support for his theory that homophobia constitutes an element of natural selection in human beings, and that anti-homosexual sentiments reduce the possibility of a lesbian or gay man having contact with a child or young person, which, by implication, minimises the coercive influence they may have upon that child's emerging sexuality. Various researchers have attempted to demonstrate the fallacy of such assumptions and have done so with a certain degree of success (see Dressler, 1978; Miller, 1979; Cramer, 1986; Bigner and Bozett, 1990; Gottman, 1990; Patterson 1992; Jenny, Roesler and Poyer, 1994; Bailey *et al.*, 1995; Golombok and Tasker, 1996; Rivers *et al.*, 2008). But if, as Morrison *et al.* (1997) suggest, teachers remain silent about what they know, see or feel, the second and third assumptions underpinning Gallup's (1995) research will, more than likely, continue to go unabated from generation to generation.

In the UK, in a study of homophobic bullying and its long-term effects Rivers (2001), also explored the nature of homophobia, particularly the names and labels that were used to victimise young lesbians and gay men. Among gay and bisexual men, names tended to focus on conceptions of illness (e.g. 'AIDS victim'), abnormality (e.g. 'pervert', 'queer'), gender atypicality (e.g. 'mary', 'queen', 'him-she-geezerbird') and sexual behaviour (e.g. 'bum bandit', 'rapist', 'shirt lifter'). Rigby (1997) suggests, in his brief discussion of the impact HIV/AIDS has had upon bullying, that those names and labels that refer to aspects of gay sex deflect criticism away from the boys who use them and draw attention to the actions, behaviours or demeanour of their targets who, by virtue of their acquired 'deviant' status, are unable to challenge their persecutors. Thus, calling another boy 'gay' is not only a method by which other boys identify and label those who do not conform, it is also a means by which they highlight the fact that they themselves are conforming.

Theoretically, this view of name-calling is somewhat reminiscent of Goffman's (1968) belief in the existence of a subliminal 'ideal' within society where all must accentuate it or seek to attain it, or otherwise face ridicule and criticism. Indeed, as Rigby pointed out, following the advent of HIV/AIDS during the early 1980s, names that are associated with homosexuality have become much more potent in terms of their impact upon victims of bullying, and thus those who do not accentuate the heterosexual 'ideal' are relegated to the group labelled 'faggots', marking them as individuals from whom others should stay clear.

ADOLESCENCE, SEXUALITY AND POPULARITY AMONG PEERS

During adolescence, the emergence of sexual identity and all that it entails becomes of paramount importance to the individual in her or his social group (Duncan, 1999; Rivers *et al.*, 2007). Within the unofficial hierarchy of the school yard, playground, gang or club, power is determined by the ability of one person or a small group to belittle or otherwise subjugate the majority. Name-calling is a particularly potent weapon in the tormentors' armoury, and those names that are sexually loaded tend to be the most powerful. They not only attack an individual's identity at a fundamental level, they are also, more of than not, impossible to challenge effectively. Names such as 'slut', 'homo', 'gay boy', 'faggot' or 'dyke' have connotations that young people know devalue an individual's status within the social and, more importantly, moral hierarchy of the world outside.

Sexual behaviour and sexual orientation become weapons in the competition for pole position within the peer group. For young men, the sexual conquest of young women becomes a means of attaining status while, for young women, the ensnaring of the 'alpha' male or one of his cohorts ensures a high position in the pecking order. Thus, for those young men who cannot lay claim to the sexual conquest of at least one young woman, labels such as 'wimp' give way to those that suggest the absence of manliness, potency and inevitably heterosexuality. Concomitantly, for a young woman, the inability to attract a high-ranking male not only ensures that she is marked for 'out' group status, it almost inevitably ensures that questions will be raised about her conduct around other young women (i.e. she is lesbian) and young men (i.e. she is a slut).

A second factor that should not be overlooked when considering adolescents' preoccupation with sexuality comes from its high profile within western culture and, particularly, its utilisation as a marketing tool by the mass media (Reichert and Lambiase, 2005). Sex has become the primary tool we use to sell anything from cars to magazines. It is, we are told by columnists, agony aunts and uncles, the key to lifelong fulfilment. As adults, we buy into this message, purchasing more and more magazines that claim to have the secrets to successful love-making, or the fabled 5-minute work-out that will make us more desirable. Yet we fail to appreciate that young people have been sold this message through adult consumerism. By the time they have reached adolescence, they have already learnt that sex sells, and that popularity lies in providing peers with an affirmative assessment of their own sexual behaviour, together with a negative exposé of the behaviour of others.

THE PSYCHOLOGICAL CONSEQUENCES OF HOMOPHOBIA IN ADOLESCENCE

The consequences of allowing homophobia to continue unabated have been well documented. For example, in the US Hershberger and D'Augelli (1995) found that 42 per cent of their sample of LGB youth said that they had attempted suicide on at least one occasion – a figure confirmed by the California study in 2004 (California Safe Schools Coalition, 2004). In the UK, in a retrospective study of homophobic bullying, Rivers (2001) reported that 53 per cent of the former victims surveyed recalled contemplating self-harm or suicide: 40 per cent made at least one attempt, and three-quarters of those (30%) made two or more attempts.

In their study, Hershberger and D'Augelli (1995) found that some participants reported symptoms indicative of depression and anxiety. In the California study, 55 per cent of those who were bullied because of their actual or perceived sexual orientation also reported symptoms of depression. However, it should be noted that rates of self-reported depression were similar for those young people bullied because of their special needs (55%), their faith or belief (48%) or their black and minority ethnic status (48%). Data from a study of 116 former victims of homophobic bullying (compared to three comparison groups – heterosexual and bullied, heterosexual not-bullied and LGB not-bullied) also found higher rates of depression, anxiety and hostility among former victims but only when compared to heterosexual non-victims (Rivers, 2006).

The studies cited so far in this chapter suggest that bullying, particularly that which is homophobic in nature, can have a significant impact upon a victim's well-being and psychological health. Equally, evidence suggests that it can also have a profound effect upon the way in which a young LGBT person daily negotiates her/his identity. For example, in one of the early qualitative investigations of the impact homophobia has upon the lives of victims of homophobic bullying, Rivers (unpublished PhD thesis) explored the coping strategies used by 16 lesbians and gay men to avoid peer harassment when they were growing up. Interviews revealed that, for the majority, memories of wanting to disappear were very vivid. At school, some tried to physically hide themselves away during lunch- and break-times, while others tried not to stand out (in some cases this was attained by under-achieving academically at school):

> For almost a year of my school life I spent every break and every dinner break sitting in the back of the ... of the toilet area reading because I knew I was safe there, that I was isolated, and no-one would give me any hassle. (Paul)

> I think my aim in life was to keep as low a profile as possible ... so, wanting to ... to merge with the background. I suppose I had a few friendships, but they weren't particularly close. That's how it went on. There were flashes where, you know, merging into the background didn't actually work. So, that's how the five years passed I suppose. (James)

Some gay men recalled attempts to prove their heterosexuality, either by fighting other boys or by taking girlfriends in the hope that it would allay questions or suspicions by peers about their sexual orientation:

> I used to have so many fights in school because the other boys would pick on me because I was a poof and then I would be fighting for survival to kind of keep up my ... my reputation – for want of a better word – as a heterosexual ... as a normal boy. (Paul)

I always pretended to be heterosexual ... it was ridiculous ... there was this girl in my class ... I pretended she was my girlfriend and she went along with the pretence. (Matthew)

Years later, feelings of anger and fear remained, which were intertwined with persistent feelings of helplessness, vulnerability and humiliation at being unable to challenge their tormentors:

I think [I felt] partly frustrated because I couldn't do anything about it ... Angry as well I think. Annoyed at the fact I was being shouted at. Getting all the attention. I didn't like that. (Liam)

I spent the first ... I would say ... two or three years in secondary school frightened on most days to go in. I was frightened of certain groups of girls. (Susan)

For the majority of those interviewed, school was a lonely experience and one that can only be described as a hostile and alien environment. Those who did establish friendship networks did so independently:

I can't call them 'mates' because I didn't really have any friends at school. There was one or two that I tended to hang around. (Marcus)

I suppose I had a few friendships, but they weren't particularly close ... I am basically quite shy and ... not confident and maybe even though other people have these traits, I had them a lot more than other people. (James)

Overall, the interviews showed that the primary concern for young people who are LGBT and who are not 'out' at school is one of being discovered. Attempts are made to disguise those behavioural traits or mannerisms that may alert peers to their sexual orientation. Frable, Platt and Hoey (1998) have argued that the degree to which a person is a 'visible' member of a minority group will have an impact upon self-acceptance, affective state and susceptibility to long-term mental health problems. The more 'identifiable' a person is the better her/his mental health. Yet, despite their best efforts to remain hidden, as Duncan (1999) argues, perceived sexuality is often a matter of public knowledge and discussion at school resulting in anger, fear, and feelings of helplessness and vulnerability.

CHALLENGING HOMOPHOBIA: LEGISLATIVE ISSUES AND CURRICULUM GUIDANCE

In the US, schools and local education authorities (districts) have found themselves before the courts as a result of their failure to act when homophobia occurs. For example, one school in California made an out-of-court settlement of over $1 million after a group of young people began legal proceedings. In this case, one of the young people who filed the suit was so badly hurt that he required hospitalisation. However, none of the perpetrators was disciplined, even though the incident had been witnessed by a district employee. The district argued that as public servants they were immune from court proceedings because their legal obligation to protect students against homophobia was unclear and, thus, could not be realistically enforced. The district's legal team also claimed that the efforts it (the district) made to address the issues raised by the plaintiffs absolved it of any liability. Unfortunately the 9th US Court of Appeals disagreed, and a settlement was obtained before the judges ruled. It seems the judges had come to the decision that the lack of action on the part of school administrators to stop the harassment was tantamount to intentional discrimination.

In the UK, local education authorities (LEAs) have also been fined for their failure to protect young people from harassment, including homophobic harassment. In October 2000, Trafford LEA was ordered to pay a pupil compensation amounting to £1,500 because his school did not prevent him from being subjected to homophobic bullying. In this case, the judge determined that the school's inaction was in effect a breach of its duty of care. Despite these and other cases reported by the media, there remains a great deal of reticence in addressing issues of homophobia both within schools and within wider communities on both sides of the Atlantic. Yet, resources are available for teachers and youth and community workers in the UK and the US that provide guidance on relevant legislation, discussion topics and activity plans that address homophobia and homophobic bullying. A list of some of the most useful resources is provided in the appendix to this chapter.

For some people, homosexuality is a subject that they believe should never be discussed at school, even when discussion seeks to bring to an end bullying and harassment. Failure to address these issues does not preserve the innocence of children and young people: it promotes ignorance, and that ignorance is the foundation upon which discrimination thrives. We must all acknowledge that there are different points of view and, within the context of school for example, this means that pupils should be provided with an opportunity to discuss the different views people hold about homosexuality, and to explore those views in relation to their own emerging beliefs and value systems. As a starting point, Smith (2000) offers guidance that suggests that school governors and teachers should seek to:

- include homophobia in a school's anti-bullying policy – so pupils know that discrimination is wrong and the school will act;
- discuss homophobia in INSET training days on bullying in general;
- guarantee confidentiality and appropriate advice to lesbian and gay pupils;
- challenge homophobic language;
- explore issues of diversity and difference – discussing what school and society can do to end discrimination;
- explore pupils' understanding of their use of homophobic language – they may not understand the impact.

To support this endeavour, in 2004, the Health Development Agency launched *Stand Up For Us*, a resource for schools to challenge homophobia through the development of inclusive, safer and more successful educational environments for young people. The resource was designed for those working in 'early years' settings, primary, secondary and special schools, off-site units, and pupil referral units (PRUs). It assists teachers in meeting their statutory obligations under the Children Act 2004 and *Every Child Matters* (Department for Education and Skills, 2004). It includes information about homophobia (its nature and correlates), relevant legislation and guidance, and various materials for teachers working in the classroom, as well as outlines for staff training sessions.

CONCLUSION

Current evidence suggests that we have yet to tackle homophobia effectively both at school and within peer youth culture. Reticence about discussing homosexuality in the classroom is a correlate if not the cause of the continued rise of homophobia in our schools and in wider society. As Hunt and Jensen's (2007) study showed, in the UK only one-quarter of the schools that participants attended included homophobia in anti-bullying policies. Our failure to take action to stop homophobia has significant implications for the safety of all young people at school, not just young LGBTs. In California, for example, just under one-fifth of the young people who had been bullied because of their actual or perceived sexual orientation said that they carried a weapon to school for the purpose of protection, and over one-quarter said that they had been assaulted by another person wielding a weapon (California Safe Schools Coalition, 2004). It is noteworthy that, in response to concerns relating to the rise of gun-related crimes perpetrated at school, the Illinois State Board of Education (2001) reported that between 1996 and 1999 six of the eight perpetrators of gun violence had been regularly teased by peers, and that four had been specifically subjected to homophobic abuse.

ISSUES FOR PRACTICE

- Include homophobia in anti-bullying and non-discrimination policies.
- Check if homophobia is a topic colleagues feel confident in addressing.
- Make homophobia a topic for INSET or in-house training.
- Consider using or adapting existing resources in your work with young people (see the appendix to this chapter).
- Record and monitor incidents of homophobia and homophobic bullying.
- Remember, the government committed local authorities to providing services for all young people including LGBTs in *Youth Matters: Next Steps* (Department for Education and Skills, 2006).

REFERENCES

Bailey, M.J., Bobrow, D., Wolfe, M. and Mikach, S. (1995) Sexual orientation of adult sons of gay fathers. *Developmental Psychology*, **31**, 124–9.

Bigner, J.J. and Bozett, F.W. (1990) Parenting by gay fathers, in *Homosexuality and Family Relations* (eds F.W. Bozett and M.B. Sussman), Harrington Park Press, New York.

California Safe Schools Coalition and 4-H Centre for Youth Development (2004) *Consequences of Harassment Based on Actual or Perceived Sexual Orientation and Gender Non-conformity and Step to Making Schools Safer*, California Safe Schools Coalition, University of California, Davis, San Francisco, CA.

Chan, R. W., Raboy, B. and Patterson, C.J. (1998) Psychosocial adjustment among children conceived via donor insemination by lesbian and heterosexual mothers. *Child Development*, **69**, 443–57.

Cramer, D. (1986) Gay parents and their children: a review of research and practical implications. *Journal of Counseling and Development*, **64**, 504–7.

Department for Education and Skills (DES) (2004) *Every Child Matters: Change for Children*, DES, London.

Department for Education and Skills (2006) *Youth Matters: Next Steps*, DES, London.

Dressler, J. (1978) Study of law student attitudes regarding the rights of gay people to be teachers. *Journal of Homosexuality*, **4**, 315–29.

Duncan, N. (1999) *Sexual Bullying*, Routledge, London.

Ellis, V. and High, S. (2004) Something more to tell you: gay, lesbian or bisexual young people's experiences of secondary schooling. *British Educational Research Journal*, **30**, 213–25.

Flaks, D.K., Ficher, I., Masterpasqua, F. and Joseph, G. (1995) Lesbians choosing motherhood: a comparative study of lesbian and heterosexual parents and their children. *Developmental Psychology*, **31**, 105–14.

Frable, D.E.S., Platt, L. and Hoey, S. (1998) Concealable stigmas and positive self perceptions: feeling better around similar others. *Journal of Personality and Social Psychology*, **74**, 909–22.

Gallup, G.G. (1995) Have attitudes towards homosexuals been shaped by natural selection? *Ethology and Sociobiology*, **16**, 53–70.

Gartrell, N., Rodas, C., Deck, A. and Peyser, H. (2005) The national lesbian family study: 4. Interviews with the 10-year-old children. *American Journal of Orthopsychiatry*, **75**, 518–24.

Gershon, T.D., Tschann, J.M. and Jemerin, J.M. (1999) Stigmatization, self-esteem, and coping among adolescent children of lesbian mothers. *Journal of Adolescent Health*, **24**, 437–45.

Goffman, E. (1968) *Stigma: Notes on the Management of Spoiled Identity*. Penguin, Harmondsworth.

Golombok, S. and Tasker, F. (1996) Do parents influence the sexual orientation of their children? Findings from a longitudinal study of lesbian families. *Developmental Psychology*, **32**, 3–11.

Gottman, J.S. (1990) Children of gay and lesbian parents, in *Homosexuality and Family Relations* (eds F.W. Bozett and M.B. Sussman), Harrington Park Press, New York.

Hershberger, S.L. and D'Augelli, A.R. (1995) The impact of victimization on the mental health and suicidality of lesbian, gay and bisexual youths. *Developmental Psychology*, **31**, 65–74.

Hunt, R. and Jensen, J. (2007) *The School Report: The Experiences of Young Gay People in Britain's Schools*. Stonewall, London.

Illinois State Board of Education (2001) Bullying: bad behaviour is not just 'kids being kids'. *Education Insight*, **1** (1), 1–11.

Jenny, C., Roesler, T.A. and Poyer, K.L. (1994) Are children at risk from sexual abuse by homosexuals? *Pediatrics*, **94**, 41–4.

Miller, B. (1979) Gay fathers and their children. *Family Coordinator*, **28**, 544–52.

Morrison, T.G., McLeod, L.D., Morrison, M.A., Anderson, D. and O'Connor, W.E. (1997) Gender stereotyping, homonegativity, and misconceptions about sexually coercive behavior among adolescents. *Youth and Society*, **28**, 351–82.

Patterson, C.J. (1992) Children of lesbian and gay parents. *Child Development*, **63**, 1025–42.

Reichert, T. and Lambiase, J. (2005) *Sex in Consumer Culture: The Erotic Content of Media and Marketing*, Routledge, New York.

Rigby, K. (1997) *Bullying in Schools and What To Do About It*, Jessica Kingsley, London.

Rivers, I. (2001) The bullying of sexual minorities at school: its nature and long-term correlates. *Educational and Child Psychology*, **18** (1), 33–46.

Rivers, I. (2006) Homophobic bullying and mental health. *Health Psychology Update*, **15**, 20–3.

Rivers, I. and Cowie, H. (2006) Bullying and homophobia in UK schools: a perspective on factors affecting resilience and recovery. *Journal of Gay and Lesbian Issue in Education*, **3**, 11–43.

Rivers, I. and Noret, N. (2007) Tackling homophobic bullying: practical solutions, paper presented at the NASUWT seminar 'Tackling prejudice-related bullying', Europa Hotel, Belfast, 20 November.

Rivers, I., Duncan, N. and Besag, V.E. (2007) *Bullying: A Handbook for Educators and Parents*, Greenwood/Praeger, Westport, CT.

Rivers, I., Poteat, V.P. and Noret, N. (2008) Victimization, social support, and psychosocial functioning among children of same-sex and opposite-sex couples in the United Kingdom. *Developmental Psychology*, **44**, 127–34.

Smith, P.K. (2000) (ed.) *Bullying: Don't Suffer in Silence*. HMSO, London.

Tasker, F.L. and Golombok, S. (1997) *Growing Up in a Lesbian Family: Effects on Child Development*. Guilford, New York.

Wainright, J.L., Russell, S.T. and Patterson, C.J. (2004) Psychosocial adjustment, school outcomes, and romantic relationships of adolescents with same-sex parents. *Child Development*, **75**, 1886–98.

Warren, H. (1984) *Talking About School*. London Gay Teenage Group, London.

APPENDIX

The following resources are suggested for teachers and parents in dealing with homophobia at school (adapted from Rivers *et al.*, 2007, p. 91):

An Administrator's Guide to Handling Anti-Gay (LGBTQ) Harassment, www.safeschoolscoalition.org/guide_administrator_handleharass2005.pdf (accessed 10 July 2010).

An Educator's Guide to Intervening in Anti-Gay (LGBTQ) Harassment, www.safeschoolscoalition.org/guide_educator_interveneharass2005NAT.pdf (accessed 10 July 2010).

A Family's Guide to Handling Anti-Gay (LGBTQ) Harassment, www. safeschoolscoalition.org/guide_family_handleharass2005NAT.pdf (accessed 10 July 2010).

A Student's Guide to Surviving Anti-Gay Harassment and Physical or Sexual Assault, www.safeschoolscoalition.org/guide_student_surviveharass2005NAT. pdf (accessed 27 July 2010).

Gay, Lesbian and Straight Education Network (GLSEN) – this aims to ensure that every child learns to respect and accept all people, regardless of sexual orientation or gender, identity or expression, www.glsen.org (accessed 10 July 2010).

Human Rights Campaign – information on workplace policies and law surrounding sexual orientation and gender identity, www.hrc.org/worknet (accessed 10 July 2010).

National Association for Multicultural Education (NAME) – bullying resources, www.nameorg.org (accessed 10 July 2010)

National Union of Teachers (NUT) – guidance that includes information and advice on supporting pupils who are lesbian, gay, bisexual or transgender (LGBT), and on tackling homophobia within schools, www.chooselife.net/ web/site/Resources/Toolkit/TacklingHomophobicBullyingAnissuefor everyteacher.asp (accessed 26 July 2010).

Part III Understanding Peer Violence

11 Impact of Child Maltreatment and Domestic Violence

VERONICA M. HERRERA AND JEFFREY STUEWIG

INTRODUCTION

In 2005, the US Department of Health and Human Services reported that 3.6 million cases of child abuse and neglect were investigated, with 899,000 of them resulting in substantiated cases of child maltreatment. Over half (51%) of identified victims in child abuse and neglect cases were girls, with estimates increasing to 70 per cent for cases of child sexual abuse (Finkelhor and Baron, 1986). Although this is an alarmingly high number, official reports are generally considered to be underestimates with only a fraction of cases of maltreatment coming to the attention of social or judicial agencies (Straus *et al.*, 1998).

In addition to the direct, immediate harm done to children, the long-term effects of child maltreatment on children's future lives is of increasing concern for policy makers and researchers alike. Research has found that maltreated children are more likely to express problems in a wide array of developmental domains, including mental health (Cicchetti, Rogosch and Toth, 1994), social development and peer relations (Salzinger *et al.*, 1993; Jouriles *et al.*, 2001; Baldry, 2003), school achievement (Eckenrode, Laird and Doris, 1993) and delinquent behaviour (Smith and Thornberry, 1995; Herrera and McCloskey, 2001).

There is pressing concern that youth who have been maltreated or exposed to violence in the home will grow up to be aggressive and violent. Attachment theory suggests that children internalise important aspects of caregiving relationships that then influence their behaviour in later relationships with peers (Sroufe and Fleeson, 1986). Patterson and colleagues (e.g. Patterson, 2002) have shown that harsh, erratic, physical discipline promotes coercive exchanges in the family, and provides an environment for the child to learn aggressive and anti-social behaviour patterns. If these patterns of coercive exchanges persist in the family, they are likely to be incorporated into adolescents' repertoires of behaviour because they recognise the inherent reinforcing potential

Children Behaving Badly? Peer Violence Between Children and Young People
Edited by Christine Barter and David Berridge
© 2011 John Wiley & Sons Ltd.

of physical aggression. Marital violence, which often co-occurs with child abuse, has also been linked to aggression in children and adolescents. It could be that exposure to marital violence establishes patterns of behaviour modelled by their parents and generalised to behaviour within the wider peer network. By witnessing the imbalance of power and aggression between family members, some children learn to dominate others and may even be encouraged to do so (Baldry and Farrington, 1998).

Although much of the research has focused on how child maltreatment increases children's aggression, there is evidence to suggest that maltreated children are also at an increased risk of becoming targets of peer harassment and victimisation (Schwartz et al., 1993; Shields and Cicchetti, 2001). Some maltreated children adopt a submissive and ingratiating posture with their parents in an effort to maintain their safety in violent, chaotic homes (Cicchetti and Toth, 1995). They may come to expect that coercion, violence and exploitation are fundamental to all relationships and adopt an over-submissive style of interaction to appease others, making them an easy mark for exploitation and victimisation by peers (Schwartz et al., 1993; Shields and Cicchetti, 2001). Research has found that submissive social behaviour is associated with the emergence of chronic victimisation by peers (Schwartz et al., 1993). It is also true, however, that aggression and victimisation often go hand in hand. Those who are bullied may in turn bully others (Barker et al., 2008).

Maltreated children may be at risk of progressing down a path towards increasing maladjustment, marked by limited social competence with the potential of continued aggression and anti-social behaviour (Teisl and Cicchetti, 2008). Aggression against peers is probably the most common form of adolescent aggression. Dishion and colleagues (1991) found that the tendency towards peer aggression among boys both in childhood and adolescence could be traced to early coercive and neglectful parenting. Studies have demonstrated that maltreated children have serious difficulties with peer relations; physically abused children especially tend to show heightened levels of physical and verbal aggression in their interaction with peers (Mueller and Silverman, 1989). In an investigation of peer relations of school-aged children, Salzinger and colleagues (1993) found that peers viewed maltreated children as evidencing more anti-social behaviour, such as aggressiveness, meanness, disruptiveness and fewer pro-social behaviours such as leadership and sharing. Similarly, Rogosch and Cicchetti (1994) found that maltreated children were rated as lower in social competences and higher in externalising behaviours both by teachers and peers. Longitudinal studies have confirmed that the association between child maltreatment and aggressive and victim behaviour continues into adolescent relationships with peers and romantic partners (Wolfe et al., 1998; McCloskey and Lichter, 2003).

A meta-analysis of studies of the effects of child sexual abuse found that sexual victimisation accounted for 43 per cent of the variance in measures of aggression when comparing abused and non-abused children (Kendall-Tackett,

Williams and Finkelhor, 1993). A growing body of work focusing on girls' aggression and violence has identified physical and sexual abuse as especially salient pathways for girls' aggressive, violent and delinquent behaviour (Kendall-Tackett *et al.*, 1993; Belknap and Holsinger, 1998; Chesney-Lind and Shelden, 1998; Herrera and McCloskey, 2003). There is also evidence showing that girls exposed to marital violence are more likely to directly bully others, compared with girls who have not witnessed marital violence (Baldry, 2003). It is argued that girls' development may be more contingent on family circumstances than that of boys, given families' greater propensity to keep daughters closer to home while allowing sons more freedom (Pepler and Craig, 2005). Given that relationships are of central importance in the lives of girls and women (Maccoby, 1998), exposure to violence, abuse, rejection or indifference would be particularly devastating for girls' emotional and developmental well-being.

The purpose of this chapter is to examine the impact of three forms of child maltreatment – exposure to marital violence, child physical abuse and child sexual abuse – on aggression, bullying and peer victimisation in a community sample of adolescent boys and girls. Because different forms of child maltreatment tend to overlap in families, disentangling the unique effects of specific maltreatment types has proven difficult. To date, few studies have examined gender differences in the effects of early maltreatment on later bullying (generally conceived of as a subtype of aggressive behaviour) or feelings of victimisation. For that reason, the main focus of this chapter is to examine if different forms of child maltreatment are related differentially to later peer aggression and peer victimisation depending on the gender of the child.

THE PRESENT STUDY

The present study utilised data from an 8-year longitudinal study designed to examine the impact of marital violence on children's mental health. A volunteer community sample of abused and non-abused mothers and their children were recruited to participate in the study (see McCloskey, Fuguerdo and Koss, 1995). Women responded to posters and advertisements located throughout the city requesting participation of mothers with school-aged children for a university study on the family. Abused women were uniquely contacted from battered women's shelters as well as through targeted posters in the city asking for women who had been abused in an intimate relationship during the past year. Upon contacting the project, all women who had co-resided with a male partner within the last 12 months and had a child between the ages of 6 and 12 years were recruited for the study. One child from each family was selected to participate. The interviewer alternated between choosing a boy or girl from each family, resulting in an approximately equal number of boys and girls interviewed.

The original sample interviewed in 1990–91 comprised 363 mother–child dyads representing families with domestic violence (n = 166) and comparison families (n = 197). All mothers provided informed consent and children provided written assent prior to participating. Although confidentiality was guaranteed, for ethical reasons, reports of ongoing child abuse were reported to Child Protective Services. Women and children were re-interviewed at two later time points completed in 1997 (Time 2) and 1999 (Time 3). More than 80 per cent of the original sample was retained during the 8-year course of the study. The present analyses focus on data collected at Times 1 and 2. Our final sample size was 313 for analytic purposes.

Mothers were 33 years old on average (standard deviation [SD] = 5.2) at the time of the first interview (1990–1) and 39 (SD = 5.2) at Time 2. The target child was between 6 and 12 at initial assessment (average [mean – M] = 9 years, SD = 1.9). At Time 2 they were on average 15 years old (SD = 2.1). The ethnic distribution was approximately 53 per cent Anglo-European and 35 per cent Hispanic, with the remainder self-identified as Native American (5%), African American (5%), Asian American (1%) or other (1%). The average yearly family income during the youth's childhood (1990–1) was $17,320.80 ($SD$ = $11,432.40), although the median was $14,436.00, only slightly above the poverty threshold for a family of four ($13,404) established by 1992 Arizona guidelines.

MEASURES OF CHILD MALTREATMENT

Three aspects of child maltreatment were assessed during the first wave of data collection – exposure to marital violence, child physical abuse and child sexual abuse. Exposure to marital violence was measured via mothers' reports of the extent of marital violence they had experienced using selected items from an abridged version of the Conflict Tactics Scale (CTS; Straus, 1979). The CTS assessed the mean frequency women experienced physical violence by their current partners, ranging from being slapped to having a knife or gun used against them. The frequency of violent episodes reported by women in this sample ranged from 0 to 18.4 or more times (M = 2.8, SD = 4.2).

Child physical abuse was assessed using items from the CTS (Straus, 1979). Children responded to questions about escalated forms of physical abuse (e.g. 'kicked or hit with a fist' and 'burned') that they had experienced from either their mother or their mother's partner. Each mother also received an expanded list of questions about her partner's abusive tactics towards the child. The frequency of escalated abuse reported by children and their mothers ranged from 0 to 6.4 (M = 42, SD = 1.0).

Child sexual abuse was assessed using coded transcripts of narratives describing the child's sexual abuse experiences collected from both the child and the mother. If either the mother or the child confirmed a sexual abuse incident, the child was considered sexually abused. Based on this criterion, 33 children (10.5%) were coded as sexually abused. There was, however, a large sex difference in reports of sexual abuse, in that only 4 males (2.6%) but 29 females (18.4%) were classified as sexually abused.

MEASURES OF ADOLESCENT AGGRESSION AND VICTIMISATION

Physical aggression was measured using the Buss-Perry Aggression Questionnaire (Buss and Perry, 1992), a widely used self-report measure of trait aggression. Aggression in adolescence was measured using three items: 'Once in a while I can't control the urge to strike another person'; 'Given enough reason, I may hit another person'; and 'If somebody hits me, I hit back.' Responses to items ranged from 1 = 'extremely unlike me' to 5 = 'extremely like me' ($\alpha = .75$, $M = 2.9$, $SD = 1.0$).

Bullying was measured using four items: 'Other people think of me as someone to watch out for', 'I think that it's someone's own fault if other kids tease or make fun of them', 'I like to make certain other kids are afraid of me', and 'I feel better after beating someone up' ($\alpha = .70$, $M = 2.0$, $SD = .77$). Feeling victimised by peers was measured using three items: 'I have felt like I want to drop out of school because of people teasing me or beating me up', 'I am often afraid that other kids might hit, kick or shove me', and 'I often feel picked on by other people' ($\alpha = .76$, $M = 1.7$, $SD = .76$).

RESULTS

Bivariate correlations between the childhood victimisation variables and adolescent outcomes split by gender are presented in Table 11.1. In general, *for*

Table 11.1 Correlations between child victimisation variables and outcome variables by gender

	Girls ($n = 156$)			Boys ($n = 155$)		
	Aggression	Bullying	Feeling victimised by peers	Aggression	Bullying	Feeling victimised by peers
Escalated physical abuse	.20*	.29**	.23**	.03	.05	−.10
Marital violence	.20*	.14+	.17*	.18*	.10	−.10
Sexual abuse	.24**	.15+	.17*	.13	−.08	−.02

$+p < .08$, $*p < .05$, $**p < .01$.

girls, all three forms of childhood victimisation were positively related to aggression, bullying and feelings of victimisation. *For boys*, however, only marital violence in the home was positively related to aggression. The rest of the correlations were non-significant for boys. At least at the bivariate level, it seems as if childhood victimisation may have an influence on girls' later aggressive behaviour and feelings of victimisation.

In order to examine this in a more multivariate model, controlling for the different types of childhood victimisation, and to directly test whether there were differences between boys and girls in these relationships, we conducted three multiple regressions. Each of the adolescent outcomes (aggression, bullying, feeling victimised by peers) were regressed onto the three child maltreatment variables (escalated abuse, sexual abuse, marital violence in the home) as well as the interaction of each of these with gender. Variables were centred and two steps were evaluated: (Step 1) the main effects of gender and the child maltreatment variables; and (Step 2) the interaction term between gender and each of the three predictor variables.

AGGRESSION

Results from the multiple regressions are presented in Table 11.2. Examining Step 1 (Table 11.2, far left) we found that females generally reported lower levels of aggression than did males. Controlling for the other forms of childhood victimisation, sexual abuse in childhood was positively related to aggression in adolescence. Results also showed that households with higher levels of marital violence tended to have children who were higher on aggression in adolescence. The lack of significant interactions between the main predictor variables and gender in Step 2 of the analysis indicated that girls and boys were equally vulnerable to the effects of marital violence and sexual abuse. In other words, girls and boys who were sexually abused or exposed to violence in the home were more aggressive in adolescence than non-abused youth.

BULLYING

When examining Step 1 predicting bullying (Table 11.2, centre) we found again that females reported lower levels of bullying than males. Of the three child maltreatment variables tested, escalated physical abuse emerged as the only significant predictor of bullying behaviour in adolescence. In Step 2 we found a marginally significant effect $(p = .057)^1$ for the interaction of gender by escalated physical abuse, demonstrating that the relationship between escalated physical abuse and later bullying behaviour differed for boys and girls.

---

[1] This calculation refers to the probability ('p') of results occurring by chance. Usually, researchers conclude that results of less than .05 ($p = <.05$) (that is, 1 in 20) are unlikely to have arisen by chance but are 'statistically significant'.

Table 11.2   Multiple regressions including the main effects of gender and child maltreatment and the interaction terms between gender and each of the predictor variables

	Aggression			Bullying			Victimisation		
	B	SE	Beta	B	SE	Beta	B	SE	Beta
Step 1									
Sex	−.17	(.06)	−.17**	−.19	(.04)	−.25**	−.04	(.05)	−.05
Physical abuse	.05	(.06)	.05	.10	(.04)	.13*	.04	(.04)	.05
Sexual abuse	.57	(.19)	.17**	.12	(.14)	.05	.27	(.15)	.11+
Marital violence	.04	(.01)	.16**	.01	(.01)	.08	.00	(.01)	.02
	Adj. R^2 = .07			Adj. R^2 = .08			Adj. R^2 = .01		
Step 2									
Sex	−.18	(.06)	−.18**	−.17	(.05)	−.23**	−.02	(.05)	−.03
Physical abuse	.05	(.06)	.05	.11	(.04)	.14*	.05	(.04)	.07
Sexual abuse	.63	(.27)	.19*	−.12	(.20)	−.05	.11	(.21)	.05
Marital violence	.04	(.01)	.16**	.01	(.01)	.08	.00	(.01)	.01
Sex x physical Abuse	.08	(.06)	.08	.08	(.04)	.11+	.10	(.04)	.13*
Sex x sexual abuse	−.10	(.27)	−.03	.31	(.20)	.12	.16	(.21)	.06
Sex x marital violence	−.01	(.01)	−.03	−.01	(.01)	−.03	.02	(.01)	.09
	Adj. R^2 = .07			Adj. R^2 = .09			Adj. R^2 = .03		

Further analyses were conducted in order to interpret the significance of this interaction. Results indicated that for girls, history of escalated physical abuse was related to bullying behaviour. Girls who had been physically abused in childhood reported higher levels of bullying behaviour in adolescence than did non-abused girls. This pattern of results, however, was not found for boys. Although boys in general reported higher levels of bullying than girls, rates of bullying among abused boys were similar to those of non-abused boys.

FEELING VICTIMISED BY PEERS

In contrast to the previous two regressions, we did not find a gender difference for feeling victimised by peers (Table 11.2, far right). Overall, girls and boys reported similar levels of peer victimisation. Examining the main effects of the three child maltreatment variables, we see a trend where children who were sexually abused in childhood report more feelings of peer victimisation in adolescence than do those who were not sexually abused ($p = .07$). In Step 2, we found a significant effect for gender by escalated physical abuse. Again, as we found for bullying, subsequent analyses revealed that girls who had been physically abused in childhood reported higher levels of feeling victimised by peers in adolescence than did non-abused girls. This pattern of results was not found for boys.

DISCUSSION AND RECOMMENDATIONS

The relationships children experience in their families are said to provide a crucial foundation for later social interactions (Shields and Cicchetti, 2001). Attachment theory suggests that children internalise important aspects of caregiving relationships that then influence their behaviour in later relationships with peers (Sroufe and Fleeson, 1986). Families where children are maltreated characteristically provide fewer supports and opportunities for children to learn to function effectively outside the family. This chapter highlights the impact of different forms of child maltreatment on peer relationships, specifically adolescent aggression, bullying and peer victimisation. Although research has consistently identified a link between child maltreatment and aggression, fewer studies have examined whether bullying and victimisation are also evident in maltreated children's relationships with peers. The inclusion of girls is a unique strength that allowed us to examine whether gender moderated maltreatment's effects.

By comparing the relative impact of three forms of childhood victimisation, we were able to identify the independent effects of physical abuse, exposure to marital violence and sexual abuse on aggression, bullying and peer victimisation. Of the three maltreatment variables tested, physical abuse emerged as being more strongly related to girls' outcomes than boys'. Results showed that being a victim of physical abuse influenced girls' bullying behaviour as well as their feelings of victimisation by peers. Although boys engage in higher levels of bullying behaviour than girls in general, physical abuse emerged as a significant pathway to girls bullying.

It is suggested that girls' victimisation and their response to that victimisation are specifically shaped by their status as young women (Chesney-Lind and Shelden, 1998). Girls, in comparison with boys, are more frequently socialised to attend to the needs and well-being of others and to judge their self-worth in terms of others' opinion of them (Cross and Madson, 1997). Abuse at the hands of a parent can distort a child's expectation about her own role and those of others in relationships. Girls' experiences of physical abuse within the family may limit their capacity to form trusting relationships. To protect themselves from what they expect to be a pervasive social threat, some maltreated girls may adopt bullying tactics in social interactions in order to assert a position of power, or some may assume an over-passive and non-assertive behaviour style to avoid attention or appease others. These behaviours may then place them at risk of bully or victim status (Shields and Cicchetti, 2001), or even both.

A large body of research has demonstrated that exposure to family violence contributes to the development of behaviour problems in children (Wolfe *et al.*, 1988; McCloskey *et al.*, 1995). We found that exposure to marital violence increased adolescent aggressive behaviour. According to social learning theory, children learn through observation and imitation of adult models (Bandura, 1977). It is likely that exposure to a high degree of family conflict in childhood may constitute 'aggression training' that may extend into peer group interactions (Mohr, 2006). It has also been suggested that exposure to marital violence can lead to later aggressive behaviour through the suppression of pro-social adaptations such as empathy (Miller and Eisenberg, 1988). Gender did not moderate the relationship between exposure to marital violence and later aggression, suggesting that the influence of marital violence functions similarly for boys and girls.

Lastly, childhood sexual abuse was found to increase aggressive behaviour in adolescence. There was also some evidence to suggest that children who had been sexually abused were more likely to report feeling victimised by peers. Child sexual abuse can launch a life course where maladaptive beliefs shape self-perceptions and perceptions of others. Processes related to stigmatisation, shame and self-blaming attribution styles have been described as being important for understanding the adjustment of victims of child sexual abuse (Feiring, Miller-Johnson and Cleland, 2007). It has been suggested that shame can motivate retaliation such as defensive anger (Tagney *et al.*, 1996). In other words, individuals who experience stigmatisation may try to avoid this negative state by displacing shame with anger, which can increase the likelihood of aggressive behaviour (Feiring *et al.*, 2007). Child sexual abuse has also been linked to internalising behaviour problems such as depression, anxiety and low self-esteem (Finkelhor and Browne, 1985), which may leave a child vulnerable to victimisation by peers. Gender did not moderate the relationship between child sexual abuse and later aggression. Because of the small number of sexually abused boys, there was perhaps insufficient power in the analyses to detect gendered effects.

Research has shown that maltreated children may be at risk of progressing down a path towards increasing maladjustment, influencing how they interact with others and how others respond to them. We believe more research is needed to fully understand the mechanisms through which child maltreatment affects later behaviour. We also need to identify individual risk factors (e.g. attention deficit disorder, conduct disorder) that may contribute to the development of aggression and bullying in adolescents, and then to test for gender differentiated effects. Lastly, we need to further investigate how girls' experiences of, and responses to, child maltreatment differ from those of boys in order to develop appropriate and effective intervention and treatment programmes.

We close this chapter by proposing several recommendations:

- When assessing child maltreatment, it is important to assess not just direct forms of maltreatment, such as physical and sexual abuse, but also exposure to violence between parents. Children who have witnessed violence appear just as vulnerable to developing behaviour problems as are children who have been direct victims.
- When working with adolescents who exhibit problem behaviours, such as aggression and bullying, youth workers should address prior victimisation that the young people may have experienced in the home.
- Similarly, when working with adolescents who report feeling bullied and victimised by peers, it is important to address not only the impact of current experiences of victimisation, but also prior victimisation that the young people may have experienced in the home.
- Given the evidence for differential risk factors for girls versus boys in bullying behaviour, prevention programmes need to be evaluated as to whether a 'one size fits all' approach is appropriate, or whether programmes should be modified to the specific needs of boys and girls.
- It may be especially important to be aware of experiences of child victimisation when tailoring interventions for aggressive and bullying girls.

REFERENCES

Baldry, A.C. (2003) Bullying in schools and exposure to domestic violence. *Child Abuse and Neglect*, **27**, 713–32.

Baldry, A.C. and Farrington, D.P. (1998) Parenting influences on bullying and victimisation. *Criminal and Legal Psychology*, **3**, 237–54.

Bandura, A. (1977) *Social Learning Theory*. Prentice Hall, Englewood Cliffs, NJ.

Barker, E., Arseneault, L., Brendgen, M., Fontaine, N. and Maughan, B. (2008) Joint development of bullying and victimization in adolescence: relations to delinquency and self-harm. *Journal of the American Academy of Child and Adolescent Psychiatry*, **47**, 1030–8.

Belknap, J. and Holsinger, K. (1998) An overview of delinquent girls: how theory and practice have failed and the need for innovative changes, in *Female Offenders: Critical Perspectives and Effective Interventions* (ed. R. Zaplin), Aspen Publishers, Inc., Gaithersburg, MD.

Buss, A. and Perry, M. (1992) The aggression questionnaire. *Journal of Personality and Social Psychology*, **63**, 452–9.

Chesney-Lind, M. and Shelden, R. (1998) *Girls, Delinquency, and Juvenile Justice*, 2nd edition, Wadsworth, Belmont, CA.

Cicchetti, D. and Toth, S.L. (1995) A developmental psychopathology perspective on child abuse and neglect. *Journal of the American Academy of Child and Adolescent Psychiatry*, **34**, 541–65.

Cicchetti, D., Rogosch, F.A. and Toth, S.L. (1994) A developmental psychopathology perspective on depression in children and adolescents, in *Handbook of Depression in Children and Adolescents* (eds W.M. Reynolds and H.F. Johnston), 123–41. Plenum Press, New York.

Cross, S.E. and Madson, L. (1997) Models of the self: self-construals and gender. *Psychological Bulletin*, **122**, 5–37.

Dishion, T.J., Patterson, G.R., Stoolmiller, M. and Skinner, M.L. (1991) Family, school, and behaviour antecedents to early adolescent involvement with antisocial peers. *Developmental Psychology*, **1**, 172–80.

Eckenrode, J., Laird, M. and Doris, J. (1993) School performance and disciplinary problems among abused and neglected children. *Developmental Psychology*, **29**, 53–62.

Feiring, C., Miller-Johnson, S. and Cleland, C.M. (2007) Potential pathways from stigmatization and internalizing symptoms to delinquency in sexually abused youth. *Child Maltreatment*, **12**, 220–32.

Finkelhor, D. and Baron, L. (1986) Risk factors for child sexual abuse. *Journal of Interpersonal Violence*, **1** (1), 43–71.

Finkelhor, D. and Browne, A. (1985) The traumatic impact of child sexual abuse: a conceptualization. *American Journal of Orthopsychiatry*, **55**, 530–41.

Herrera, V.M. and McCloskey, L.A. (2001) Gender differences in the risk for delinquency among youth exposed to family violence. *Child Abuse and Neglect*, **25**, 1037–51.

Herrera, V.M. and McCloskey, L.A. (2003) Sexual abuse, family violence, and girls' antisocial behaviour: findings from a longitudinal study. *Violence and Victims*, **18**, 319–34.

Jouriles, E.N., Norwood, W.D., McDonald, R. and Peters, B. (2001) Domestic violence and child adjustment, in *Interparental Conflict and Child Development: Theory, Research, and Applications* (eds J.H. Grych and F.D. Fincham), 315–36. Cambridge University Press, New York.

Kendall-Tackett, K.A., Williams, L.M. and Finkelhor, D. (1993) Impact of sexual abuse on children: a review and synthesis of recent empirical studies. *Psychological Bulletin*, **113**, 164–80.

Maccoby, E.E. (1998) *The Two Sexes: Growing- up Apart, Coming Together. Family and Public Policy*. Belknap Press/Harvard University Press, Cambridge, MA.

McCloskey, L.A. and Lichter, E.L. (2003) The contribution of marital violence and adolescent aggression across different relationships. *Journal of Interpersonal Violence*, **18**, 390–412.

McCloskey, L.A., Figuerdo, A.J. and Koss, M.P. (1995) The effects of systematic family violence on children's mental health. *Child Development*, **66**, 1239–61.

Miller, P.A. and Eisenberg, N. (1988) The relation of empathy to aggressive and externalizing/antisocial behaviour. *Psychological Bulletin*, **103**, 324–44.

Mohr, A. (2006) Family variables associated with peer victimization: does family violence enhance the probability of being victimized by peers. *Swiss Journal of Psychology*, **65**, 107–16.

Mueller, E. and Silverman, N. (1989) Peer relations in maltreated children, in *Child Maltreatment: Theory and Research on the Causes and Consequences of Child Abuse and Neglect* (eds D. Cicchetti and V. Carlson), 529–78, Cambridge University Press, New York.

Patterson, G.R. (2002) The early development of coercive family process, in *Antisocial Behaviour in Children and Adolescents: Developmental Analysis and Model for Intervention* (eds J.B. Reid, G.R. Patterson and J. Snyder), 25–44. American Psychological Association, Washington, DC.

Pepler, D.J. and Craig, W.M. (2005) Aggressive girls on troubled trajectories: a developmental perspective, in *The Development and Treatment of Girlhood Aggression* (eds D.J. Pepler, K.C. Madsen, C. Webster and K.S. Levene), 3–28. Lawrence Erlbaum Associates, Mahwah, NJ.

Rogosch, F.A. and Cicchetti, D. (1994) Illustrating the interface of family and peer relations through the study of child maltreatment. *Social Development*, **3**, 291–308.

Salzinger, S., Feldman, R.S., Hammer, M. and Rosario, M. (1993) The effects of physical abuse on children's social relationships. *Child Development*, **64**, 169–87.

Schwartz, D., Dodge, K.A. and Coie, J.D. (1993) The emergence of chronic peer victimization in boys' play groups. *Child Development*, **64**, 1755–72.

Shields, A. and Cicchetti, D. (2001) Parental maltreatment and emotion dysregulation as risk factors for bullying and victimization in middle childhood. *Journal of Clinical Child and Adolescent Psychology*, **30**, 349–63.

Smith, C. and Thornberry, T.P. (1995) The relationship between childhood maltreatment and adolescent involvement in delinquency. *Criminology*, **33**, 451–77.

Sroufe, L.A. and Fleeson, J. (1986) Attachment and the construction of relationships, in *Relationships and Development* (eds W. Hartup and Z. Rubins), 51–76. Earlbaum, Hillsdale, NJ.

Straus, M.A. (1979) Measuring intrafamily conflict and violence: the conflict tactics scales. *Journal of Marriage and the Family*, **41**, 75–88.

Straus, M.A., Hamby, S.L., Finkelhor, D., Moore, D.W. and Runyon, D. (1998) Identification of child maltreatment with parent–child conflict tactics scales: development and psychometric data for a national sample of American parents. *Child Abuse and Neglect*, **22**, 249–70.

Tagney, J.P., Wagner, P.E., Hill-Barlow, D., Marschall, D.E. and Gramzow, R. (1996) Relation of shame and guilt to constructive versus destructive responses to anger across the lifespan. *Journal of Personality and Social Psychology*, **70**, 797–809.

Teisl, M. and Cicchetti, D. (2008) Physical abuse, cognitive and emotional processes, and aggressive/disruptive behaviours problems. *Social Development*, **17**, 1–23.

US Department of Health and Human Services (2007) *Child Maltreatment 2005. Administration on Children, Youth and Families*, US Government Printing Office, Washington, DC.

Wolfe, D.A., Jaffe, P., Wilson, S. and Zak, L. (1988) A multivariate investigation of children's adjustment to family violence, in *Family Abuse and its Consequences* (eds G.T. Hotaling, D. Finkelhor, J.T. Kirkpatrick and M.A. Straus), 228–41. Sage, Beverly Hills, CA.

Wolfe, D.A., Wekerle, C., Reitzel-Jaffe, D. and Lefebvre, L. (1998) Factors associated with abusive relationships among maltreated and nonmaltreated youth. *Development and Psychopathology*, **10**, 61–85.

12 Media Representations of Youth Violence

SHARON L. NICHOLS

INTRODUCTION

In early April 2008, there were two incidents of youth violence that captured the national spotlight in America. The first involved a group of adolescent girls who had beaten up another girl in the Florida basement of one of the assailants (Cave, 2008; Reyes and Townsend, 2008; Townsend, 2008). The incident was taped by one of the girls who participated in the assault and who intended to distribute it on Youtube.com as revenge for the victim having smeared their names on another online networking site. The subsequent release of the video tape into the national news cycle dominated the airwaves for a few days as newscasters, enthralled by the 'outrageous' event, played the video over and over again all the while pointing to the event as 'shocking', 'unbelievable' and 'hard to watch'.

The second incident involved a group of half a dozen third graders (9–10-year-olds), who were involved in a 'plot' to kill their teacher in a Georgian elementary school (Standora, 2008). There was no video of this incident, so newscasters had to rely on police reports and photographic evidence to recount the story. The plot involved various weapons and tools including a paperweight to knock the teacher down, duct tape to tie her up and a knife to stab her. The students were cunning in their plot, assigning roles to each other as one student was to keep watch, another to use the paperweight, another to cover the windows and another to 'clean up'.

These events were already shocking to an American public unaccustomed to images of girls beating up one another or of children with murderous inclinations. Still, this was the exact reason why these incidents, and not other forms of youth violence, preoccupied the media landscape. The more outrageous the event, the more likely it will dominate media coverage. But the problem isn't that it gets covered. The problem is *how* it is covered (Edelman, 1988). When it comes to youth violence, analyses suggest that the media coverage slants towards distortion, exaggeration and misrepresentation.

Children Behaving Badly? Peer Violence Between Children and Young People
Edited by Christine Barter and David Berridge
© 2011 John Wiley & Sons Ltd.

FRAMING IN THE MEDIA

Temporal and spatial restrictions in a highly competitive news environment, where TV, newspapers, magazines and now the internet are vying for profit and a loyal consumer base, mean that shock value is a critical ingredient to any news story.[1] In framing newsworthy events, specific aspects, it is argued, are made more salient to consumers than others and, thereby, more 'noticeable, meaningful, or memorable to audiences' (Entman, 1993, p. 51). Of course, saliency does not necessarily predict *how* readers or consumers interpret events but, at a minimum, an event is more likely to be remembered (e.g. Fiske and Taylor, 1991; Halpern, 2003). The strategic use of saliency, as in the 'if it bleeds, it leads' philosophy of reporting, is meant to grab (and hopefully sustain) readers' attention.

Yet media analysts find that framing does so much more than just grab our attention. The way a story is framed offers a specific version of events that is characterised by the language used as well as the perspective taken (e.g. Kahneman and Tversky, 1984). Entman (1993) defines it this way:

> To frame is to *select some aspects of a perceived reality and make them more salient in a communicating text, in such a way as to promote a particular problem definition, causal interpretation, moral evaluation, and/or treatment recommendation* for the item described. Typically frames diagnose, evaluate, and prescribe …Frames, then, *define problems*– determine what a causal agent is doing with what costs and benefits, usually measured in terms of common cultural values; *diagnose causes*–identify the forces creating the problem; *make moral judgments*– evaluate causal agents and their effects; and *suggest remedies*– offer and justify treatments for the problems and predict their likely effects (p. 52).

Thus, mass media define social problems for audiences – presenting the who, what, where, why and when. The strategic choices of how to discuss story knowns and unknowns not only influence the beliefs and attitudes of consumers (e.g. Iyengar and Kinder, 1987) but, in turn, also help to shape how social problems are addressed through policies and legislation (Gamson, 1992; Surette, 1992).

Media expert David Altheide makes this point when it comes to how violence against children, in this case child kidnappings, get framed. He argues the following:

> Focusing on 'stranger kidnappings' of which there were very few each year (e.g. 67 in 1983), sparked an unprecedented multi-media barrage of 'missing child' photos and pleas on milk cartons, billboards, network news, millions of pieces of mail, and of course numerous movies and documentaries. The children of America

---

[1] Importantly, in this chapter, I focus on work that largely examines print and television news stories. Currently, there is a paucity of studies examining the role, nature and impact of the internet in framing youth violence.

were reportedly under siege. Such action fuelled legislation, policy changes, increased criminal sanctions and budget allocations in the millions of dollars. Ignoring the far more numerous 'runaway' and 'throwaway' children left most cities with paltry resources to help and protect several hundred thousand children 'on the road'.

Altheide, 1997, p. 655

In this case, the slanted emphasis on stranger abductions in an environment where the problems of youth runaways are significantly more prevalent played a significant role in subsequent resource allocations and policy implementation.

FRAMING AND YOUTH VIOLENCE: HOW ARE EVENTS CONSTRUCTED?

There is evidence to suggest that, when it comes to youth violence, the media (which often works in concert with politicians), exaggerate in ways that suggest youth violence is more prevalent than actually is the case. For example, in the late 1980s, American policy makers predicted that society should prepare for the onslaught of the teenage 'superpredator', who in growing numbers would commit serious violent crimes (e.g. assault, rape and murder) without remorse (Snyder and Sickmund, 1999; US Department of Health and Human Services *et al.*, 2000). These predictions were based on two salient factors. First, the 1990s were about to experience one of the largest adolescent populations ever seen. Also, gun violence was increasing in the late 1980s, leading experts to predict that violent crimes would increase substantially with a growing youth population. However, these predictions never materialised. Youth crime actually dropped off (e.g. Blumstein and Wallman, 2000; Butts, 2000) and yet media coverage increased, giving the impression that youth violence rates were rising (Males, 1996, 2000).

Analyses of media coverage of youth violence highlighted this discrepancy. Research on Hawaiian coverage revealed that there was an *11 per cent decrease* in juvenile arrests during the period 1987–96, and yet between 1991 and 1996 the number of articles about juvenile delinquency increased *690 per cent*, while the number of articles about gangs specifically increased *720 per cent*. And these percentages increased respectively to 2,800 per cent and 4,000 per cent when a 10-year time period was studied (Perrone and Chesney-Lind, 1997). Males (2000) found that in the 1997 *Los Angeles Times* Orange County edition, youth were 3.2 times more likely to be featured in violent crime stories than were adults. Or, put another way, Males (2000) found that half the stories on crime featured youth – 6 to 10 times more frequently than actual youth violence rates (Males, 2000).

US isn't alone in its exaggerated reporting. Elsewhere, Body-Gendrot (2005) argues that the prevalence and severity of urban violence among youth in Paris is dramatically overblown, pointing to cultural, ideological and political forces that may explain the misconstruction. In short, data suggest that the media perpetrates an image that youth violence is more common and more likely than actual crime data suggest. The result of this capitalisation on a fear-based approach to youth violence (Altheide, 1997, 2002) is a public that embraces a pessimistic, fearful and unsympathetic view of youth (Farkas and Johnson, 1997; Nichols and Good, 2004).

EPISODIC VERSUS THEMATIC

However, framing choices delivers so much more than a distorted notion of the prevalence of youth violence. News framing delivers a complete story including information about the who, what, where, why and when of events. Either implicitly or explicitly, news framing captures some type of message that in the absence of facts is laden with insinuations of what happened and who is to blame (e.g. Edelman, 1988; Cerulo, 1998).

One major distinction, often made in analyses of news media coverage to capture framing effects, is its *episodic* or *thematic* focus (Iyengar and Kinder, 1987; Iyengar, 1991). Episodic reporting focuses on a single event at a time that is void of any contextual information relating to that event. Thematic reporting, on the other hand, emphasises multiple viewpoints of stories while providing more nuanced contextual information regarding the event or events. Researchers agree that newspaper coverage of youth violence is largely episodic (Iyengar, 1991; McManus and Dorfman, 2002). For example, in an analysis of local TV news coverage about violence in California, Dorfman *et al.* (1997) found that 80 per cent of stories were episodic in nature and emphasised the role of personal individual responsibility. Only one story (out of 1,800) emphasised the role of societal responsibility.

One problem with episodic reporting rests with the attributions that are often associated with the event. When the news focuses on a specific event or case (e.g. boy shoots mom) without attending to the circumstances or context (e.g. family loses job, parental abuse, poverty), it tends to frame responsibility in terms of the individual being highlighted rather than the context in which the event occurred. Dodge (2008) argues that youth violence frames commonly involve metaphors that elicit familiar assumptions about the origin and nature of youth violence. For example, the metaphors of youth as 'superpredator' or as 'morally defective' shape beliefs about youth violence as a problem of 'bad' youth instead of bad conditions. Ultimately, these attributional frames lessen policymakers' responsibilities for having to invest in youth programs (perhaps strategically) because they construct images of calculating youth (e.g. Iyengar and Kinder, 1987; Gamson, 1992; Weiner, 2006).

Some analysts argue that media representations of youth violence are more complex and maybe not as episodic as others believe. Spencer's (2005) analysis of media crime coverage in 1994, when youth crime was at its highest in

America, found that the media regularly placed the blame of youth violence on social causes of poverty, broken homes and drugs. Thus, rather than individualise the causes of youth violence, the media casts a net over the problem, associating it with common social problems of child abuse, single-parent families, drugs and poverty.

Spencer's analysis also paints an interesting paradox about the framing of youth violence – that is, by constructing the story of youth who commit violence as a story of 'lost youth' (those who were robbed of their childhood through sexual abuse, poverty or other familiar social problem), it tends to raise three questions: 'What are these lost youth like? How are we to orient to them emotionally? And how are we to attribute responsibility for their actions? ' (pp. 54–5). According to Spencer (2005), the answers led to two very distinct images of youth:

> On the one hand, these youth were portrayed as cold-blooded, calculating predators, incapable of remorse. On the other hand, they were portrayed as innocent victims of the social conditions that had robbed them of youthful innocence.
>
> p. 55

SCHOOL SHOOTINGS

Media coverage of school shootings changed across the years as the 'look' of the 'typical' school shooter changed. In the early 1990s, the media mostly focused on inner-city school gang violence among males, often pointing to conditions associated with poverty in urban areas (drugs, violence, gangs) as the cause of these problems. However, coverage of school shootings in the late 1990s seemed to abandon the problems of inner city youth in preference for the newer, seemingly more unexpected spate of rural and suburban shootings. The media jumped on the fact that school shooters seemed to be changing and, therefore, crafted a 'new' image of youth violence:

> The new face of the threat to school safety was a clean-cut rural teenaged boy, a boy who did not look like a killer. And the stories described communities that were stunned that such crimes could happen in their small, rural, or suburban hamlets, the lesson being that it can – and does – happen anywhere. Finally, increasing throughout the year, the stories suggested that administrators, students, parents, and teachers ignored warning signs of impending violence. The shootings, and the warnings that preceded them, came to represent a cautionary tale, so that, by the end of the examination period, articles were pointing out how school were now *planning* on shootings, building such scenarios into their school crisis plans (Herda-Rapp, 2003, p. 555).

This new threat, it was implied, meant violence was possible, even probable, and that no school was safe. Herda-Rapp continues:

> Communities previously thought to be sheltered from the violence of the urban world were now the playgrounds of young male assassins. In its reconstruction,

the threat of school violence had been transfigured, magnified, and relocated, upsetting old notions of criminality and the tranquility and safety of small towns.

2003, p. 557

The changing nature of the media's framing of school violence positioned youth as reckless, anti-social beings who were inevitably bad and could 'strike' anywhere – a view that dramatically distorts the reality that such extreme violence in schools is rare and not as unpredictable as we are led to believe (e.g. Nichols and Good, 2004).

Media attention to school shootings was particularly heightened in the aftermath of a particularly devastating incident that has come to be known as 'Columbine'. Columbine refers to a shooting rampage at Columbine High School in Littleton, Colorado, perpetrated by two teenagers, Eric Harris and Dylan Klebold. On one April morning in 1999, Harris and Klebold enacted a plan that involved bombs, guns and a great deal of ammunition. As videos would later reveal, over the course of about an hour, Harris and Klebold casually walked through their school shooting at their classmates with what appeared to be an absolute absence of emotion or remorse. They killed 14 students (including themselves) and one teacher, and hurt dozens more. Media coverage of this event was extensive, yielding a wealth of data to examine how news stories framed the events that unfolded on that day.

One interesting study on how Columbine was covered came from Ogle, Eckman and Leslie, (2003), who conducted a content analysis of all print media coverage for a year after the tragedy. Their analysis focused on the ways in which the gunmen's and victims' appearances (dress, physical characteristics) had an impact on how the events around the tragedy were described. Their data suggested that references to 'appearance cues' shaped journalists' reporting of the events.

One aspect of reporting was the way in which appearance cues became entangled with speculation about the cause of the Columbine violence, among which Ogle *et al.* identified three major themes. The first had to do with a 'sub-cultural group' claim, wherein the media extrapolated on the meaningfulness of the black trench coat worn by the gunmen as symbols of belonging to a culture of devil worshippers and death-loving outcasts who were preoccupied with death and hatred of mainstream society. This 'trench coat mafia', it was reported, was a clique of deviant teens who worshipped Adolf Hitler and who:

tested friendships by cutting each other with knives, engaged in endless hours of macabre internet chatter and relished in a bloody fantasy game called Doom on their computers.

p. 14

In the months following the tragedy, these ascriptions were debunked, but the damage had already been done to persuade local and national audiences that the teens, on the basis of their attire, could be characterised as calculating and evil.

The important implication of this story telling was the suggestion then that 'appearance could be used as a reliable predictor of one's proclivity for violence' (Ogle *et al.*, 2003, p. 14). That is, any student who wore black, or a long trench coat, was assumed to belong to a group of anti-social teens who would be violent and, therefore, should be viewed with suspicion. Indeed, this played out not only in Littleton in the days following the tragedy, but throughout the country. Teens in many high schools were being picked up on the basis of their clothing alone – an act that was fuelled by the media's interpretation of the gunmen's choice of black trench coat. The fear of youth who didn't dress 'mainstream' spread like wildfire.

Of course, the assumption that kids who wear black are would-be killers is absurd. Still, a national debate ensued that focused on a potential solution to the problem of black attire in the form of a clothing ban in some schools. But as opponents to this proposal accurately point out, this notion distracts from addressing the real problems associated with violence, to which 'dress' has very little value or meaning:

> If Eric Harris and Dylan Klebold had been wearing Denver Broncos jerseys with No. 7 on the back, would school systems be so quick to ban those? This banning of trench coats is a ridiculous response promoted by people who refuse to deal with the real underlying causes of violence.
>
> Ogle *et al.*, 2003, p. 21

The same authors identified two other themes that were used to construct the motives for the shooting. One was the social tension experienced by the two shooters, who even themselves reported feeling insecure as a result of the constant teasing and ridicule they experienced. Here, the media also capitalised on reports about the victims' dress that conjured up images of the 'jocks' or the 'popular' kids. In this analysis, the media allowed for some culpability on the part of the school that had failed to identify and remedy problems of bullying, teasing and harassment among its students.

A further construction Ogle *et al.* (2003) identified had to do with the choice of a trench coat not as a symbol of evil, but as a practical choice that would conceal weapons. The endless speculation about the meaningfulness of the gunmen's and victims' appearances in the immediate aftermath of the tragedy constructed a certain version of events that was difficult to deconstruct when the facts came out.

Coverage of 2007 and 2008 shootings in Finland reveal some differences in how media violence coverage might compare internationally. On 7 November 2007, Pekka-Eric Auvinen, an 18-year-old student, killed eight people including the principal and a school nurse before killing himself at Jokela High School in Tuusula, Finland (*Helsingin Sanomat*, 2007). Nearly a year later, on 23 September 2008, Matti Juhani Saari, a 22-year-old student killed 10 people, including one teacher, at the Kauhajoki School of Hospitality in Kauhajoki, Finland. Saari set the building on fire, burning his victims before fatally shooting himself (*Helsinki Times*, 2008). An informal review of media headlines suggests that Finnish coverage seemed to focus more on the facts of the events instead of on endless speculation of its causes. In the absence of such speculation, the media coverage more aptly contextualised the event rather than providing insinuations about what these rare acts of violence might have to say about every other Finnish youth.

GENDER

In the past decade or so, we have seen increasing media attention towards females who commit violence. Perhaps not surprisingly, this coverage has also utilised frames that distort both the prevalence and nature of female violence. One suggestion by these framing devices is that females are more violent. In spite of data suggesting that female violence rates have been consistent throughout the years (e.g. Zahn *et al.*, 2008), the sensationalistic reporting of one or two horrifying events strategically implies that females, by their very nature, are not just capable but inevitably more likely than previously to commit violent acts (Barron and Lacombe, 2005).

A more troubling problem when it comes to females, however, is that the preoccupation with a masculinised definition of violence (as an act of physical aggression) diminishes the very real and pervasive problem of relational violence among girls. Data suggest that females are much more likely than their male counterparts to engage in other forms of violence, especially relational assaults that include behaviours such as backstabbing, gossiping and verbal bullying (Simmons, 2002). However, these incidents are grossly under-reported and under-examined unless, of course, they are connected to actual violence. A recent tragic incident reminded us of the horrors of verbal assaults when one teen, who had been 'cyber-bullied' by an anonymous 'peer' (who, as it turned out, was the mom of one of her friends), committed suicide (Steinhauer, 2008).

INTERNATIONAL PERSPECTIVE

Most of the research reviewed here is confined to the US media. However, there is reason to believe that coverage of youth violence assumes a similar form in other westernised nations. My own unsystematic look at headlines from major world newspapers reveals an episodic line of reporting about youth violence that cast youth as troublemakers. For example, consider these headlines from major newspapers around the world:[2]

---

[2] Revealed by using LexisNexis and scouring all major US and world newspapers with the search term 'youth violence' covering the past 2 years.

- 'Teenage carnage' (27 January 2008, *The People*, UK);
- 'Gang teen had history of violence' (22 September 2006, *The Courier Mail*, Australia);
- 'Terrorised community suffers 450 crimes a year by one gang' (4 March 2008, *The Daily Mail*, London);
- 'Youth "torch 50 homes"' (20 August 2006, *The Sunday Mail*, Australia);
- 'Flashpoints where a third of teenagers are in gangs' (28 January 2008, *The Evening Standard*, London);
- 'Judge attacks "do-gooder" obsession with rights that has left Britain bedeviled by feral youths' (18 January 2008, *The Daily Mail*, London);
- 'Youth violence on the rise' (7 May 2007, *The South China Morning Post*, China);
- 'End bail for "feral youths"' (18 January 2008, *The Daily Post*, Liverpool);
- 'Bullying has spread like wildfire: latest wave of violence involves children as young as 4-years-old' (3 April 2007, *The Toronto Star*, Canada);
- 'Urban gangs wreak havoc in islands' (27 January 2007, *The Press*, New Zealand);
- 'Youth gangs triple child murder rate' (27 January 2008, *The Sunday Telegraph*, London);
- 'The girl crimewave' (18 November 2007, *The Sunday Mercury*, UK).

Building upon the analyses from American coverage, it seems reasonable to suspect that media coverage assumes a similar type of sensationalistic and distorted framing. Still, the lack of cross-national analysis of youth violence coverage makes it impossible to make any meaningful conclusions about how it is represented or the ways in which consumers interpret that representation.

Coverage of other types of social problems, however, such as international conflicts, provides some insight into the ways in which youth violence coverage may vary. In general, data seem to show that cultural differences influence the way in which international conflict gets covered (Aday, Livingston and Hebert, 2005; Dimitrova and Strömbäck, 2005). For example, Dimitrova and Connolly-Ahern (2007) compared the ways in which Arab and coalition countries (UK and US) covered the 2003 Iraq War. They concluded that the 'tales of war' by these disparate news outlets were by nature different from one another, and thereby reflective of their own cultural stance towards the war:

> The 'tale of war' in the Arab media was one of destruction and violence. The 'tale of war' in the Coalition media was one of military conflict leading to rebuilding for the people of Iraq. Whereas the Arab media in this study focused on the personal toll of war in the present, the Coalition media focused on the 'greater good' in Iraq's future.
>
> Dimitrova and Connolly-Ahern, 2007, p. 165

Thus, international coverage of youth violence is likely to vary according to cultural beliefs about the value and importance of its youth. The US, having one of the highest rates of poverty among its children in international comparisons as well as a lack of willingness to invest in the education of its youth, demonstrates the low value placed on its youth (Berliner, 2006). It is unsurprising, then, that coverage of youth violence assumes more of a 'blame the child' frame versus 'blame the lack of resources, opportunities, socialization' type of perspective. Future studies may reveal a similar type of culture-related-to-reporting connection.

CONCLUSION

Three major conclusions are drawn from this review of how youth violence is represented in the media. First, media's coverage tends to mislead consumers about actual rates of youth violence. This was especially the case through the 1990s when Americans were warned to 'look out' for youth superpredators. On the basis of population data, it was predicted that youth violence would increase substantially but, instead, youth violence *coverage* increased substantially. This misled many into believing youth were more violent than was the case.

Second, media coverage employs frames that strategically position the causes and consequences of youth violence in simplistic yet distorting ways. Over and over, youth violence gets cast as a problem of 'bad youth'. This attribution simplistically blames youth instead of the complex interaction of effects connected with youth violence (US Department of Health and Human Services *et al.*, 2000). Lastly, and related to the previous two points, is that framing influences subsequent policies aimed at addressing youth violence (Dodge, 2008). A 'blame the youth' position leads to attitudes that are more punitive and reactionary than supportive and proactive (Nichols and Good, 2004).

Most of the work examined here comes from analyses of the American media. In the absence of international studies, it is difficult to conclude how countries compare. Still, anecdotal evidence seems to suggest a similar phenomenon elsewhere. That is, when youth commit violence, media coverage assumes a perspective that tends to be more episodic in nature. Similarly, coverage takes the rate and intensity of violence out of perspective, giving readers the illusion that it is somehow a more prevalent problem than might otherwise be the case.

Consumers must be weary of how the media constructs stories about youth in general, and youth violence specifically. If it is true that 'fear is part of social control' (Altheide, 2002, p. 13), then the media is doing a good job shaping an image of youth who are to be feared. Such a construction legitimises policy actions that work to control and react to youth violence rather than to support and guide young people before violence occurs. Perhaps that is why, in America at least, the last few decades have seen an unprecedented set of hostilities towards our youth in the form of a harsher juvenile justice system and harsher penalties to youth who commit violence (Dilulio, 1996). Consumers must be critical consumers of reports about youth violence so as to protect the important perspective that youth are a group worthy of our support, guidance and proactive socialisation instead of societal fear, hostility or, even worse, indifference (Nichols and Good, 2004).

POINTS FOR PRACTICE

• It is critical that media consumers understand that reporting on youth violence tends to distort events in ways that lead to erroneous generalisations about youth. Practitioners should be critical consumers of the way in which youth violence is portrayed and not let these insinuated generalisations determine how they see the youth with whom they work.
• Media consumers must be aware that the media uses 'framing' devices in selling stories about youth violence. Frames tend to posit causes and solutions of youth violence in over-simplistic ways. Practitioners must be careful not to rely on media representations of youth violence for making attributions about the causes of youth violence when it comes to the youth with whom they work.
• Male and female violence tend to receive the same type of media coverage. Practitioners must be sensitive to the very real differences between males and females in how they engage in violence.

REFERENCES

Aday, S., Livingston, S. and Hebert, M. (2005) Embedding the truth. A cross-cultural analysis of objectivity and television coverage of the Iraq War. *Harvard International Journal of Press/Politics*, **10** (1), 3–21.
Altheide, D.L. (1997) The news media, the problem frame, and the production of fear. *The Sociological Quarterly*, **38** (4), 647–68.
Altheide, D.L. (2002) *Creating Fear: News and the Construction of Crisis*, Aldine DeGruyter, New York.
Barron, C. and Lacombe, D. (2005) Moral panic and the nasty girl. *Canadian Review of Sociology and Anthropology*, **42** (1), 51–69.
Berliner, D.C. (2006) Our impoverished view of educational research. *Teachers College Record*, **108** (6), 949–95.
Blumstein, A. and Wallman, J. (eds) (2000) *The Crime Drop in America*, Cambridge University Press, New York.
Body-Gendrot, S. (2005) Deconstructing youth violence in French cities. *European Journal of Crime, Criminal Law and Criminal Justice*, **13** (1), 4–26.
Butts, J.A. (2000) *Youth Crime Drop*, Urban Institute, Justice Policy Center, Washington, DC.

Cave, D. (2008k) Eight teenagers charged in Internet beating have their day on the web. *New York Times*, A11.

Cerulo, K.A. (1998) *Deciphering Violence: The Cognitive Structure of Right and Wrong*, Routledge, NEW YORK.

Dilulio, J.J. (1996) How to deal with the youth crime wave. *The Weekly Standard*, **2**, 30–5.

Dimitrova, D.V. and Connolly-Ahern, C. (2007) A tale of two wars: framing analysis of online news sites in coalition countries and the Arab world during the Iraq War. *The Howard Journal of Communications*, **18**, 153–68.

Dimitrova, D.V., and Strömbäck, J. (2005) Mission accomplished? Framing of the Iraq War in the elite newspapers in Sweden and the United States. *Gazette: The International Journal for Communication Studies*, **67**, 401–20.

Dodge, K.A. (2008) Framing public policy and prevention of chronic violence in American Youths. *American Psychologist*, **63** (7), 573–90.

Dorfman, L., Woodruff, K., Chavez, V. and Wallack, L. (1997) Youth and violence on local television news in California. *American Journal of Public Health*, **87** (8), 1311–6.

Edelman, M. (1988) *Constructing the Political Spectacle*, University of Chicago Press, Chicago, IL.

Entman, R.M. (1993) Framing: toward clarification of a fractured paradigm. *Journal of Communication*, **43** (4), 51–8.

Farkas, S. and Johnson J. (with Duffett, A. and Bers, A.) (1997) *Kids These Days: What Americans Really Think about the Next Generation*, Public Agenda, New York.

Fiske, S.T. and Taylor, S.E. (1991) *Social Cognition*, McGraw Hill, New York.

Gamson, W.A. (1992) *Talking Politics*, Cambridge University Press, New York.

Halpern, D.F. (2003) *Thought and Knowledge: An Introduction to Critical Thinking* (4th edition), Erlbaum, Mahwah, NJ.

Helsingin Sanomat (2007) Death toll in school shooting reaches nine, www.hs.fi/english/article/BREAKING+NEWSDeath+toll+in+school+shooting+reaches+nine/1135231614979, 9 November (accessed 25 June 2010).

Helsinki Times (2008) Finland left reeling by another school massacre, www.hs.fi/english/article/BREAKING+NEWSDeath+toll+in+school+shooting+reaches+nine/1135231614979, 24 September (accessed 21 October 2008).

Herda-Rapp, A. (2003) The social construction of local school violence threats by the news media and professional organisations. *Sociological Inquiry*, **73** (4), 545–74.

Iyengar, S. (1991) *Is Anyone Responsible? How Television Frames Political Issues*, University of Chicago Press, Chicago, IL.

Iyengar, S. and Kinder, D.R. (1987) *News that Matters: Television and American Opinion*, University of Chicago Press, Chicago, IL.

Kahneman, D. and Tversky, A. (1984) Choices, values, and frames. *American Psychologist*, **39** (4), 341–50.

Males, M. (1996) *The Scapegoat Generation: America's War on Adolescents*, Common Courage Press, Monroe, ME.

Males, M. (2000) *Kids and Guns: How Politicians, Experts, and the Press Fabricate Fear of Youth*, Common Courage Press, Monroe, ME, www.commoncouragepress.com (accessed 25 June 2010).

McManus, J. and Dorfman, L. (2002) Youth violence stories focus on events, not causes. *Newspaper Research Journal*, **23** (4), 6–20.

Nichols, S. and Good, T.L. (2004) *America's Teenagers – Myths and Realities: Media Images, Schooling, and the Social Costs of Careless Indifference*, Erlbaum, Mahwah, NJ.

Ogle, J.P., Eckman, M. and Leslie, C.A. (2003) Appearance cues and the shootings at Columbine High: construction of a social problem in the print media. *Sociological Inquiry*, **73**, 1–27.

Perrone, P. and Chesney-Lind, M. (1997) Representations of gangs and delinquency: wild in the streets? *Social Justice*, **24** (4), 96–116.

Reyes, R. and Townsend, B. (2008) YouTube adds to melee in videotaped beating case. *Tampa Tribune*, 10 April, 1.

Simmons, R. (2002) *Odd Girl Out: The Hidden Culture of Aggression in Girls*, Harcourt, Inc., New York.

Snyder, H.N. and Sickmund, M. (1999) *Juvenile Offenders and Victims: 1999 National Report*, Office of Juvenile Justice and Delinquency Prevention, Washington, DC.

Spencer, J.W. (2005) It's not as simple as it seems: ambiguous culpability and ambivalent affect in news representations of violent youth. *Symbolic Interaction*, **28**, 47–65.

Standora, L. (2008) Third-graders' plot to attack teacher foiled. *Daily News*, 2 April, 10.

Steinhauer, J. (2008) Woman indicted in MySpace suicide case. *New York Times*, www.nytimes.com/2008/05/16/us/16myspace.html, 16 May (accessed 25 June 2010).

Surette, R. (1992) *Media, Crime and Criminal Justice: Images and Realities*, Brooks/Cole Publishing Co., Pacific Grove, CA.

Townsend, B. (2008) 8 charged as adults in beating case. *Tampa Tribune*, April 22, 1.

US Department of Health and Human Services, Centers for Disease Control and Prevention, National Institutes of Health, and Substance Abuse and Mental Health Services Administration (2000) *Youth Violence: A Report of the Surgeon General*, US Department of Health and Human Services, Washington, DC.

Weiner, B. (2006) *Social Motivation, Justice, and the Moral Emotions: An Attributional Approach*, Erlbaum, Mahwah, MJ.

Zahn, M.A., Hawkins, S.R., Chiancone, J. and Whitworth, A. (2008, October) *Girls Study Group: Understanding and Responding to Girls' Delinquency*, U.S. Department of Justice, Office of Juvenile Justice and Delinquency Prevention, Washington, DC, www.ncjrs.gov/pdffiles1/ojjdp/223434.pdf (accessed 10 November 2008).

13 Boys, Girls and Performing Normative Violence in Schools: A Gendered Critique of Bully Discourses

JESSICA RINGROSE AND EMMA RENOLD

INTRODUCTION

Recently there has been heightened public awareness and government concern around school bullying, and intensified anti-bullying policy development, implementation and evaluation in the DCSF/DCELLS.[1] Increasing resources have been devoted to standardising anti-bullying work in schools UK-wide in line with the *Every Child Matters* (Department for Education and Skills, 2004) mandates and the *Staying Safe* consultation (Department for Children, Schools and Families, 2007) on the safety and well-being of children and young people. In this chapter we respond, however, to the prominence of what is often an unproblematised concept of 'bullying' in use in psychological and educational policy and research (see also Walton, 2005). We suggest the dominant 'bullying discourses' are untenable for understanding and coping with the complex range of experiences of peer aggression and violence in school.

We argue that the categories 'bully' and 'victim' operate to individualise, demonise and pathologise children and young people. As we will explore through our respective research with girls and boys in school, discourses of 'bully' and 'victim'[2] are embedded in and reinforce the power relations of gender norms – that is, dominant sets of understandings which connect 'femininity' with girls' bodies and powerlessness, and 'masculinity' with boys'

---

[1] Department for Children, Schools and Families, UK government (renamed Department for Education in 2010); Department for Children, Education, Lifelong Learning and Skills, Welsh Assembly Government.
[2] We are using the term 'discourse' as socially organised frameworks of meaning that regulate our behaviour and can determine the 'conditions of possibility' of what can be said and done at particular moments in time (Foucault, 1978).

Children Behaving Badly? Peer Violence Between Children and Young People
Edited by Christine Barter and David Berridge
© 2011 John Wiley & Sons Ltd.

bodies and powerfulness. Moreover, we argue that the individualising logic of bully discourses work to obscure the many different ways through which gender and sexualised conflicts are organised and experienced, and to position bullies and victims as gender deviants and therefore as socially failing. As such, bully discourses, or the sets of understandings and meanings in popular use around bullying, offer few symbolic resources or practical tools for addressing and coping with everyday interpersonal conflict.[3]

To illustrate our claims, we map some of the difficult effects upon girls and boys who are positioned as bullies and victims. These include heightened defensiveness, anxiety, guilt and feelings of failure. We begin, however, by deconstructing the conceptualisation of bullying elaborated in school psychology literature.

THE ROLE OF 'GENDER' IN RESEARCH ON SCHOOL BULLYING

After over two decades of research on bullying in schools, bullying continues to be conceptualised as a developmental psychological problem among children (Smith and Brain, 2000; Ma, Stewin and Mah, 2001). Almost without exception, the majority of this literature draws upon a binary framework of bullies/bullying and victims/victimisation. Power in definitions of bullying is conceived of as an individual and intentional acting-out of aggression from bully to victim (Olweus, 1999). Explanations for bullying behaviours are frequently attributed to the psychological characteristics of either the bully or the victim, and there is a search for personality and family causes so that bullying and victimisation become both individualised and pathologised, and constructed in relation to non-bullies or un-afflicted children (Connolly and O'Moore, 2003).

With little attention paid to the social and cultural context, most research on school bullying, until very recently, has been 'gender blind', focusing implicitly on boys as both perpetrators and victims of bullying (Olweus, 1993, 1999; Rigby, 1998). This traditional focus stemmed from definitions of bullying as mostly physical with research studying male cultures of peer abuse (Duncan, 1999). Research, however, is now attempting to foreground gender, but in ways that emphasise gender difference and set up a further binary (boys versus girls). This research draws on a psychological literature of gender-differentiated aggression to suggest that boys aggress in physically direct ways, while girls are aggressive in 'indirect', 'covert' and 'relational' ways (Owens, Slee and Shute, 2000a, 2000b; Shute, Owens and Slee, 2002; Woods and Wolke, 2003).

---

[3] We use the term 'symbolic' to refer to the historically embedded cultural meanings that people hold, and that shape how they see and act in the world.

The psychological literature on bullying, which has now filtered widely into fields of education, childhood and behaviour management, tends to simplify and reduce the relationship between gender, victimisation and bullying, suggesting repeatedly that, while boys use 'direct counter-aggression' and 'fighting', girls 'manipulate', 'use threats' and are 'covert bullies' (Bjorkqvist, Lagerspetz and Kaukiainen, 1992; Salmivalli, Karhunen and Lagerspetz, 1996; Koch and Irby, 2005). But what does it mean to suggest self-evidently or as 'truth' that boys physically fight and girls psychologically manipulate? Our argument is that such understandings of gendered aggression and bullying simply re-invoke gender and sexual stereotypes. These arguments and analyses also gloss over the unequal power relations associated with masculinity (power) and femininity (lack). As such, these bully discourses not only heavily regulate a wide range of affects, like aggression, but they do so in ways that draw on and perpetuate hierarchical gender relations and norms.

BULLYING AS NORMATIVE GENDERED 'PERFORMANCE'?

Our feminist post-structural position is influenced by the social and cultural queer theorist Judith Butler, who illustrates how much of the 'doing' of gender, be it 'masculinity' or 'femininity', involves repetitive practices of performing the norms of gender (Butler, 1990; Renold, 2005). As Youdell (forthcoming) explains in a useful introductory chapter on 'performativity', Butler's gender theories illustrate how 'classificatory systems, categories, and names that are used to designate, differentiate and sort people [like gender categories] ... work performatively to create the people they name ... [but] demand "repetition"' to sustain their normative force and give off the illusion of a 'proper', 'natural' or 'fixed' gender. Normative gender performances are so insistent and repetitive that they are legitimised and taken for granted. So the 'normal' ways of 'performing' and enlivening or 'doing' 'girl' and 'boy' in everyday life, including gendered norms of aggression (e.g. boys are violent, girls are indirectly aggressive), are passed over in the classroom and schoolyard as natural practice. In contrast, we have found in our research that what is identified as bullying tends to be that which dramatically transgresses normative gendered behaviour. Thus, the position of bully marks out both boys and girls as gender deviants, and there are demands to recoup appropriate masculinities and femininities, embedded in children's schooling and parental responses to conflicts.

As we proceed, we shall use a feminist post-structural approach to analyse performative and discursive constructions of gender identity (Davies, 1989; Walkerdine, 1990), and how this informs what is then constituted as bullying. We draw on our respective research with boys and girls in primary and secondary schools. Jessica's research is from a focus group and individual interview-based study with girls (aged 12–14) attending an inner-city secondary school in South Wales, UK. Emma's data are from a year-long ethnographic study exploring gender and sexual relationship cultures with 10- and 11-year-old boys and girls in two semi-rural primary schools in the East of England.[4]

BOYS AND NORMATIVE VIOLENCE

Research on school-based masculinities has illustrated how gendered and sexualised forms of aggression, harassment and violence are central in the production of 'hegemonic',[5] heterosexual masculinities across primary and secondary schooling (Epstein and Johnson, 1998; Duncan, 1999; Skelton, 2001; Renold, 2004). For example, Emma's data illustrate the routinisation of young masculine violence and aggression in the battlefield of the school playground. Here, fighting games (e.g. the 'tripping-up' game), embodied rituals (such as showing marks or scars) and re-living past fights (e.g. 'Did you see that fight?') were all ways in which tough masculinities were performed (Best, 1983; Connolly, 2004):

> (Discussing the 'tripping-up' game)
> Ryan: It's quite fun if you don't get hurt.
> ER: So who ...
> Ryan: It's not like really mad violence, you just trip 'em up.
> Jake: Yeah yeah and we were standing there and Sean and Sam comes in and goes 'stop fighting' and kicked him right at the same time and they go 'aaaagh' [they all laugh].
> ER: How do you get away with all this fighting in the playground, don't the dinner ladies stop you?
> Sean: Yeah, but if they do, if they see you and if they're like looking and someone says 'stop it', you like walk to another place, like you walk over to the other side and start again.

As Sean's comments in the extract illustrate, violent fighting 'games' were rarely framed as problematic or as 'bullying'. If they were told (by staff) to 'stop', the fighting would be moved to a space with less surveillance. In most cases, systemic physical violence was normalised through the blurring of boundaries between games, play-fighting and violence, with dominant mascu-linities both tolerated and legitimised:

---

[4]Emma's research explores children's constructions of gender and sexuality in their final year of primary school (two classes of 30, aged 10–11). This doctoral research, funded by Cardiff University, took place in two contrasting primary schools situated in a small semi-rural town in the east of England: Tipton Primary (white, working and middle-class catchment) and Hirstwood Primary (white, predominantly middle-class catchment). All the data presented in this chapter are from ethnographic observation and conversations (anonymised) with the pupils attending Hirstwood Primary.

[5]We are using the term 'hegemony' to refer to the ways in which belief systems and values are embedded in everyday life and come to appear as 'common sense' (Connell, 1995).

(Rick confronts Ryan on how he used to 'beat him up' in Year 5)
Rick: You used to beat me up.
Ryan: No I didn't.
Rick: Yes you did, you did body slams on me.
Ryan: That was because we were *playing* fights.
Rick: Were we? [sounds unsure]
Ryan: Yeah.

When Emma repeatedly pointed out to staff during her fieldwork that boys' violent games looked like bullying, developmental, social and cultural norms were invoked to legitimise these as 'just playing' or legitimate forms of defence of self or others. The 'super-vision' of boys' experiences of physical violence was hardly 'super'. Rather, they worked to normalise and sustain the culture of masculine violence:

ER: What about the dinner ladies? Can you tell them?
Neil: They're not bothered, they're not bothered ...
Simon: Yeah because if someone kicks you or something, they ...
Neil: You need to be crying before they take any notice.
Graham: They call you a wimp.
Simon: You have to be either crying or lying on the floor with loads of people round you.
ER: For ...?
Simon: To get any attention.

We return to the cycle of performative normative masculinities later in this chapter.

As feminist research on masculinities and schooling has long illustrated, violent masculinity is not merely sanctioned, it is demanded and usually couched within a discourse of 'heroic masculinity' (Reay, 2002). This dynamic was evident in Jessica's data, where girls used the discourse of heroic masculinity to call upon boys to normatively discipline other boys who violated appropriate modes of heterosexualised appearance and/or behaviour:

Lucy: William Brown, he's got long hair, like girl long hair, about that long, all blond. Gwyneth walked past him and as a joke she just like ...
Gwyneth: I just like went like that to his hair like [makes flicking motion].
Lucy: Because you touched his luxury flowing locks! [laughing]
Faiza: He ... got up, grabbed her by her neck and smacked her against the wall and then she couldn't breathe, that's how boys react. And then, and then I was there, I saw everything and I told a couple of boys in my year who are like the hard boys.
Lucy: So I told this boy called Patrick Dunsmuir and they had the guts to go up to William Brown and teach him a lesson.
JR: What did they do?
Faiza: Physically and mentally?
Lucy: They pulled him!
Girls: [all laughing]

JR: So you told them what they had done to Gwyneth and they retali-
               ated ...
Lucy: Yeah because they thought it was wrong like what he done.
Elizabeth: Because he hits girls!

In this excerpt, a boy who enacts public violence against girls, thereby violating the norm of heroic masculinity, is punished. Degrees of excess were required to mark masculine violence as deviant, and for boys to differentiate a boy as going 'over the top' or enacting, in the words of Ryan, 'mad violence'. If a boy enacts 'unmerited' violence against boys or girls, this is constituted as dysfunctional and over-aggressive in ways that are read through gender, sexuality, class and culture to establish particular boys as bullies. As Emma has noted (Renold, 2005), 'severe' forms of violence, where there is a clearly demarcated victim and perpetrator, were typically necessary for any official school sanctions to be implemented. To be explicitly positioned as a 'bully' either by the school or by other children was neither desirable nor powerful. A label of 'bully' could operate to position a boy as weak, pathological and sexually deviant, as illustrated in the following extract where Stu's friends position him as a low-class wife-beater for thumping girls in the chest:

(The initial question was prompted by Sam's comment that Stu 'beats girls up'.)
ER: So Stu, you don't hit the girls at all?
Stu: No.
ER: So are they just making it all up?
Sam: I do.
ER: I know you do.
Sam: 'Cos they're always going like this [hair ruffling].
ER: So you hit them back?
Sam: Yeah.
ER: They were telling me that sometimes you thump them in the chest. [I
           obtained the girls' consent to confront the boys]
Sam: Yeah, yeah he does [laughing].
Stu: No.
James: He's, he's a women-beater he is.
Sam: Man slaughter.
Jake: He's like someone out of Cracker.[6]
James: Stu can't beat up boys so he beats up girls.
Stu: Oh yeah, I could beat you up [Sam laughs].
James: Come on then [holds up his clenched fists].

Much like Jessica's data on teenage boys and girls, when Stu violently retaliates to having his hair ruffled by the girls, his peers position both the challenge posed by the girls and Stu's retaliation as ambiguously masculine. Stu's violence becomes a signifier of a class-based, pathological version of young

[6] *Cracker* is the title of a mid-1990s UK television crime drama series in which the central protagonist is a criminal psychologist.

domestic violence, and thereby sets up a dichotomy of abnormal/normal masculine violence.

BOYS AND THE PERFORMATIVE CYCLE OF NORMATIVE 'HARD', VIOLENT MASCULINITY

Normative gender discourses constitute boy 'victims' as transgressing or breaching young hegemonic masculinity. To be constituted as victims is to position boys as 'feminine', as sexual deviants (e.g. as questionably 'heterosexual') and therefore as abject subjects to a normative gender/sexual script. Responses to this positioning by parents and teachers to 'stop complaining' and 'toughen up' draw upon the very same discourses and performances of masculinity that position boys as 'victims' in the first place. In peer, teacher and parental cultures where there is extreme investment in competitive, violent masculinities, and where the everyday violence between boys is normalised as 'boys being boys', this leaves those positioned at the gender margins with few options:

ER:	Have you told, or can you tell your parents what goes on sometimes?
Graham:	No.
Neil:	No, 'cos they'd go mad.
ER:	Even though it's not you doing it?
Neil:	Yeah but they said 'Well you shouldn't carry on doing it, you should just go away.'
ER:	What if ...?
Simon:	My mum and dad don't say you shouldn't have done that ...
ER:	Can you tell them, would they come up to the school if they found out you'd been hit and teased?
Graham:	No probably not.
Neil:	I don't bother telling my mum and dad because they don't really hurt me.
Graham:	My dad told me to stick up for myself, but he doesn't know them like I do (almost in tears).
ER:	I know it's very difficult [he nods].
Simon:	If I do tell my mum and dad, what happens, 'cos my dad, he teaches me some moves, he teaches me how to block, by putting two arms in front of me.
ER:	So they tell you either to stick up for yourself, or in your case, Simon show you how to do that, but they wouldn't ...
Graham:	If if if I do something to them, they just carry on, they do it again.
Neil:	My mum and dad just say 'Just walk away'.
Graham:	But you can't [exasperatedly].
Neil:	Yeah.
ER:	But it's difficult, because they can still come after you.
Graham:	I know.

Simon: ... and if I do get into a fight and I tell my mum and dad and say 'Well
              I just thumped them and I just ran off so and my dad says 'So you
              won the fight then? ' and I go 'Yeah' [unconvincingly] and my mum
              and dad go 'Good for you'.

The desire of Graham's and Simon's fathers for their sons to 'fight' and 'stick
up' for themselves illustrate that hard, retaliatory, violent masculinity is the
norm. The bully discourses formalise and entrench a set of unviable subject
positions (bully/victim) for boys to take up. Both bully and victim are viewed
as signs of failed masculinity. A bully is a pathologically violent boy and a
victim is a weak loser, rendered invisible for the most part by both school and
parents. Those practices of normalised masculine violence we may wish to
challenge as oppressive are defined outside the purview of bullying, so that
bullying is not a symbolic or practical resource that boys can call upon for help
in negotiating violence and conflict (from dinner ladies' avoidance of violence
to parents' demands to 'toughen up', heteronormative masculinity prevails).

    In the wake of such impossibilities, it is no surprise that by Year 6, boys like
Simon, Graham and Neil no longer sought 'help'. They reverted to silence or
ditched their gender misfit friends and hooked up with the dominant boys in
their class by helping them with academic work or trying valiantly to master
football. As we explore next, the performative cycle of normative masculinities, through which bully discourses support the institutionalised structures
and power hierarchies of gender and sexuality, were also evident in the stories
we heard from girls.

NORMATIVE FEMININITY: GIRLS AS 'COVERT BULLIES'

In line with decades of feminist work inquiring into the binary symbolic structures of masculinity and femininity, feminist work on femininity, aggression
and violence has explored cultural mandates upon girls and women to be
passive, nurturing and accommodating in contrast to the normative condition
of direct masculine aggression (Gilligan, 1982; Campbell, 1993). Multiple
studies on girlhood have illustrated the cultural expectations that to adequately perform the normative subject position of a girl in the contexts of
compulsory heterosexuality means to enact the qualities of niceness, goodness,
pre-maternal caring, innocence etc. (Walkerdine, 1990, 1997; Hey, 1997; Driscoll,
2002). Jessica's data illustrate how girls must balance being 'supportive', 'there-
for-you', non-competitive (by not making others 'feel small') and to be friends
with everybody:

JR: So what's the perfect girl?
Faiza: Sporty, pretty, funny, intelligent, friendly, kind and fits it ... gets along
         with everybody, not just in one group, she is like in everybody's group.
JR: Do you know any girls like that?
Faiza: No.

This list of idealised qualities means the painful realities of navigating human relationships, conflicts and anger are formidable, often impossible. Against this obviously repressive dynamic of what femininity must emulate, bitchiness and mean-ness become a demonised, yet expected, eventual outcome for girls (Hadley, 2003; Ringrose, 2006). Indeed, Jessica's participants also maintained that girls were not nice, suggesting repeatedly that girls were 'mean', 'two-faced' and 'could not keep secrets'. Girls are *expected*, then, to aggress in covert ways, as is evident in the developmental psychology research on gender bullying we critiqued earlier (Currie, Kelly and Pomerantz, 2007). It follows from this expectation that, when girls violate these normative conditions of practising 'indirect aggression' and secret/private rituals of 'mean-ness', they risk being constituted as gender deviants, as we now explore.

THE PERFORMATIVE CYCLE OF NORMATIVE 'INDIRECTLY AGGRESSIVE' FEMININITY

In the case of girls, we found bully discourses were only mobilised when direct, open conflict came under the register of the school, usually through the interventions of parents. The following focus group extracts illustrate girls' responses to being subject to an anti-bullying intervention at their school over a conflict with a girl (Katie) in their friendship group:

JR: So I just want to try and understand how this first happened that you got into this disagreement.

Elizabeth: [Katie] thought she was better than us ... like, Oh who fancies you? No-one, oh well I guess they all fancy me then ...

Gwyneth: Like she would say really horrible stuff to me and Elizabeth like, make us feel all small and that and like, then one day we were talking we realised she'd been saying it to both of us ... because we thought she had just like to one of us like, so we thought we'll talk to her about her and then she went ... and told her mum.

JR: So when you talked to her at school what happened?

Elizabeth: We got her by herself like because we didn't want to say it in front of everyone ...

Gwyneth and Elizabeth describe how Katie made them 'feel small', how they confronted her at school and how Katie told her mum, who complained to the school afterwards. The school then treated it as an incident of bullying, holding a meeting with the girls as explained by Gwyneth:

Gwyneth: It probably would have blown over, it probably would have been just a little fight and we wouldn't have talked for a few days and then make friends. But then her mum got involved and like rang up the school and said that we were bullying her … But then when we told them what happened they said, 'Oh, okay, you weren't bullying her' and everything, but 'Just like be friends'.

Our reading of the scenario is that it was only because the girls engaged in a confrontation with Katie, and an external adult lodged a complaint, that they were sanctioned. The open conflict transgresses what are middle-class codes of appropriate feminine behaviour as hidden, silent, secretive, covert – and thus repressive (Ringrose, 2006). By openly challenging Katie, the girls actually called into question the normative enactment of 'hyper-feminine' 'girly girl' (Renold, 2005) and heterosexualised competition (Ringrose, 2008a) particularly consonant with normative ways of 'doing girl'. However, this direct form of confrontational aggression can constitute girls as gender deviants, and they are often demanded to recoup 'good' and nice femininity and 'just be friends' (Ringrose, 2008b). Indeed the girls describe at various points the need to 'be nice' and to 'talk it out' with one another. Girls are incited to *get along* no matter what the context or cost.

What we want to suggest, therefore, is that, against the normative model of feminine aggression organised around a binary of being either nice or indirectly mean, to be involved in *open* conflict and confrontation is to be rendered deviant, which brings abjection and shame for girls. Katie's mother responded dramatically by removing her from the friendship group and school, and transferring her to a higher performing comprehensive, indicating further dynamics and levels of race and class regulation at work. Defensiveness and anger simmered among the remaining friendship group, in the wake of being positioned as bullies:

Faiza: I personally thought that we had sorted it. We all gave each other hugs, we walked home the same way and then suddenly she didn't come to school anymore … all of a sudden she'd want to change school … and then on MSN she'd be so scared to say it to our faces, she'd go on MSN 'Oh, you stupid cow, dur, dur, dur, dur, dur'. I didn't care about that. If she had guts, she would say it to my face. And every time she was around me she would be like, 'Oh god, I'd never want to start a fight with you.'

Faiza: She said to us that her mum made her change school … Make up your mind mum. She took her daughter off school for three months, so she can find her another school … Her mum would have been arrested, put in jail for not letting her daughter to go to school.

JR: It seems like it was … a difficult situation.

Faiza: She brought it onto herself. She talked about Gwyneth to me, she talked about me to Gwyneth, she talked about Lucy to Lizzy, she talked about Lizzy to Lucy, how stupid is that? If you are going to talk to someone about someone else, it would be someone … we weren't best friends with. Then at last, she just left. And that had to be the happiest bit of Herbert for us four girls. She made us go through all that trouble of coming into a classroom and the teacher locking us in and we had to sort it out and then she left. Good.

Faiza describes with great anger and frustration how Katie called her a 'stupid cow' within the virtual space of MSN,[7] and as someone to be feared whenever they spoke in person. In exploring class and race dynamics, it is significant that Faiza is a racially marginalised, Muslim subject here,[8] which intersects in complex ways with being positioned as a threatening, masculinised, bully girl, whom Katie and her mother appear to openly fear. Faiza is very defensive in the wake of the events, calling Katie 'a two-faced pig', 'slut', 'weird', 'ugly' and 'making herself small' during our interviews. She also fantasises about Katie's mother being put in jail as a response to 'locking us in' a classroom, during the anti-bully intervention.

What we have also found is that following such anti-bully interventions, much like the boys, girls develop fears of either telling adults about their problems or having their conflicts discovered by adults, reverting instead to silence and secrecy:

JR: ... do you think you have learned anything from this or ...?
Gwyneth: Probably it's best to like, not to say it in front of people because it might make them feel that people are ganging up on like the person you are talking to, just get them by themselves and say it ... We learned to like talk to them quietly by themselves.

After their engagement in the anti-bully intervention, the girls' convictions that they must keep conflict totally secret from the school and their parents shows the ineffectiveness of the strategy and how it worked to reinforce the gender norms of indirect feminine aggression. We found a great deal of shame and stress in negotiating the type of public spectacle incited through the schools' bully discourses and the performative cycles of normative masculinity and femininity. As with the boys, renewed silence and denial surrounding violence and aggression resounded.

CONCLUSION

In this chapter, we have illustrated how bully discourses organised around binaries of bully and victim enact rigid gender norms, which support unequal

---

[7] For a more sustained exploration of friendship and conflict in the context of digital mediums like instant messaging or social networking sites, please see Willett and Ringrose (2008).

[8] The raced and 'religioned' (Youdell, 2006) aspects of Faiza's identity work in a 'constellation' with her gendered and sexualised identity. Discourses of Islamophobia are highly visible in the UK press and popular culture (Khan, 2006). While a detailed analysis is beyond the scope of this chapter, Faiza is in some senses masculinised through events in ways that unsettle ideas of pathologised, masculine, ethnicised/Muslim violence typically set in opposition to ethnicised/Muslim feminine passivity (Shain 2003; Werbner, 2007). Faiza unsettles mythologies of the passive/victim Muslim girl/woman, but this transgression is swiftly pathologised (through the anti-bully intervention) and has ongoing emotional effects for her as we describe (see also Ringrose, 2008b).

heterosexualised power relations. We want to expose and challenge these effects of power, and have attempted here to map out and critique the bully discourses in operation. Through feminist and post-structural analyses of gendered power, which outline how norms and symbolic structures of gender are performative (Butler, 1990; Youdell, forthcoming), we have illustrated how bully discourses reinforce the institutionalised structures of normative femininity and masculinity, offering no symbolic resources for breaking out of these binds. Indeed, when bullying discourses are invoked, they position those who violate normative femininity and masculinity as gender deviants through class- and race-specific discourses of pathologisation and 'otherisation', as we have illustrated.

The problem is that these discourses have gained 'hegemonic' (Gramsci, 1971) status in both popular and schooling cultures, which means that they have become so normalised and 'common sense' for considering issues of aggression, bullying and violence among young people that they are unquestioningly adopted. Our goal in this chapter has been to raise questions about the practices and performances of the bully discourses, alongside some other critical educational researchers who have begun to problematise the conceptual underpinnings of the notion of bullying in order to understand or intervene into peer violence (Walton, 2005). Further research that critically explores the impacts of anti-bullying interventions in practice would be helpful to continue in understanding and addressing the complexity of gendered and indeed racialised and classed peer conflict, aggression and violence at school and beyond.

POINTS FOR PRACTICE

Working with children and young people meaningfully around issues of conflict, aggression and violence requires confronting normative assumptions (from staff, parents and young people) about how girls and boys are assumed to enact aggression or fight both within and between gender groups.

The following are what we consider to be some useful starting points and related questions in critically thinking through approaches for understanding and addressing the relationship between school-based aggression and violence, and cultures and performances of 'masculinity' and 'femininity':

- As a practitioner or researcher, critically explore your own and your institution's gendered assumptions around femininity and masculinity and aggression:
  - What stereotypes of feminine and masculine aggression do you as a teacher or practitioner hold (also around girls and boys of different ages, ethnicities, faiths, sexualities, class groups etc.)?
  - What kinds of dominant images of femininity and masculinity does the school itself reflect to the children in the school?

- Learn from girls and boys about how they understand femininity and masculinity as it relates to aggression and conflict:
  o What kinds of images of feminine and masculine aggression do girls and boys bring with them into the school context?
  o How are different kinds of femininity and masculinity acted out in different contexts (inside school and beyond the school gates)?
- When planning interventions, participation and dialogue are crucial. Involve young people (as far as possible) in the planning and design of those interventions. Reflect with them on the anticipated positive and negative effects of such interventions upon girls and boys and their lives:
  o What do young people themselves think about gendered conflict and fighting?
  o What do young people think works and doesn't work around coping with conflict and violence?

USEFUL RESOURCES

Womankind: this charity works with young people and teachers to identify sexual bullying in the school environment, define it in school policies, raise awareness across a school and work on whole-school preventative strategies (www.womankind.org.uk/Stop-sexual-bullying-UK.html [accessed 6 July 2010]).

'Stand up for us: challenging homophobia in schools' is a downloadable government resource to help schools challenge homophobia. It is one of the few documents that explore the ways in which gender and sexuality intersect (e.g. the relationship between sexist and homophobic abuse) and adopt a whole-school approach to preventative strategies. It is aimed at anyone who works in early years settings, primary, secondary and special schools, off-site units and pupil referral units. It also offers a series of 10 practical resources, which include information about homophobia and the relevant legislation and guidance, a range of material for teachers and an outline staff training session. These are available at http://publications.teachernet.gov.uk/default.aspx?PageFunction=productdetails&PageMode=publications&ProductId=challenge-homophobia& (accessed 6 July 2010).

REFERENCES

Best, R. (1983) *We've All Got Scars: What Girls and Boys Learn in Elementary School*, Indiana University Press, Bloomington.
Bjorkqvist, K., Lagerspetz, K. and Kaukiainen, A. (1992) Do girls manipulate and boys fight? Developmental trends in regard to direct and indirect aggression. *Aggressive Behavior*, **18**, 117–27.

Butler, J. (1990) *Gender Trouble: Feminism and the Subversion of Identity*, Routledge, New York.

Campbell, A. (1993) *Men, Women and Aggression*, Basic Books and HarperCollins, New York and London.

Connell, R.W. (1995) *Masculinities: Knowledge, Power and Social Change*, Polity Press, Cambridge.

Connolly, I. and O'Moore, M. (2003) Personality and family relations of children who bully. *Personality and Individual Differences*, **35** (3), 559–67.

Connolly, P. (2004) *Boys and Schooling in the Early Years*, RoutledgeFalmer, London.

Currie, D.H., Kelly, D.M. and Pomerantz, S. (2007) The power to squash people: understanding girls' relational aggression. *British Journal of Sociology of Education*, **28** (1), 23–37.

Davies, B. (1989) *Frogs and Snails and Feminist Tales: Pre-school Children and Gender*, Unwin Hyman, London.

Department for Children, Schools and Families (DCSF) (2007) *Staying Safe: Action Plan*, HMSO, London.

Department for Education and Skills (DFES) (2004) *Every Child Matters: Change for Children*, HMSO, London.

Driscoll, C. (2002) *Girls: Feminine Adolescence in Popular Culture and Cultural Theory*, Columbia University Press, New York.

Duncan, N. (1999) *Sexual Bullying: Gender Conflict and Pupil Culture in Secondary Schools*, Routledge, New York.

Epstein, D. and Johnson, R. (1998) *Schooling Sexualities*, Open University Press, Buckingham.

Foucault, M. (1978) *The History of Sexuality: An Introduction* (trans. R. Hurley), Penguin, Harmondsworth.

Gilligan, C. (1982) *In a Different Voice: Psychological Theory and Women's Development*, Harvard University Press, Cambridge, MA.

Gramsci, A. (1971) *Selections from the Prison Notebooks*, Lawrence and Wishart, London.

Hadley, M. (2003) Relational, indirect, adaptive or just mean: recent work on aggression in adolescent girls – Part I. *Studies in Gender and Sexuality*, **4** (4), 367–94.

Hey, V. (1997) *The Company She Keeps: An Ethnography of Girls' Friendships*, Open University Press, Buckingham.

Khan, H. (2006) The bad news: British Muslims have been let down, and extremism is the result. *The Independent*, 12 February.

Koch, J. and Irby, B. (2005) *Gender and Schooling in the Early Years*, Information Age Publishing, Charlotte, NC.

Ma, X., Stewin, L.L. and Mah, D. (2001) Bullying in school: nature, effects and remedies. *Research Papers in Education*, **6** (3), 247–70.

Olweus, D. (1993) *Bullying in Schools: What We Know and What We Can Do*, Blackwell Publishers, Oxford.

Olweus, D. (1999) *Bullying Prevention Program*, Center for the Study and Prevention of Violence, Institute of Behavioral Science, University of Colorado, Boulder, CO.

Owens, L., Shute, R. and Slee, P. (2000a) Guess what I just heard! indirect aggression among teenage girls in Australia. *Aggressive Behavior*, **26** (1), 67–83.

Owens, L., Slee, P. and Shute, R. (2000b) It hurts a hell of a lot: the effects of indirect aggression on teenage girls. *School Psychology International*, **21** (4), 359–76.

Reay, D. (2002) Shaun's story: troubling discourses of white working class masculinities. *Gender and Education*, **14** (3), 221–34.

Renold, E. (2004) Other boys: negotiating non-hegemonic masculinities in the primary school. *Gender and Education*, **16** (2), 247–67.

Renold, E. (2005) *Girls, Boys and Junior Sexualities: Exploring Children's Gender and Sexual Relations in the Primary School*, RoutledgeFalmer, London.

Rigby, K. (1998) Gender and bullying in schools, in *Peer Relations Amongst Children: Current Issues and Future Directions* (eds P. T. Slee and K. Rigby), Routledge, London.

Ringrose, J. (2006) A new universal mean girl: examining the discursive construction and social regulation of a new feminine pathology. *Feminism and Psychology*, **16** (4), 405–24.

Ringrose, J. (2008a) Just be friends: exposing the limits of educational bully discourses for understanding teen girls' heterosexualized friendships and conflicts. *British Journal of Sociology of Education*, **29** (5), 509–22.

Ringrose, J. (2008b) Every time she bends over she pulls up her thong: teen girls negotiating discourses of competitive, heterosexualized aggression. *Girlhood Studies: An Interdisciplinary Journal*, **1** (1), 33–59.

Salmivalli, C., Karhunen, J. and Lagerspetz, K.M.J. (1996) How do the victims respond to bullying? *Aggressive Behavior*, **22** (2), 99–109.

Shain, F. (2003) *The Schooling and Identity of Asian Girls*, Trentham Books, Stoke on Trent.

Shute, R.H., Owens, L. and Slee, P. (2002) You just stare at them and give them daggers: nonverbal expressions of aggression in teenage girls. *International Journal of Adolescence and Youth*, **10**, 353–72.

Skelton, C. (2001) *Schooling the Boys: Masculinities and Primary Education*, Open University Press, Buckingham.

Smith, P.K. and Brain, P. (2000) Bullying in school: lessons from two decades of research. *Aggressive Behavior*, **26**, 1–9.

Walkerdine, V. (1990) *Schoolgirl Fictions*, Verso, London.

Walkerdine, V. (1997) *Daddy's Girl*, Verso, London.

Walton, G. (2005) Bullying widespread: a critical analysis of research and public discourse on bullying. *Journal of School Violence*, **4** (1), 91–118.

Werbner, P. (2007) Veiled interventions in pure space: honour, shame and embodied struggles among Muslims in Britain and France. *Theory, Culture & Society*, **24**, 2, 161–86.

Woods, S. and Wolke, D. (2003) Does the content of anti-bullying policies inform us about the prevalence of direct and relational bullying behaviour in primary schools? *Educational Psychology*, **23**, 381–401.

Youdell, D. (forthcoming) Performativity: making the subjects of education, in *Handbook of Cultural Politics in Education* (ed. Z. Leonardo), Sense Publishers, Rotterdam.

Part IV Responding to Peer Violence

14 Bullets, Blades and Mean Streets: Youth Violence and Criminal Justice Failure

PETER SQUIRES AND CARLIE GOLDSMITH

INTRODUCTION

The tabloid media had a field day in 2008 when Sir Al Aynsley-Green, the government's Children's Commissioner, cautioned against what he called the heavy-handed police tactics being proposed by the government to tackle the carrying of weapons, chiefly knives, by young people. A triumph of contrived misunderstanding likened his comment to a suggestion that the police might 'go easy' on criminals for fear of antagonising them. Yet Sir Al's comments were a not entirely unfamiliar notion that the criminal justice system should seek, first, to do less harm and avoid demonising young people in general and, second, to address more effectively the underlying causes of youth exclusion and the issues – conflict, fear and violence – so closely associated with it. Indeed, Sir Al had courted controversy only a few months earlier by suggesting a ban on the recently marketed ultrasonic 'mosquito' youth repellent device but, apparently, criticising the police during a 'knife crisis' was a press release too far.

The Children's Commissioner was by no means the first to make such points, although the angry media-led reaction spoke volumes about the politics of youth justice today. When the Centre for Crime and Justice Studies released its 10-year verdict on New Labour's failure to develop a more effective and preventive youth justice system (Solomon and Garside, 2008), nothing like the same outcry resulted. Yet the failures of contemporary youth justice that the report documented, and the apparent increase in the willingness of largely disadvantaged young people to carry weapons and use them to victimise their peers, share some common and familiar roots. They are also connected by an intolerant and often uninformed populist politics of punitiveness that still appears to believe we can 'police' our way out of a social and cultural crisis. This is not to claim that the criminal justice system is primarily *responsible* for

Children Behaving Badly? Peer Violence Between Children and Young People
Edited by Christine Barter and David Berridge
© 2011 John Wiley & Sons Ltd.

the problems of youth violence on our streets, far from it. For as Garside (2006) has argued, the criminal justice system has nowhere near the purchase on the broader social issues necessary to meaningfully dent our crime and disorder problems. In that sense, the real social problems lie elsewhere. But criminal justice processes are increasingly implicated in the predicament of young marginalised youth as their socially excluded status and identity are intensified and recycled through seemingly unavoidable encounters with the police, a wider cadre of new community safety agents, and the cold climate of public fear and alarm.

In this chapter, we begin by setting this 'contemporary crisis' of youth violence in the British context. We try to explore what is known about the nature and scale of this supposed epidemic of violence, how concern shifted from guns to knives to the 'weaponisation' of youth social relations in more general terms. We then move on to explore the meanings that this violence is said to invoke, before considering the social groups and contexts in which it appears most prevalent and the ways in which it is being addressed. For us, a sense of criminal justice failure pervades the entire account: not that it is causing the problems in the first place, simply that it is making them worse.

DECIVILISING CONTEXTS

In an introduction to *Respect in the Neighbourhood*, an edited collection of articles about civility, community development and social capital, through which he hoped to 'decriminalise' the debate about anti-social behaviour in contemporary Britain, Harris (2006) describes a disturbing future with, as he puts it 'civility in freefall'. He continues:

> Society implies civil relations – relationships which by their degree of respect, the informality of their exchanges, and the generation of trust and cooperation, make other things possible ... So if we were to pay less attention [to these issues] it would put a great deal of pressure on all sorts of other social structures and resources ... Anti-social behaviour and physical disorder would increase, probably stimulating crime and increased fear. We would gradually become less inclined to venture out unless armed and protected, we would move in fear of others because actions of disrespect would be acceptable and expected. In time, civilisation – the complexities of co-existing cultures – could not exist.
>
> p. x.

Harris is not the first to articulate this dystopian vision. The key point is that, for *some* young people, the future has already arrived, the 'nightmare' is already a reality. While it is right and appropriate to exercise caution in the use of emotive labels, about youths, gangs, weapons and violence (the media being far too willing to fan the flames of sensation, typically generating more heat than light about these issues) (see Young *et al.*, 2007), a study by Broadhurst, Duffin and Taylor (2008) on behalf of the teacher's union,

NASUWT, produced testimonies from some young people about the protective and self-defensive practices they already followed (or maybe just subscribed to) – even on the way to school:

> It's not a bad thing to bring a weapon into school. You might get attacked on the way to school, on the way back. It's protection.

> I can protect myself with a knife or a gun. I would rather be arrested than dead.

> It's not a bad thing to bring weapons into school because of the area you are going to on the way to school. (pp. 15–16)

FROM BULLETS TO BLADES?

Writing on the BBC News website as long ago as November 2003, in one of the opening forays into this issue, journalists Megan Lane and Brian Wheeler (2003) commented: 'Concern about violent crime in Britain has swung back to knives and their availability to children.' But has the so-called 'knife culture' risen while the media's attention has been so fixed on gun crime? The point raises a number of issues. It was a timely observation for, between 1998 and 2002, recorded gun crime had risen by as much as 105 per cent (Squires, 2008a), and 2003 was the year when the steeply rising trend began to plateau. Yet the suggestion that media and public attention might be able to fixate upon only one problem at a time does give a clue to our present concerns.

Research has drawn attention to the apparently increasing numbers of young people who admit they carry knives. For instance, among other research (Lemos, 2004; Eades et al., 2007; Firmin, Turner and Gavrielides, 2007; Fitzgerald, 2007; NCH, 2008; Broadhurst et al., 2008), MORI's annual youth surveys for the Youth Justice Board (YJB) suggested that a growing proportion of young people were carrying knives. The most recent findings indicate that about a third of young people do so, a proportion rising significantly when the sample focuses upon young people excluded from school (Eades et al., 2007).

According to Young et al. (2007):

> A majority of young people excluded from mainstream education said they had carried a knife within the last year … [Moreover] in all cases, young people were more likely to carry a knife if they had been a victim of crime, but most young people who had carried a knife claimed this was only for protection and that they had never actually used them.
>
> p. 3

Knife carrying, however, has also been found to be more prevalent among those involved in more serious group-related offending. As Broadhurst et al. (2008) confirmed, 'school exclusion was regarded as an open invitation to escalation into gang culture and related issues' (p. 16).

When looking at why young people carried a knife, it was found that:

- more than 8 out of 10 (85%) of those who had carried a knife said the main reason for doing so was for protection;
- fewer than 1 in 10 (7%) of those who had carried a knife had used it to threaten someone, and 2 per cent had used the knife to injure someone (Eades *et al.*, 2007).

Furthermore, a survey conducted on behalf of the National Youth Agency (2006) revealed the following:

- One in five 16-year-old boys admitted attacking someone, intending to hurt them seriously.
- Twenty-five per cent of young people at school admitted that they had carried a penknife compared to 47 per cent of excluded students. A further 21 per cent said they had threatened someone with a knife.
- Nearly half of excluded young people (47%) admit to having carried a weapon, but say they never used it. Of these, 30 per cent have carried a flick knife, 20 per cent an air gun and 16 per cent a kitchen knife.
- Young girls are considerably less likely to have carried a knife in the last year than boys (15% of girls compared to 40% of boys).

The early months of 2008 saw a growing intensity in the media preoccupation with knife crime. With each grisly murder, the problem appears to escalate even though the trend data are, at best, ambiguous. As Young *et al.* (2007, p. 3) noted in their report for the YJB:

> Currently, there are no national trend data on knives available to support the growing concern (shared by professionals working with young people) about the extent to which knives are carried by 10–17-year-olds.

The 2007 guide on knife crime (Association of Chief Police Officers [ACPO] and Home Office) also reflected this ambiguity:

> Perhaps surprisingly, the available data indicates that the proportion of violent offences involving the use of a knife has remained relatively stable in recent years. This fact is contrary to public perception that knife crime is rising. There may also be an element of under-reporting.

Nevertheless, it continued:

> The public need to be reassured that police services in the UK and the Home Office are working together ... to make communities feel and be safer.

> p. 4

Even the *British Crime Survey* (BCS) noted that knife-enabled crime had remained stable at around 6–7 per cent of all crime, knives being employed in some 30–35 per cent of all homicides ('sharp instruments' being the most common weapon in male-on-male homicide) (Kershaw, Nicholas and Walker,

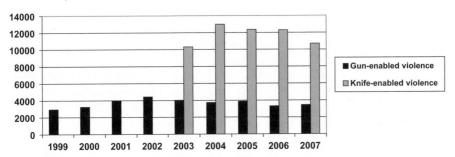

Figure 14.1 Gun- and knife-enabled crime in London
Source: Metropolitan Police Service (2007, private communication)

2008). In London, recorded knife crime appeared to have fallen by 16 per cent over the 2 years before 2007 (see Figure 14.1). How much 'knife crime' goes on in London without being reported to the police, and how effectively the BCS represents the 'knife-carrying' section of the population, remain open questions. Such misgivings have influenced the recent decision to try to extend the BCS to those aged under 16.

As Figure 14.1 indicates, at least as far as offences recorded by the police are concerned, there appears to have been no significant switch (in London at least) in the methods employed by (predominantly) young males to violently attack one another. London is chosen because the Metropolitan Police Service (MPS) records approximately three times as many knife attacks as the next highest city (Manchester) in the 'knife crime league'. Furthermore, 'stabbings' have always exceeded shootings, certainly predating the current knife crime 'crisis'. In fact, the MPS only began to record the precise weapon responsible for stab or cut injuries in 2003. Prior to this, such injuries were recorded according to the gravity of the injury (e.g. grievous bodily harm, wounding, attempted murder), or by the crime that the knife was 'enabling' (e.g. robbery) rather than the particular weapon employed (Eades *et al.*, 2007). Only from April 2007 did knife-enabled crime become part of the annual data requirement in the National Police Recording Standard (ACPO and Home Office, 2007).

These data provide no evidence of significantly increasing weapon-related violence *being recorded by the police* (although it would be far from unusual for a significant proportion of it to go unreported – especially if no, or only minor, injuries resulted [Squires, 2008a, 2008b]). However, the perceptions of increased weapon carrying reported by youth workers and police officers (Kite, 2008), not to mention the survey data cited earlier, are not without some further corroboration. For example, supplementary evidence supplied by the Home Office to the Home Affairs Select Committee Inquiry into Knife Crime during 2007 (Coaker, 2007) revealed an increasing number of weapon-carrying offences being recorded nationally by police forces (see Figure 14.2).

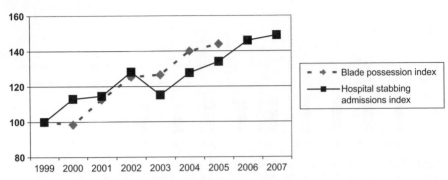

Figure 14.2   Percentage indices of weapon-possession offences recorded by the police in England and Wales 1999–2005 and hospital admissions for 'stabbing' injuries
Source: Coaker (2007) and Home Office (2008)

Figure 14.2 deals with offenders of all ages and contains data from three sets of weapon-possession offences: 'having an article with blade or point in public place', which increased by 66 per cent overall during the period represented by the graph; 'possession of offensive weapons without lawful authority or reasonable excuse', which increased by 30 per cent during the same years; and 'having an article with blade or point on school premises', which increased by over 500 per cent during the same years, although from a considerably lower base. It is accepted, however, that, to some extent, this greater evidence of knife possession to a large degree reflects the impact of police targeting of weapon carrying (Royal Armouries Museum, 2007, p. 5).

The figures on weapon-possession offences correspond much more closely to data (also presented in Figure 14.2) from hospital accident and emergency departments, where the hospital admissions were attributed to 'assault with a sharp object' rather than to the more limited recorded offence data so far available (Home Office, 2008, p. 3, figure 10).

Similarly, a hospital accident and emergency study published in 2007 confirmed that, during the period 1997–2005, the number of people admitted as a result of stab or sharp object injuries rose by 30 per cent (Maxwell *et al.*, 2007). Likewise, König and Knowles (2006) have argued that, unlike data on knife-enabled crime, hospital admissions evidence broadly supports public perceptions of increasing rates of knife violence.

Parliamentary answers provided to MPs Chris Huhne and Norman Lamb provided further information on hospital admissions for gun- or knife-related injuries in England and Wales (Department of Health, 2008a, 2008b). These figures detailed the age, sex and ethnic background of violence victims (see Figures 14.3–5) covering the decade from 1997. These figures are likely to be more reliable than police-recorded figures given the well-documented reluctance of victims to report gang-related victimisation to the police. Nevertheless, these figures still comprise only the more serious wounding where victims were

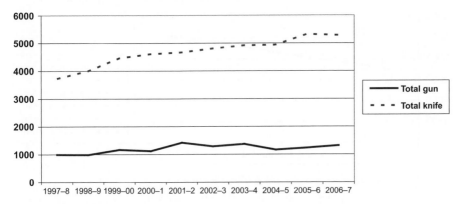

Figure 14.3   Hospital accident and emergency admissions in England and Wales, 1997–
2007 for gun- or knife-inflicted injuries
Source: Department of Health (2008a, 2008b)

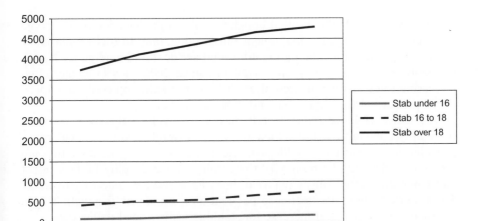

Figure 14.4   Stabbing injuries reported to hospital accident and emergency departments by age 2002–7
Source: Department of Health (2008a, 2008b)

significantly concerned about the scale of their injuries to seek medical assistance. This evidence might cause us to reflect upon the potential implications
of recent Home Office proposals to require accident and emergency departments to notify *all* suspected gun and knife injuries to the police.

Likewise, drawing upon the same accident and emergency admissions
figures, the following graph (Figure 14.4) shows the age groups reporting knife
injuries. Despite the media's preoccupation with violence occurring between
those aged under 18, the major trends for reported knife injuries involves

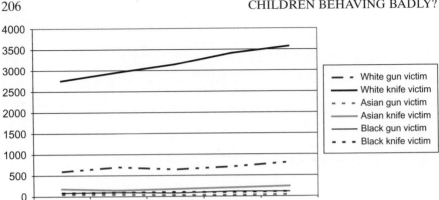

Figure 14.5 Knife violence victims by ethnicity attending accident and emergency departments in England and 2002–7
Source: Department of Health (2008a, 2008b)

victims aged *over* 18. Similarly, although a significant proportion of the media coverage, especially regarding violence in London, tend to focus upon black victims or perpetrators, the national hospital accident and emergency figures (categorised by ethnicity – only available since 2002–3) also suggest that increasing rates of weapon victimisation (gun and knife injuries) are experienced primarily by *white* people and those aged over 18.

The major violence injury trends may have involved the over 18s most frequently, but a more detailed look at the injury trends in younger age groups provides a fuller picture. Although the trends relating to under-16s and 16–18-year-olds hug the bottom of the graph, never exceeding 1,000 accident and emergency attendances per year, both have risen significantly over the 5-year period. There has been a 75 per cent increase in stabbing victims aged 16–18 and an 88 per cent increase for stabbing victims aged under 16.

Finally, Figure 14.5 indicates the knife-related violence reported by white, black and Asian victims between 2002 and 2007. Clearly knife-related victimisation of white people far exceeds that of ethnic minority groups across the country as a whole even though, especially in large conurbations (London, Birmingham, Manchester), black and Asian groups endure very disproportionate rates of weapon victimisation (House of Commons, 2007).

The evidence in Figures 14.3–5 emerged in the summer of 2008, significantly only *after* the knife crime 'moral panic' was already well under way. It was the political controversy surrounding young people, street violence and knife crime that brought the data to light. Parliamentary questions in the House of Commons brought it to the fore. Moral panics often involve 'smoke' (public reactions) and 'fire' (hard evidence), and the figures tell us something important about moral panics and evidence. It was the specific evidence of stabbings (including several murders) of persons aged under 18 and under 16, almost doubling in 5 years, that underpinned the media and public reactions. The actual frequency of injuries (fewer than 200 under-16s requiring hospital treatment for knife injury in 2006–7) may be low, but the trend is alarming. This is the spark of flame at the heart of all the smoke, but it is still only a very partial aspect of urban violence problems involving young people.

The hospital accident and emergency evidence plainly contradicted the limited police records of knife-enabled crime, suggesting that a longer term increase in knife carrying and use was under way – thereby confirming the more qualitative accounts we considered earlier. The issue is not resolved by statistics of police action against offenders for knife or blade possession simply because, as we have seen, possession offences tend, above all, to be a reflection of police activity. So it is the hospital admission figures that give us the most reliable grasp on weapon usage and its consequences. As we have seen, the data provide us with a rather different picture of the consequences of violence, for, while the media reporting drew particular attention to the relative youth of the knife crime victims (and perpetrators) and, certainly in London, the seemingly disproportionate number of victims from the black communities, the evidence clearly shows that the overwhelming majority of knife victims were white and aged over 18. It appears that factors other than statistics have been influential in driving the youth knife crime panic and it is to these issues to which we now turn.

VIOLENT INTENT, HUMAN TRAGEDY AND DANGER

A further dimension of the reporting of violent youth offending concerns the ways in which attention centres upon the tangible human tragedies when someone is killed. Each stabbing prompts a generic media-driven reflection upon the pointless waste of a promising young life, the senseless savagery of youth, the social conditions in which such brutality is allowed to flourish and the, seemingly inevitable, failures of the criminal justice system. Knife violence has become the latest in a long line of 'signal crimes' (Innes, 2004), the signals reproducing a chilling message about youth violence, depraved social contexts, the supposedly random risks we think we all run, and the collapse of civilized social relationships.

In one sense we have seen it all before. To adopt Innes's perspective, the shift to knife violence perhaps represents a kind of 'signal displacement'. It is important to be clear about this – the issue is one of 'signal shift', for there does appear to have been a shift in what knife violence is taken to mean.

When gun crime began to attract significant media attention, although there was no doubt about the brutality entailed in this new ratcheting-up of the seriousness of youth violence, attention tended to focus upon what was new – the gun. Guns were conceived of as the supreme facilitators of lethal interpersonal violence. Relatively easy to use, portable, concealable and, in

England, Wales and Scotland at least, illegal, so attention focused initially upon the problem of the gun itself and upon the illegal supply chain. One consequence of this was that all 'gun crime' tended to be lumped together as if it could largely be understood in the same way. An appreciation of the complex combination of more instrumental or more expressive motivations surrounding illegal firearm use only came later (Hales, Lewis and Silverstone, 2006; Squires, 2007).

Rising gun crime, an alien and supposedly 'un-British' form of violence, was bad enough but the guns themselves seemed the problem, less so the offenders using them. Guns offered a detached form of exercising violence: by a simple, instinctive or even seemingly effortless pull of a trigger. The results, in injuries sustained or trauma induced, when a bullet hits a human body far outweigh the effort exerted by the offender, just as it may effectively harness and multiply an offender's intentions. Indeed, some commentators have come to refer to some violent encounters as literally 'gun-driven' (Squires, 2000, 2007; Hales *et al.*, 2006) when impulsive, volatile (indeed 'hair-trigger') personalities encounter perceived insults or 'disrespect' and shoot first before being shot themselves. Even that seemingly most amoral, chaotic and destabilising form of urban gunplay, the 'drive-by shooting', when automatic or semi-automatic weapons are discharged from a moving vehicle with reckless disregard as to whether they will strike a 'target', and employed to ruthless effect in Birmingham on New Year's Eve 2004 when friends Letitia Shakespeare and Charlene Ellis were killed, might suggest a less deliberate and visceral act of purposeful violence than to plunge a knife into a fellow human at less than arm's length. In fact, as American research on drive-by shootings has confirmed (Sanders, 1994), however reckless and immoral a 'drive-by' may seem, many assume a primarily symbolic significance, chiefly targeting property (windows, doors, vehicles) rather than persons. Of course, firing guns through windows and at buildings and vehicles containing people is highly likely to produce casualties, but even this criminal recklessness may suggest a less deliberate, malicious or forceful intention to kill than the proximate, physical and immediately personal act of stabbing someone.

In this narrative, even though a knife is a technologically more limited and inefficient means of inflicting violent injury than a gun, knife crime comes to be construed as immeasurably worse *precisely* because of the meanings associated with, and the motives attributed to, the unambiguous, up-close and personal, visceral brutality of thrusting a blade into a fellow human being. Carrying and using knives implies a new brutalism of youth street life. A new low in violent de-civilising depravity is thereby signalled.

THE WEAPONISATION OF YOUTH VIOLENCE?

The response of the Home Office to these developments has involved two principal strands: the first a reassurance agenda; and, second, a twin-track strategy to tackle violent youth crime and to address the crime threat posed in some communities by the presence and activities of criminal gangs. Policy documents addressing both areas of violence prevention were published during the first part of 2008: the *Tackling Violence Action Plan 2008–11* (HM Government, 2008) and the *Tackling Gangs Action Programme* (Home Office, 2008). It is not the aim of this chapter to move into the specific area of youth gangs except of course where the two issues overlap, although debate has addressed the role of gangs as accelerators of violence and crime (Marshall, Webb and Tilley, 2005; Smith and Bradshaw, 2005; Sharp, Aldridge and Medina, 2006), exacerbating the marginalisation of young people. Perhaps it could hardly be otherwise: such accounts conform to the dominant gang suppression discourses of contemporary policing (Klein, 1995). What such accounts neglect are parallel sociological analyses of the role of gangs in offering protection, excitement and social, emotional and material support to their members; or even of their channelling, containing and restraining of violence, and mediating social conflicts. The recognition that gangs are social groupings, after all, is an important step to take here. Yet while it may be possible to harness the social processes of gang organisation for more effective crime management, more sporadic incidents of raging individual brutality seem rather less amenable to such interventions.

In a sense, in contrast to gang-related violence, acts of individual violence may fall closer to the social construct of 'mindless violence' frequently invoked in discussions of youth crime and disorder. The fact that actually such violence seldom will be 'mindless', though often much misunderstood, might alert us to a process of redefinition occurring – knife-related violence being read through the perspective of crime rather than the perspective of mental disorder. It is difficult to estimate how much of today's violent knife crime might be attributable to mental and personality disorders, or similar aetiologies about which our contemporary violence discourses appear relatively uninformed and largely uninterested. However, if research from either end of the criminal justice system is taken as a rough guide, then the high proportion of young people receiving ABCs (Acceptable Behaviour Contracts) and ASBOs (Anti-Social Behaviour Orders) with diagnosed behavioural and personality disorders (up to 50% [Stephen and Squires, 2004]) and the proportion of prison inmates with recognised behavioural and personality issues (starting at around 30% and upwards [Peay, 2002]), then the supposed 'epidemic' of knife crime presently confronting the UK might be more appropriately recast as a crisis of community mental health provision.

Moving the discussion in this direction takes us much closer to a concept of 'dangerousness', which has frequently bedevilled public safety policies (Greer, 2003). As Jewkes (2007) has noted:

> Society's obsession with dangerousness results in a tendency to view crime in wholly individualistic terms … [and] victimisation as befalling tragic innocents who happened to be in the wrong place at the wrong time.
>
> p. 585

One seldom needs to look far to find recent street murders conforming to precisely these 'types'. Yet this conception of dangerous, volatile and brutal delinquents stalking the streets with malice aforethought becomes endlessly recycled about young people, in complete contrast to the opinions of the young people cited earlier in this chapter.

From the perspective of the Home Office's *Tackling Violence Action Plan*, the issue of young people carrying weapons more frequently takes on a particular contemporary cultural dimension:

> Changing demographics in local communities can affect the nature of … violence; honour-based violence is an issue that is increasing in importance, and we will develop a national Action Plan for tackling this.
>
> Home Office, 2008, p. 7.

These issues were further elaborated in the Home Affairs Select Committee Report, *Young Black People and the Criminal Justice System* (House of Commons, 2007) where the connections between race, social exclusion and violence victimisation were explored. According to the Committee report:

> The evidence does point strongly to a much greater likelihood of young black people falling victim to violent and weapon-enabled crime, including homicide.
>
> para. 35

Furthermore, several witnesses before the Committee noted how many:

> young black people live in sustained fear of victimisation … Many people live in absolute terror, and they have armed themselves in response to that terror … the safety of young people travelling to and from schools is an issue which comes up 'continually' in some schools.
>
> paras 39–40

Of particular note were the suggestions that 'young black people primarily fear being attacked by someone of the same ethnicity' (para. 41) and 'young black people's fear of crime is typically to do with them being attacked by other young black people' (para. 42); while Lee Jasper, the then Mayor of London's race adviser, 'highlighted a "specific crisis" in black communities as regards the level of violence and death by guns and knives' (para. 58).

CONTEXTS FOR VIOLENCE AND POLICY FAILURE

When we add together the discrete elements explored so far, it becomes clear that the violence experienced by young black people in deprived inner-city areas promotes precisely the kinds of self-defensive lifestyles that can put them in conflict and opposition with other neighbouring youth groups, terrify the community at large and, just as readily, draw the attention of the police. These lifestyles can include weapon carrying, 'gang' (collective self-defence) formation, mutual suspicion and hostility towards 'outsiders', orientations towards safe 'home turf' or 'respected' neighbourhood figures, truancy (avoiding the dangerous journey to school or the bullying that follows arrival) and what Hallsworth (2005) has called 'thugging up'. In conventional social policy terms, social exclusion of this entrenched and intensified kind exposes young people to greater risks, limits their capacity for either legitimate redress or escape, while simultaneously under-protecting them and over-controlling their coping strategies. These areas are what Hope (2001) has termed 'communities of fate'. They may not be 'typical' but perhaps they represent an early- warning sign (or worst-case scenario) of the consequences of social exclusion, compounded by inequality, relative deprivation, policy failure, community fragmentation and a culture of competitive individualism.

Many deprived high crime communities that once commanded the attentions of the Downing Street Social Exclusion Unit share many of these distressing features. Policing and the criminal justice system in its entirety have relatively little to offer such communities (Garside, 2006) beyond a potentially self-defeating mix of 'force' and 'reassurance'; the rolling-out of presumptive Section 60 'stop and search powers' to tackle weapon-carrying young people; and containment policing of 'toxic mix' estates where public policy has reverted to a form of pest control (Davies, cited in Harris, 2006, p. xiii). Behind this analysis lurks a profound lesson from America that 'most gang prevention and [violence] suppression programmes have been either ineffectual or actually have made matters worse' (Klein, 1995).

CONCLUSION

We began this discussion seeking to make sense of a supposed 'epidemic' of violence in which young people, especially our more marginal and excluded young people and even more especially those of black or mixed race, are caught up as both victims and perpetrators. We tried to make some sense of the competing claims made about youth violence and what might need to be done about it. We tried to throw some light on the available facts about the scale, nature and trends relating to youth violence (in the absence of wholly reliable and consistent data) and disentangle these from the many heated fictions surrounding the issue. We explored the growing concern about the weaponisation of youth violence and the prevalence of gun and knife carrying by certain groups of young people; and we looked at some of the research reproducing the words of young people as they expressed their concerns, recounted their fears and explained the choices they made to help them negotiate the risks and dangers of their communities.

There are many themes here; yet the problems they address go to the heart of the question of youth exclusion and the violence and victimisation with which it is associated. At root, the key question concerns the purchase that the criminal justice system, and perhaps especially the police, has upon these issues. Solomon and Garside (2008) have recently concluded that the Labour government's 10-year record on youth justice (and anti-social behaviour management), a decade that began with such bold and ambitious new legislative principles (not to mention performance targets) and which has seen a major increase in expenditure, has had only a relatively marginal impact upon overall levels of youth crime and only limited preventive impact. And yet we end a decade that began preoccupied by the so-called (and certainly contested) 'persistent young offender' (Hagell and Newburn, 1994) with a seemingly more acute crisis of weapon-facilitated youth violence. Violent crimes by young people aged under 16 appear to be increasing, resisting the government's otherwise more positive criminal justice trends. The argument is not that the criminal justice system can, in any meaningful sense, 'control' the amount of criminal victimisation in a society; on the contrary, it can merely manage a small percentage of those offenders and victims that stray into its path. The major social problems influencing rates of crime largely lie elsewhere. Our argument is that in managing these groups badly, by fostering and facilitating a demonisation of young people, further ostracising and excluding them, and demonstrating a punitive lack of trust and respect, it pushes them to find their own, even more problematic and often dangerous solutions.

A vicious circle is established. Rod Morgan, the former head of the YJB, cautioned against the punitive climate of youth justice and its problematic implications – swift enforcement is not the answer, he suggested. Likewise, the Children's Commissioner's recent doubts about police-led solutions for problems of youth violence and conflict suggest that, in 10 years, we have learned relatively little.

LESSONS FOR POLICY AND PRACTICE

There are important policy and practice issues arising from an analysis of youth weapon-involved violence. While gun amnesties have symbolic and some practical merit, knife amnesties can only be educative and symbolic; emptying the cutlery drawers of the nation one knife at a time is not a practical option. This is not to say that such initiatives cannot have real value *provided* they are linked with wider attempts to educate and support key target groups about the risks involved in weapon carrying. Even so, young people are unlikely to be very receptive to these messages while their fears remain and they continue to lack confidence in 'adult authorities'.

Unfortunately, one consequence of the climate of 'moral panic' surrounding weapon-related violence has been to reinforce support for police-led, enforcement-driven activities, such as London's *Operation Blunt*, entailing lots of 'stop and search'; all these have the potential, if not sensitively handled, to further alienate and exclude the very groups whose behaviour most needs to be positively addressed.

It follows that a coordinated community safety approach needs to underpin any strategy to address 'weapon-involved' violence, targeting the most vulnerable groups. Diversion, communication and 'exit' (including protection) opportunities need to be available for young people living in fear or caught in potentially violent networks and relationships. These can include outreach, mediation and credible mentoring relationships for young people at risk. Many successful examples exist including the Manchester Multi-Agency Gang Strategy (MMAGS), Lambeth's X-it programme and gang mediation projects that have been employed in the West Midlands. A tension remains, however, in that 'community safety' and young people's rights have to be the primary consideration, whereas police involvement in such initiatives is often predicated upon their 'intelligence development' potential. Any sense that a project is serving an alternative 'policing' purpose is likely to undermine its credibility in the eyes of those who need it most (Lovell, 2008).

REFERENCES

Association of Chief Police Officers (ACPO) and Home Office (2007) *Knife Crime Best Practice Guidelines*, ACPO and Home Office, London.

Broadhurst, K., Duffin, M. and Taylor, E. (2008) *Gangs and Schools: An interim report for the NASUWT*, Perpetuity Group and NASUWT, Birmingham.

Coaker, V. (2007) Supplementary memorandum submitted by the Home Office to the Home Affairs Select Committee: Knife Possession Offences. 1 May, www.publications.parliament.uk/pa/cm200607/cmselect/cmhaff/433/433we10.htm (accessed 26 July 2010).

Department of Health (2008b) Hospital accident and emergency admissions for gunshot wounds and stab injuries by age, placed in the House of Commons Library 25 June. DEP2008-1681.XLS, www.theyworkforyou.com/wrans/?id=2008-06-25b.210404.h&s=stab+wounds#g.

Eades, C., Grimshaw, R., Silvestri, A. and Solomon, E. (2007) *Knife Crime. A Review of Evidence and Policy*, 2nd edition, Centre for Crime and Justice Studies, London.

Firmin, C., Turner, R. and Gavrielides, T. (2007) *Empowering Young People Through Human Rights Values: Fighting the Knife Culture*, Esmée Fairbairn Foundation, London.

Fitzgerald, M. (2007) Memorandum of Evidence on Knife Crime to the Home Affairs Select Committee, 26 March, www.parliament.the-stationery-office.co.uk/pa/cm200607/cmselect/cmhaff/433/433we04.htm (accessed 28 June 2010).

Garside, R. (2006) Right for the wrong reasons: making sense of criminal justice failure, in *Does Criminal Justice Work? The Right for the Wrong Reasons Debate* (eds R. Garside and W. McMahon), Crime and Society Foundation/Centre for Crime and Justice Studies, London.

Greer, C. (2003) Media representations of dangerousness. *Criminal Justice Matters*, **51**. Centre for Crime and Justice Studies, London.

Hagell, A. and Newburn, T. (1994) *Persistent Young Offenders*, Policy Studies Institute, London.

Hales, G., Lewis, C. and Silverstone, D. (2006) *Gun Crime: The Market In and Use of Illegal Firearms*, Home Office Research Study 298, Home Office, London.

Hallsworth, S. (2005) *Street Crime*, Willan Publishing, Cullompton.

Harris, K. (2006) Introduction, in *Respect in the Neighbourhood: Why Neighbourliness Matters* (ed. K. Harris). Russell House Publishing, Lyme Regis.

HM Government (2008) *Saving Lives, Reducing Harm, Protecting the Public*, An Action Plan for Tackling Violence 2008–11, Home Office, London.

Home Office (2008) *Tackling Gangs Action Programme*, Home Office, London.

Hope, T. (2001) Crime victimisation and inequality in risk society, in *Crime, Disorder and Community Safety* (eds R. Matthews and J. Pitts). Routledge, London.

House of Commons (2007), *Young Black People and the Criminal Justice System*, Home Affairs Select Committee Report, HC 181–1 and 2, The Stationery Office, London.

Innes, M. (2004) Signal crimes and signal disorders: notes on deviance as communicative action. *British Journal of Sociology*, **55** (3), 35–55.

Jewkes, Y. (2007) Regimes, rehabilitation and resettlement, in *Handbook on Prisons* (ed. Y. Jewkes), Willan Publishing, Cullompton.

Kershaw, C., Nicholas, S. and Walker, A. (2008) *Crime in England and Wales 2007/08: Findings from the British Crime Survey and Police Recorded Crime*, Home Office, London.

Kite, M. (2008) Violent crime is worse than ever, say PCs on the front line, *Daily Telegraph*, 3 March.

Klein, M. (1995) *The American Street Gang. Its Nature, Prevalence, and Control*, Oxford University Press, New York.

König, T. and Knowles, C.H. (2006) Stabbing: data support public perception. *British Medical Journal*, www.bmj.com/cgi/content/full/333/7569/652, (accessed 28 June 2010).

Lane, M. and Wheeler, B. (2003) *Is Knife Crime Really Getting Worse?* BBC News, 11 November, news.bbc.co.uk/1/hi/magazine/3244709.stm (accessed 28 June 2010).

Lemos, G. (2004) *Fear and Fashion: The Use of Knives and Other Weapons by Young People*, Lemos and Crane, London.

Lovell, C. (2008) Ex-gang members at Lambeth gang summit slate unit plan. *Community Care*, 15 February.

Marshall, B., Webb, B. and Tilley, N. (2005) *Rationalisation of Current Research on Guns, Gangs and Other Weapons: Phase 1*. Jill Dando Institute of Crime Science, University College, London.

Maxwell, R., Trotter, C., Verne, J., Brown, P. and Gunnell, D. (2007) Trends in admissions to hospital involving an assault using a knife or other sharp instrument, England, 1997–2005. *Journal of Public Health*, **29** (2), 186–90.

Metropolitan Police Service (2007) Metropolitan Police Crime Data 2007, private communication, Metropolitan Police Service, London.

National Youth Agency (2006) *Knives, Guns and Gangs*. Spotlight, 37, September.

NCH (2008) *Step Inside Our Shoes: Young People's Views on Gun and Knife Crime*, NCH, London.

Peay, J. (2002) Mentally disordered offenders, mental health and crime in (eds M. Maguire, R. Morgan and R. Reiner) *The Oxford Handbook of Criminology*, third edition, Oxford University Press, Oxford.

Royal Armouries Museum (2007) *Tackling Knife Crime: A Review of Literature on Knife Crime in the UK*, a report for the Royal Armouries Museum, Royal Armouries and the Perpetuity Group, Leicester.

Sanders, W.B. (1994) *Gangbangs and Drive-bys: Grounded Culture and Juvenile Gang Violence*, Aldine de Gruyter, New York.

Sharp, C., Aldridge, J. and Medina, J. (2006) *Delinquent Youth Groups and Offending Behaviour*: Findings from the 2004 Offending, Crime and Justice Survey, Home Office Online Report 14/06, www.law.man.ac.uk/aboutus/staff/judith_aldridge/documents/sharpEA2006.pdf (accessed 10 July 2010).

Smith, D.J. and Bradshaw, P. (2005) *Gang Membership and Teenage Offending*, the Edinburgh Study of Youth Transitions and Crime, University of Edinburgh, Edinburgh.

Solomon, E. and Garside, R. (2008) *Ten Years of Labour's Youth Justice Reforms: An Independent Audit*, Centre for Crime and Justice Studies, King's College, London.

Squires, P. (2000) *Gun Culture or Gun Control: Firearms, Violence and Society*, Routledge, London.

Squires, P. (2007) *Police Perceptions of Gang and Gun Related Offending: A Key Informant Survey*, Magnet project report, www.brighton.ac.uk/sass/contact/staffprofiles/pas1-magnet.pdf

Squires, P. (2008a) New research on gun crime, *Criminal Justice Matters*, **71**, Centre for Crime and Justice Studies, King's College, London.

Squires, P. (2008b) *Gun Crime: A Review of Evidence and Policy*, Centre for Crime and Justice Studies, King's College, London.

Stephen, D.E. and Squires, P. (2004) *Community Safety, Enforcement and Acceptable Behaviour Contracts*, Health and Social Policy Research Centre, University of Brighton, Brighton.

Young, T., FitzGerald, M., Hallsworth, S. and Joseph, I. (2007) *Groups, Gangs and Weapons: A Report for the Youth Justice Board*, Youth Justice Board, London.

15 Delivering Preventive Programmes in Schools: Identifying Gender Issues

NICKY STANLEY, JANE ELLIS AND JO BELL

INTRODUCTION

This chapter considers preventive approaches to violence in young people's relationships that have emerged in the UK over the last 10 years. In particular, we explore the evidence on preventive programmes delivered in schools and draw on two independent evaluations of such programmes to consider their achievements and the challenges they encounter. Gender differences emerge as a key factor that needs to inform both the delivery of these programmes and their content.

Programmes that aim to prevent violence in young people's intimate relationships and raise their awareness of domestic violence have been delivered in North America and Canada since the mid-1980s (Jaffe *et al.*, 1992, Avery-Leaf *et al.*, 1997; Macgowan, 1997; Foshee *et al.*, 1998; Meyer and Stein, 2001). Recognition of the widespread nature of domestic violence and its impact on all family members has developed at a slower pace in the UK generally (Stanley, 1997); however, from the mid-1990s onwards, similar programmes began to emerge in the UK. A mapping study (Ellis, 2004) undertaken in England, Northern Ireland and Wales in 2003, identified 102 local authorities where such programmes had been delivered; 82 per cent of reported programmes addressed domestic violence and 40 per cent 'dating' violence. This development was directly related to an increase in Home Office funding for community safety initiatives and to the creation of the *Children's Fund* with its prevention agenda. Government support for delivering these preventive programmes in schools is discernible (Department for Education and Skills, 2004; Home Office, 2004), although no additional resources have been allocated to schools for this task.

Children Behaving Badly? Peer Violence Between Children and Young People
Edited by Christine Barter and David Berridge
© 2011 John Wiley & Sons Ltd.

The majority of the programmes identified by Ellis's (2004) mapping study were delivered in mainstream schools with just over a third also running in special schools. The personal, social, health and economic education (PSHE) curriculum has provided a home for these programmes, although the mapping study found that the initiative for such programmes often originated in organisations outside education such as Women's Aid, multi-agency domestic violence forums or crime partnerships. The extent to which schools have contributed to or claimed ownership of these programmes has varied considerably and they have suffered from the lack of long-term sustainability that characterises voluntary sector initiatives reliant on short-term funding. For instance, the Healthy Relationships Programme, discussed later, changed ownership when the voluntary organisation where it had originated closed prematurely (Bell and Stanley, 2005).

These programmes usually embrace a range of goals that include raising young people's awareness of violence and abuse in intimate relationships; directing them to sources of advice and support; and identifying and promoting positive behaviour in relationships. The schools programmes surveyed by Ellis (2004) were targeted at pupils under 16, with 34 per cent of the programmes aimed at both primary and secondary school pupils, 11 per cent targeted on the 5–11 age group and 54 per cent directed at secondary school students. Most programmes are delivered to a mixed-gender audience, although 41 per cent of the programmes surveyed included some single-sex components (Ellis, 2004). Programmes usually draw on a small number of established and well-known models (London Borough of Islington 1994; Sandwell Against Domestic Violence, 2000; Debbonaire and Westminster Domestic Violence Forum, 2002; Protective Behaviours UK, 2004), which utilise a range of activities and techniques to engage children and young people. However, the extent to which programmes focus on gender equality and adopt explicitly feminist explanations of power and violence can vary according to the model employed and the attitudes and understandings of those delivering the programmes.

THE HEALTHY RELATIONSHIPS PROGRAMME

This programme is one of the few delivered to date in the UK that has been subjected to independent evaluation. It was delivered between 2001 and 2003 in four secondary schools with consistently low levels of achievement in an inner-city area with high levels of social exclusion. The programme was designed and delivered by an integrated domestic violence service in the same neighbourhood, which also provided services for women experiencing domestic violence and for perpetrators (Bell and Stanley, 2005). Year 8 pupils aged 12–13 were selected as the target group for the programme because this group was considered to offer an opportunity for intervention before the young people became heavily involved in intimate relationships.

Not all the schools could find time in the PSHE curriculum to deliver the programme in its full form but, for those who could, the programme included a specially commissioned drama production delivered by a theatre-in-education company, which was immediately followed by a workshop. Thereafter, five 1-hour workshops were delivered on a weekly basis by domestic violence project staff and community workers. Key workshop themes included developing self-esteem and mutual respect; stereotypical attitudes and beliefs; cultural and social influences on gender identity; sex role stereotypes; acknowledging one's own and others' feelings; and practising communication skills. A range of tools such as games, videos, role-play and quizzes were used to facilitate learning.

The programme was ambitious in its goals, aiming both to enable participants to recognise the possibility of domestic violence featuring in their parents' relationships, and to seek support in such situations and develop skills and attitudes that would protect them from abuse in their own relationships. While the drama production depicted a 12-year-old boy struggling with the effects of domestic violence in his parents' relationship, much of the material in the workshops focused on what constituted positive behaviour in young people's own relationships.

The evaluation comprised a 3-part survey, which explored young people's attitudes and understandings of relationship violence before, immediately after and 1 year after the programme (although only one school was able to administer the third stage of the survey). The first stage of the survey was completed by 450 pupils with 337 participating in the second stage and 55 in the third stage. Ten single-sex discussion groups involving 48 pupils were held to collect additional qualitative data on young people's perceptions of the programme and its impact.

The evaluation undertaken at Stage 2 found considerable gender differences in the young people's perceptions of the programme. Girls were generally more positive and more likely to consider that their ideas had been changed by the programme. Boys were less likely to report that the programme had substantially changed their thinking. All participants had enjoyed the drama production and the interactive elements of the programme, but boys were less likely to say that they had learnt a lot from the workshops and were keen to emphasise their preference for the more active elements of the programme:

> We didn't really do much moving. We had to just sit still.
> They was doing a lot of talking but we didn't understand much of it.
> It was too complicated.
> Too much talking.
> They did too much talking. Not enough acting.
>
> Discussion group 3, boys

This contrasted with the girls' views:

> I like discussing stuff.
> Yeah I like discussing in the groups. That was the best part I think.
> Especially doing about what girls like and boys like and we swapped it over.
>
> > Discussion group 2, girls

In just one of the four schools, a male facilitator was involved in delivering the workshops; boys in this school were more likely to rate the workshops positively than boys in the other schools. The programme coordinator argued that the use of a male facilitator conveyed the message that discussion of feelings and relationships, as well as the concept of gender equality in relationships, was compatible with masculinity. The boys participating in the discussion groups also emphasised the value of male role models. These boys were asked what they might say to the father in the play:

> Talk to them. 'Cos some blokes only listen to other blokes.
> Some men only listen to other men. They just think women are … just there.
> Some men might just think they can rule. Some of them like to get their own way.
>
> > Discussion group 3, boys

In one of the schools delivering the programme, the facilitators had adopted a more explicitly feminist ideology than that which informed the programmes on the other sites. This may have had an impact on how the programme was received. Following the programme in this school, students were less likely than those in the other schools to consider that domestic violence involved women bullying men and more likely to consider that domestic violence was mainly about men bullying women.

Generally, the programme seemed to be successful in conveying messages about individuals' rights to autonomy, privacy and freedom in relationships, and in emphasising themes of equality, trust, honesty and understanding:

> Both partners have an equal say. No-one should make someone do what they don't want to. No-one should get hurt.
>
> > girl

> To listen and look after my partner and try to understand her.
>
> > boy

However, the evaluation identified some difficulties in communicating messages about the need to be assertive in relationships. Prior to the programme, a small percentage of pupils said that they could think of a situation where they would agree with a man slapping his wife's face; this proportion increased slightly following the programme. The proportion who considered that they could think of situations where they would agree with a wife slapping her husband's face was even higher, with about a third of all participants in the survey signalling agreement. This proportion increased to 40 per cent following delivery of the programme in the school where the programme adopted an explicit focus on women's rights and assertiveness. An emphasis on 'girl power' may have had the unintended consequence of encouraging girls to embrace models of assertion that encompassed violence. One girl described her responsibilities in a relationship as:

> To face up to him if we start arguing or if he slaps me, slap him back.

The distinction between assertion and violence clearly needs to be clearly communicated and reinforced by examples.

THE DOMESTIC VIOLENCE AWARENESS RAISING PROGRAMME

This programme was commissioned by the local Children's Fund and delivered by Women's Aid in a Midlands city from 2003 onwards. It aimed to raise awareness of domestic violence and to enable children and young people living with domestic violence to have knowledge of and access to a range of support services, and to identify what constituted a 'healthy relationship'. Two programmes were developed – one for children in primary schools and the other for young people in secondary schools – the focus here will be on the latter in order to facilitate comparisons with the Healthy Relationships Programme described earlier. Designed as six 1-hour sessions to be delivered over a 6-week period, the programme content addressed the topics of domestic violence, children and domestic violence, gender stereotypes, power and control, conflict resolution, rights and responsibilities in relationships, healthy relationships and support services. An overtly feminist discourse of domestic violence shaped the programme. In common with the Healthy Relationships Programme, a range of methods was employed to engage young people in learning: small- and whole-group discussion, role-play, video, pair work and individual work – worksheets and writing. The programme was integrated into the wider services of Women's Aid and the schools' workers, who designed and delivered the programme, were located in Women's Aid's training team.

Every state school in the local authority was directly invited to host the programme, with three secondary schools agreeing to do so (five primary schools also hosted the programme). A girls' independent school, which heard of the programme through word of mouth, also participated. Funding was available from September 2002 to March 2004 but it took several months to recruit the two schools' worker and to gain access to schools, resulting in a slow start to the direct work with young people, which began in June 2003. Each of the four schools located the programme in the PSHE curriculum, although it was only delivered as planned in two. Table 15.1 provides

Table 15.1 Schools, pattern of delivery and number of participants

Type of school	Pseudonym	Year group	Age (years)	Number of classes	Number of young people	Number of sessions	Content
Mixed community comprehensive	North Street	9	13–14	12	227	1	Domestic violence, support services, healthy relationships
Girls' independent	Derwent	8	12–13	1	25	5	Domestic violence, date rape, grooming, sexual exploitation, support services, healthy relationships
Mixed community comprehensive	Westhill	8	12–13	1	25	6	Domestic violence, support services, healthy relationships
Mixed foundation	Lakeside	7	11–12	1	9	6	Domestic violence, support services, healthy relationships

information on the schools, numbers of sessions, participants and programme content. North Street School only agreed to the delivery of a single 1-hour session for each class; this was seen as a means of enabling every young person in one year group to take part, although this had major implications for evaluation and some unanticipated outcomes, as discussed later.

The evaluation, also commissioned by the Children's Fund, consisted of pre- and post-programme questionnaires, completed by a small sample of 74 young people, to assess knowledge, understanding and attitudes towards domestic violence and to elicit their views of the programme and its delivery. The majority of students from North Street School were unable to participate in the evaluation, because it proved too complicated to administer the survey outside the 1-hour lesson, particularly as the school had agreed to host the programme at short notice. The evaluation was multi-method and also included three single-gender focus groups with young people ($n = 15$); semi-structured interviews with six school and four Women's Aid staff; and non-participant observation of at least half of all the sessions in each school. As with many evaluations, the post-programme questionnaires were completed immediately after the end of the programme so only short-term changes were recorded (Whitaker *et al.*, 2006), which is not ideal because there is some evidence that learning is not retained beyond this. The evaluation of the Healthy Relationships Programme, for example, found that changes observed immediately after delivery of the programme, regarding which sources of help children experiencing domestic violence would access, were not sustained a year later (Bell and Stanley, 2005).

As Table 15.1 shows, because this programme took the form of a limited resource delivered by an external agency, schools faced a choice between spreading the programme 'wide and thin' or concentrating it on a single class or group of students. Gender emerged as noteworthy in relation to several aspects of the programme, but here we focus on gender as a factor in young people's responses to and learning from the programme; these are closely related because learning is more likely to occur when participants are pleased with a programme (Kirkpatrick, 1998).

The young people were not asked directly about their enjoyment of the programme. However, from comments made in response to questions about suggested changes and about whether other young people should have such lessons (97% thought that they should), it was clear that most had had a positive experience. The least enthusiastic were young men, almost exclusively those who participated in the 1-hour sessions at North Street School. A fifth of the boys at this school who completed the post-programme questionnaire left the 'suggested changes' question blank and 38 per cent did not comment on 'what they had learned'. Such high rates of abstention did not occur in the other schools where most of the young people readily completed the questionnaires.

In general, boys and girls participating in the mixed gender groups responded to the sessions differently and a gendered dynamic was evident in the observations of the programme. This pattern offered opportunities for experiential learning and, on some occasions, the group facilitators were able to use the group dynamic to enhance learning. This was particularly true in relation to the concept of gendered power relations: the tension between girls and boys was often expressed in overtly hostile ways but also in subtle ways, as seen in this extract from a girls' focus group:

Girl 1:	And everyone starts laughing.
Girl 2:	Yeah. That wasn't good.
Researcher:	So what ... how did that impact on you then?
Girl 1:	You feel embarrassed.
Researcher:	You feel embarrassed. Who do you think was laughing?
Girl 1:	Um. [boy's name].
Girl 2:	The boys.
Girl 1:	All the boys.
All together:	All the boys.
Girl 2:	When they [schools' workers] kept reading that piece ... the boys were being very stupid and everything.

Girls' focus group

A complex picture emerged in relation to the learning of young people, which might be attributable to the programme being delivered in three formats with different content, in schools with distinctive differences, to young people living with diverse circumstances and experiences. The complexity of the findings seemed to relate predominantly to gender because the young women at the girls' independent school appear to have learned most from the programme. A paired t-test, to measure changes between responses on the pre- and post-questionnaires, revealed a statistical significance in relation to 6 of closed 12 statements that examined knowledge of, and attitudes towards, gendered violence.

However, gender alone cannot account for these changes because the young women at the three other schools participating in the programme showed considerably less attitudinal change than the girls at the independent school. The question clearly arises as to what factors might have produced such marked changes in learning in this group. Several possible factors, combined together, might account for the difference: first, the young women from the independent school were highly motivated, confident learners, many of whom were extremely articulate and so able to engage more easily in discussion and debate. Moreover, they were taught in single-gender groups, creating a safer, less confrontational setting. In addition, violence as an abuse of power was discussed more often and more overtly in this school. The material was new and challenging for these students, and both the students and a woman teacher reported that some had been 'shocked' by it, although all the girls reported it had been valuable.

In respect of the young people's knowledge and understanding of interpersonal violence, there was evidence of positive change following the programme, with the exception of their views concerning minority ethnic men and domestic violence. The accumulated figures hide gender differences, however. The most positive changes, along with the group at the independent girls' school, were found among young men at Westhill and North Street schools, although some started from a low baseline particularly in relation to their attitudes towards women leaving violent relationships. Young women appeared more likely to have a broader understanding of violence and to see it as encompassing aspects of violence other than physical assault. Their readiness to identify psychological forms of violence may be drawn from their experiences of bullying, which are more commonly verbal, relational and exclusionary, as compared to the physical violence of young men. Young women also seemed more able to relate the learning from the programme to their own feelings:

Girl 4:   … I don't have anyone I know that's in a situation similar to that [in an abusive relationship]. So like I think if I did or I think that I'd feel more comfortable with the fact that I could cope if they were being abused or anything like that. Anything around that sort of… But um I'd hope that I'd be able to help because …

Researcher: Yeah.

Girl 4:   And I think it's good to tell somebody. Because it's important because otherwise they [friend] could get you down. And if you didn't know what to do if you have a friend going through it. And you can't do anything about it. Then that's just like really horrible.

Gender differences were also important in the young people's understandings of gender and violence; young women almost overwhelmingly disagreed with the statement 'some women deserve to be hit', while the young men at Westhill School showed both positive and negative changes in relation to this statement (an additional 9 per cent disagreed and a further 3 per cent agreed after the programme), suggesting that the attitudes of some boys had become entrenched.

Some young women expressed strong views about gender inequality; one young woman was very clear that the lessons were about women's rights – although this was never expressly discussed – and thought that this was good to talk about because some of the boys had learnt how to treat women better. However, other girls did not agree on that point and thought that, because their expectations of how to be treated as young women had been raised, they were more critical of how the boys treated them. Alternative femininities were implicitly discussed, which had reinforced one young woman's view that it was possible for a woman to 'live your own independent life'.

Overall, the findings were mostly positive and showed that the lessons had been thought-provoking for the young people participating, and had encouraged them to reflect on their own conduct as gendered and to contemplate gender relations. For some, it had a profound positive effect.

CONCLUSION

It is notable that both the programmes described here were delivered in schools by external agencies; teachers 'sat in' on both programmes and the level of their participation varied with the individual. This raises questions about the extent to which the programmes were embedded in the schools' cultures and whether the messages would be sustained in the long term. The young people themselves talked about the value of having messages about positive relationships repeated and reinforced:

> I would like to have it again – in Year 11 so I could keep it in mind – to learn it again in case I forgot.
>   boy participating in the Healthy Schools Programme

While such programmes remain outside the mainstream of schools' activities and the core curriculum, their marginalised nature is likely to convey a significant message to the young people participating in them. On a positive note, the government (Department of Children, Schools and Families, 2008) announced in October 2008 that PSHE lessons in schools were to be made statutory in England, although this did not guarantee that work on gender-based violence would be included in the curriculum.

Gender emerged as a significant factor in the delivery, content and impact of these programmes. There was some evidence from both evaluations that young men were more likely to respond to them with cynicism or apathy, and that the delivery of programmes could influence their response. The use of a male facilitator in delivering the Healthy Relationships Programme on one site was considered to be an important factor in engaging with young men. While research with boys about which teachers should deliver sex education has found that they considered a teacher's confidence and ability to evoke trust more important than gender (Hilton, 2003), it may be that male facilitators who can convey acceptable images of masculinity, together with a willingness to discuss relationships and emotions, are particularly valued in the context of programmes that address young people's relationships. Other aspects of programme delivery that appeared to contribute to engaging young men included the use of action-focused or kinetic learning approaches, which were explicitly valued by boys.

The preventive programmes described here adopted different approaches to the question of whether they should be delivered to single or mixed-gender groups. The Domestic Violence Awareness Raising Programme was delivered to mixed groups in mixed schools although, as an outcome of the evaluation, the programme was to be delivered to the next class at Westhill School in single-gender groups. The Healthy Relationships Programme used single and mixed-gender groups for different activities. While there is general agreement in the literature that programmes should target both boys and girls, there has been some debate, particularly in Canada, about whether programmes should be delivered to single or mixed-gender groups (Cameron *et al.*, 2002; Tutty and Bradshaw, 2002). There is no consensus, and both adults and young people identify the benefits of each approach. Using a combination of single and mixed groups affords opportunities to discuss issues in different settings and offers a flexibility that enables programmes to be more responsive to the needs of particular groups (Pacifici, Stoolmiller and Nelson, 2001; Debbonaire, 2002; RESOLVE Alberta, 2002; Weisz and Black, 2006).

The ideology that informed the programmes' content appeared to matter, and there were suggestions that a more explicitly feminist agenda that emphasised gender inequalities contributed to young people developing a view of interpersonal violence that acknowledged gender differences. However, the evaluation of the Healthy Relationships Programme identified risks that messages about young women asserting themselves in relationships could be interpreted as condoning the use of violence by girls.

While delivery emerged as a key factor in determining the impact of the programmes, other issues such as the students' level of educational attainment were clearly relevant. There has been little work done to assess the optimum age at which such programmes should be delivered. There is increasing enthusiasm for offering preventive programmes at the primary school stage, particularly in the UK and Canada (Haskell, Randall and Chen, 1999; Day *et al.*, 2002; Ellis, 2004). However, the evaluation of the Awareness Raising Programme delivered in a primary school to children aged 9–11 years found that it was difficult for some children to understand domestic violence; it is a complex concept and, to help younger children, the schools' workers referred to it as 'bullying in the home'. This message was potentially confusing because 'home' focuses attention on place and the key message in the programme was about non-violent 'relationships'. The local environment as well as cultural and social factors will also play key roles in shaping young people's attitudes towards both violence and sexual behaviour (Batchelor, Burman and Brown, 2001; Stanley, 2005; Alldred and David, 2007).

It is useful to acknowledge that girls and boys may approach this sort of learning from different starting points. Girls are likely to have had more experience of open discussion of these issues in their friendship groups, and are able to draw on the modes of expression developed through the problem pages and articles in girls' magazines. However, the evaluation of the Healthy Relationships Programme found that representations of violence in television 'soaps' provided a wealth of material familiar to both boys and girls (Bell and Stanley, 2006). Young people who might not have had personal experience of interpersonal violence were able to cite examples from their favourite show – *EastEnders* (a long-running television soap set in east London). Depiction of domestic violence in the relationship between the characters Mo and Trevor was cited by students from both the evaluated programmes – and these popular narratives allowed for discussion of violence in relationships 'at arm's length'. There is evidence that such programmes can make a major contribution to young people's learning about violence in intimate relationships. The 'Jake and Nancy' storyline on the UK soap, *Hollyoaks*, a television series aimed specifically at young people, generated considerable debate about the violence in the characters' relationship on the programme's discussion fora; and an awareness-raising survey of young people's views of the programme was undertaken by Trust, an educational project aiming to prevent violence in young people's relationships (CRG Research, 2009).

The evaluations of these preventive programmes suggest that well-facilitated and well-resourced work in schools can help young people learn that they have the right to expect non-violent relationships and the potential to achieve this in their own lives. A gender-sensitive approach appears helpful but needs to be delivered thoughtfully. However, if more young people are to benefit from these programmes, they need to be delivered more widely and to be more fully integrated into the work of schools.

PRACTICE POINTS

• Gender needs to be taken into account in planning both the delivery and content of preventive programmes.
• Storylines depicting relationship violence in television soaps can provide useful learning material.
• Preventive programmes addressing violence in young people's relationships should be fully integrated into schools' curricula and delivered on an ongoing and regular basis.

REFERENCES

Alldred, P. and David, M. (2007) *Get Real About Sex. The Politics and Practice of Sex Education*, Open University Press, Maidenhead.
Avery-Leaf, S., Cascardi, M., O'Leary, K.D. and Cano, A. (1997) Efficacy of a dating violence prevention program on attitudes justifying aggression. *Journal of Adolescent Health*, **21**, 11–17.
Batchelor, S., Burman, M. and Brown, J. (2001) Discussing violence: let's hear it for the girls. *Probation Journal*, **48** (2), 125–34.
Bell, J. and Stanley, N. (2005) *Tackling Domestic Violence at the Local Level: An Evaluation of the Preston Road, Domestic Violence Project*, University of Hull, Hull.
Bell, J. and Stanley, N. (2006) Learning about domestic violence: young people's responses to a healthy relationships programme. *Sex Education*, **6** (3), 237–50.
Cameron, C. and the Creating Peaceful Learning Environments Schools' Team (2002) Worlds apart ... coming together: gender segregated and integrated primary prevention implementations for adolescents in Atlantic rural communities, in *In the Best Interests of the Girl Child Phase II Report* (eds H. Berman and Y. Jiwani), The Alliance of Five Research Centres on Violence, Canada.

CRG Research (2009) An Independent Evaluation of the TRUST Education Project, www.tender.org.uk/files/TRUST%20Project%20External%20Evaluation%20 Report.doc (accessed 7 July 2010).

Day, D., Golench, C., MacDougall, J. and Beals-Gonzaléz, C. (2002) *School-based Violence Prevention in Canada: Results of a National Survey of Policies and Programs 1995–2002*, Earlscourt Child and Family Centre, Toronto, Available http://ww2.psepc-sppcc.gc.ca/publications/corrections/pdf/199502_e.pdf (accessed 30 June 2004).

Debbonaire, T. (2002) *Building Healthy Relationships and Safer Communities: Report of Westminster Domestic Violence Forum (WDVF) Schools Domestic Violence Prevention Project*, WDVF, London.

Debbonaire, T. and Westminster Domestic Violence Forum (WDVF) (2002) *Domestic Violence Prevention Pack for Schools*, WDVF, London.

Department of Children, Schools and Families (DCSF) (2008) *All Pupils to Get Healthy Lifestyle Lessons*, www.dcsf.gov.uk/pns/DisplayPN.cgi?pn_id=2008_0235 (accessed 7 November 2008).

Department for Education and Skills (DfES) (2004) *Safeguarding Children. Child Protection: Guidance about Child Protection Arrangements for the Education Service*, DfES, London.

Ellis, J. (2004) *Preventing Violence Against Women and Girls. A Study of Educational Programmes for Children and Young People*. WOMANKIND Worldwide, London.

Foshee, V., Bauman, K., Arriaga, X., Helms, R., Koch, G. and Linder, G. (1998) An evaluation of safe dates, an adolescent dating violence prevention program. *American Journal of Public Health*, **88**, 45–50.

Haskell, L., Randall, M. and Chen, L. (1999) *Educating for Change 2. Recommended Materials on Violence Against Women and Children*, Centre for Research and Education on Violence Against Women and Children, Ontario, Canada.

Hilton, G. (2003) Listening to the boys: English boys' views on the desirable characteristics of teachers of sex education. *Sex Education*, **3** (1), 33–45.

Home Office (2004) *The Role of Education in Enhancing Life Chances and Preventing Offending*, Development and Practice Report 19, Home Office, London.

Jaffe, P.G., Sudermann, M., Reitzel, D. and Killip, S.M. (1992) An evaluation of a secondary school primary prevention program on violence in intimate relationships. *Violence and Victims*, **7**, 129–46.

Kirkpatrick, D. (1998) *Evaluating Training Programmes: The Four Levels*, Berrett-Koehler, San Francisco, CA.

London Borough of Islington (1994) *STOP: Striving to Prevent Domestic Violence – Resource for Working with Children and Young People*. Women's Equality Unit, London Borough of Islington.

Macgowan, M. (1997) An evaluation of a dating violence prevention program for middle school students. *Violence and Victims*, **12**, 223–35.

Meyer, H. and Stein, N. (2001) 'Relationship violence prevention education in schools: what's working, what's getting in the way, and what might be some future directions', paper presented at the 7th International Family Violence Research Conference, Portsmouth, NH.

Pacifici, C., Stoolmiller, M. and Nelson, C. (2001) Evaluating a prevention program for teenagers on sexual coercion: a differential effectiveness approach. *Journal of Consulting and Clinical Psychology*, **69** (3), 552–59.

230 CHILDREN BEHAVING BADLY?

Protective Behaviours UK (PBUK) (2004) www.protectivebehaviours.co.uk (accessed 10 April 2008).

RESOLVE Alberta (2002) *School-based Violence Prevention Programs: A Resource Manual*, RESOLVE Alberta, University of Calgary, Calgary. www.ucalgary.ca/resolve/violenceprevention/English/index.htm (accessed 6 February 2004).

Sandwell Against Domestic Violence Project (SADVP) (2000) *Violence Free Relationships: Asserting Rights. A Programme for Young People*, SADVP, Sandwell.

Stanley, N. (1997) Domestic violence and child abuse: developing social work practice. *Child and Family Social Work*, 2 (3), 135–46.

Stanley, N. (2005) Thrills and spills: young people's sexual behaviour and attitudes in seaside and rural areas. *Health, Risk and Society*, 7 (4), 337–48.

Tutty, L. and Bradshaw, C. (2002) *Preventing Violence Against Girls and Young Women: Should Programs Highlight Gender?* Proceedings of the conference 'Prevention of violence against girls', Montréal, Canada.

Weisz, A. and Black, B. (2006) 'State of the art: research on programs that work to reduce dating violence and sexual assault', paper presented at international conference 'Violence against Women: Diversifying Social Responses', Montréal, Canada, 22–24 October.

Whitaker, D., Morrison, S., Lindquist, C. *et al.* (2006) A critical review of interventions for the primary prevention of perpetration of partner violence. *Aggression and Violent Behaviour*, 11 (2), 151–66.

16 Conclusion

DAVID BERRIDGE AND CHRISTINE BARTER

Having featured such an array of chapters and topics, it is a challenging task to attempt to pull it all together. In one sense, each of our authors has written about different things and approached their tasks in diverse ways; yet it is important here to try to assess the overall picture and take stock of what it all means. This includes any commonalities and recurrent themes but also differences and disagreements.

Initially, it is useful to revisit our starting point and remind ourselves why we wanted to produce this edited book and adopt the approach that we did. In our research collaborations over many years with NSPCC and in our other studies, we have sought to highlight children's perspectives on their own lives and the difficulties that confront them. One strand of this concerns children's protection and welfare and, in a context of great public and research concern about the harm that *adults* pose to children's well-being, children themselves have told us that they are also – if not sometimes *more* – concerned about the hurtful experiences inflicted by their *peers*. In fact the two often coexist.

Our natural inclination is to approach these issues broadly rather than narrowly. In the short-term this undoubtedly complicates matters and requires familiarity with different debates and a variety of academic traditions. However, to us this represents the true spirit of intellectual endeavour. Indeed, multidisciplinary research such as ours is often encouraged but with little discussion about what it actually entails. Collaboration *per se* is not inherently beneficial: it depends on whom one collaborates with and what they have to offer. We tried to choose our partners here carefully and we believe that this book makes an original contribution because of its breadth as well as its academic rigour. In addition, we feel that other researchers, students and professionals working with children, as well as other readers, will welcome complementary issues being presented in a single volume. After all, the domineering boy in the nursery may well grow up to mistreat his girlfriend as a teenager. They are one and the same.

We are pleased to have been able to produce a book that covers such a diverse range of topics as nurseries and knife crime; conflicts between siblings

Children Behaving Badly? Peer Violence Between Children and Young People
Edited by Christine Barter and David Berridge
© 2011 John Wiley & Sons Ltd.

and gangs; and teenage partner violence and racist murder. There is some British and international (US) variation. Our authors, leading figures in their fields, refer to the wider international literature and there is much new thinking with work discussed here that previously was not in the public domain. Our authors are concerned with the practical implications of their applied research, rather than developing knowledge for its own sake (which is nonetheless valuable), and ultimately aim to contribute something to improving children's lives.

Of course it may be that these qualities are shared to some degree because we, as editors, invited the contributions based on our own predilections. Yet this group of researchers write from a number of disciplines including sociology, psychology, criminology, social work and education. They adopt a range of theoretical and methodological approaches, depending on the field in question, their own backgrounds and preferences. We do not seek to evaluate the merits of these contrasting paradigms and there is little to be gained from uniformity. Instead it is interesting to see the arguments juxtaposed, and to reflect on how the different conclusions relate to the preferred approach. Our task as editors is to help present these varied contributions and debates, and to try to assess, overall, what they tell us.

Another reason for this book and the perspective we adopted concerns misgivings currently expressed in the UK about the situation and depiction of children and childhoods. Despite the overall comparative wealth of the UK nations and scientific and technological advances, we saw in our Introduction (Chapter 1) that, compared with many other countries, growing up in the UK can be very problematic: children report high levels of dissatisfaction, and youth especially are often negatively perceived and associated with 'toxic childhoods', to repeat Palmer's (2007) cogent phrase. We have tried to set the record straight.

THE PREVALENCE OF PEER VIOLENCE

CONCEPTUALISATIONS

In this concluding chapter, we return to the questions posed at the outset of the book and consider issues such as 'How great a social problem is peer violence between children and young people?' 'Is the problem reducing or worsening?' 'Who is involved and affected?' and 'How well are children safeguarded?'

Concerning prevalence, as is often the case with researchers, the situation becomes more confused before it hopefully becomes clearer. It is not just that researchers avoid answering direct questions. We informed authors at the outset about our own assumptions as editors and the general influence of the sociology of childhood literature (see Introduction). However, it is interesting to observe that the different chapters adopt different terms and concepts. It is impossible to gauge the extent of a social problem without knowing exactly what is being scrutinised. As editors, our generic preference for the peer conflict we are discussing, as reflected in the book's title, is 'violence'. Euphemisms sometimes conceal the reality of behaviour and its effects on those involved (such as perhaps 'the Troubles' and 'Unpleasantness' to refer to armed resistance or war). Brown's Chapter 2 argues that 'peer violence' is an inappropriate term for preschool settings and children at an early developmental stage, preferring instead '"energetic" or "lively" play'.

The term 'bullying' is often used regarding school-based behaviour (see Chapter 3). The concept has been criticised (Chapter 13), including its gender implications. Conceiving bullying as a sub-set of 'aggressive', rather than 'violent', behaviours might reflect more of an individualistic, educational, psychological or even biological approach, which nevertheless acknowledges the social context. Although perhaps an accurate description, not all sociologists would be comfortable with the idea, or possible oxymoron, of a 'provocative victim'.

Some authors prefer the terms 'abuse' or 'maltreatment' (Chapters 4 and 11), which perhaps imply children's experiences within *families*. Children's *sexualised* behaviour is described as 'problematic', 'harmful' or 'abusive' (Chapter 9). For Back's powerful Chapter (7) on the Stephen Lawrence murder, *racism* is the over-riding concern as in 'violent racism'. The majority of chapter authors use the term 'violence'. Perhaps all these variations are alternative 'discourses', which reflect important underlying assumptions and differences (Chapter 13).

INCIDENCE

So, having hopefully not muddied the waters too much, how much 'peer violence' of different forms is there? In view of the previous discussion, this may be an impossible question to answer. But how common in modern society are coercive and harmful behaviours between children of different types?

As argued in the earlier chapter, preschool issues are distinct in important respects. Nonetheless, 'noisy, boisterous boys' are commonplace in nurseries and other preschool settings. They dominate activities and spaces and often determine girls' group, social experiences. However, research has concluded that staff can over-react and exaggerate the degree to which developmental exuberance spills over, such as when pretend fighting develops into real fighting.

Although under-researched, in US studies between a third and half of those with siblings report having been bullied by them. In Britain, probably about a quarter of teenage girls experience some form of physical violence from their boyfriends, and three-quarters said that it affected their welfare. A third had experienced 'emotional violence' in which they had been called hurtful names, or had a partner shout at them or scream in their face. There are over 60,000 racist incidents reported annually in Britain and violence is used dispropor- tionately against young people from minority ethnic groups. There were a further 68 racist murders reported in just over a decade following Stephen Lawrence's murder. As Back argues (Chapter 7), racist violence poisons the lives of minority ethnic children and youth.

In another virulent form of discrimination, US and British studies have suggested that some 8 per cent of the *whole* school population have been bullied due to homophobia (including heterosexuals). Two-thirds of those who identified themselves as gay or lesbian experienced homophobic bullying.

Family and community violence had also been a dominant feature of the lives of youths engaged in street-based activities, few of whom, as we saw, recognised their friendship groupings as 'gangs'. Current violence in which they were engaged was usually low-level and confined mainly within peer groups or with people whom they knew. The organised groupings they had formed had social and friendship benefits, as well as contributing to their own protection. They added that young people would seldom choose to become involved in street-based activities but did so because of social and economic necessities, including lack of leisure alternatives. More specifically, a comple- mentary chapter revealed that about a third of young people in Britain admit- ted to carrying penknives or knives: of these, 8 in every 10 knives were solely for protection, 1 in 10 young people had used one to threaten someone and 2 per cent had used one to injure someone. This is a low figure but high enough for anyone on the receiving end.

Paradoxically perhaps, the state is unable to guarantee protection for chil- dren separated from their families mainly because of parental abuse and neglect, and now living in public care in foster or residential homes. In the US, a quarter of separated youth reported that they had been treated unfairly or picked on. The proportion is greater in England with its smaller residential sector and high thresholds for entry (Thoburn, 2007). 'Verbal violence', includ- ing harmful name-calling and impugning of reputations, is commonplace in children's residential homes, which shelter those who have already been rejected or otherwise experienced family breakdown.

CHANGES IN PEER VIOLENCE?

Clearly then, there is a significant number of different forms of peer violence between children and large minorities of young people are affected. The rationale for this book is justified. The romantic vision of childhood as a trouble-free, enjoyable, exploratory phase unencumbered by responsibilities is untrue and probably always was. Many children in the UK and the US lead troubled and stressful lives (UNICEF, 2007) and it is not just adults who are the cause but their peers as well. Given this disconcerting overall picture, are there signs that the situation is improving or deteriorating? Our authors were not asked to map changes systematically over time but several provided evidence of the changing nature of the problems concerned.

One of the most influential ideas to emerge from British sociology and enter common parlance is that of 'moral panic': the notion that certain social behaviours are exaggerated, and that this arises at certain times for a specific social purpose (Cohen, 1972) (see Introduction). Moral panics serve to unite fragmented societies against a defined or created, relatively defenceless, target. Youth offenders are one common source of moral panics; social workers are probably another (Parton and Berridge, forthcoming). As with all successful research dissemination, ideas can be misunderstood or misused and there is a risk of 'moral panic' becoming something of a cliché. The idea has been further refined in the literature to bring it up to date after nearly 40 years (McRobbie and Thornton, 1995). Squires and Goldsmith (Chapter 14) refer to the 'smoke' (public reactions) and 'fire' (hard evidence) of moral panics.

We were pleased to be able to encourage Sharon Nichols to write the chapter (12) for us on media representations of youth violence, which provided an academic analysis and update of this field, including international evidence. She demonstrated that 'shock value' is a critical ingredient of media news stories. International media exaggerates the prevalence of youth violence and has given much greater attention to youth crime even in periods during which it has declined. In the US, following a series of school shootings, it has been suggested that young people's dress and demeanour can be a reliable indicator of proclivity for violence. Media especially overstates the incidence of *female* violence. Nichols argues that fear is an important part of social control.

Bearing in mind, therefore, that political and media portrayals of the extent and nature of peer violence are unlikely to be reliable, what did our chapters tell us about the changing nature of the problem over time? Has it improved or worsened? Once again we need to be circumspect and most of the areas in question have received little research in the first place, let alone comparative or validated studies over time. In the preschool chapter (2), for example, it is not so much that behaviour has deteriorated but that society is now less tolerant of games that would have been acceptable in the past, such as imaginary gun play and war games. Exuberant 'rough and tumble' play in day care settings is now more likely to be channelled into more structured, acceptable learning opportunities as part of the preschool curriculum. Children's play generally is expected to be more risk averse and anxieties over 'health and safety' can become obsessive.

Two of our authors supplied evidence to show that peer violence has worsened in the two fields of discrimination – racial and homophobic violence. It was argued that these have been exacerbated by the absence of government action in the case of the former; and by restrictive legislation in the latter. We return to this later.

In the chapter on the perceived 'epidemic' in youth violence, particularly knife crime, evidence demonstrated that general youth crime over the decade has not increased; however, violent crimes involving under-16s appear to have done. There seems to be some evidence of an increase in knife-carrying but police statistics reveal no increase in knife-related crime. There is likely to be an element of under-reporting, as in many official statistics. Hospital accident and emergency admissions for stabbing have increased. However, it is important to bear in mind that knife crimes overwhelmingly concern the *over-* (not under-) 18s, and mainly involve *white* not black youths.

Apart from these findings, there is no evidence that problems have worsened: the moral panic is unjustified. But then again, there are no signs that the significant areas of concern outlined earlier have been successfully tackled.

WHO IS INVOLVED IN PEER VIOLENCE?

From the different levels of evidence available to our authors, what emerges from our chapters, as one might have anticipated, is that boys and young men are mainly responsible for the bulk of peer violence. Harmful sexual behaviours are mostly undertaken by boys, again often linked with the onset of puberty. Young men are responsible for most, and the most harmful, teenage partner violence. Referring back to the previous point, partner violence appears to be worse in same-sex relationships (boy/boy and girl/girl), although other factors intervene. Young men embark on the worst street-based violence and are more likely to carry and use knives.

Several of our authors have referred to the way in which 'masculinities' or 'hegemonic masculinities' shape boys' behaviour. This is evident even with nursery-age boys, although researchers have shown how entry to the social world of the nursery is complex for young children, which can exaggerate certain behaviours such as monopoly of play areas and toys. Nonetheless, a significant part of the peer violence discussed in our chapters seems linked to children's responses to how society defines appropriate male behaviour as assertive dominance. This can arise especially at particular phases of status changes and sexual development. It can be trite to suggest that this needs to be addressed, because its origins are deeply culturally embedded over decades and centuries, and reinforced throughout the media and in the social organisation of everyday life. However, examples are offered throughout the book of successful interventions to address gender exploitation and inequalities, such as in schools. Professionals working with children have limited influence compared with broader social and political factors. But, as our interest is in applied research, our authors drew together some of the suggestions for how professionals locally might attempt to confront some of the issues.

Some of the other problems we have discussed are more equally distributed. For example, boys and girls alike appear to bully siblings, although sexual abuse is mainly undertaken by boys. School bullying is undertaken by both boys and girls, although gender stereotyping needs to be taken into account (Chapter 13).

Probably the clearest message from our chapters concerns the increased victimisation of discriminated minorities on the grounds of racism and homophobia. Back's chapter (7) describes violent racism as an underlying feature of everyday life. Racism circumscribes physical and social space, and restricts the boundaries of minority ethnic/black young people (and adults). Rivers' contribution (10) on homophobia demonstrates how this form of discrimination often coincides with the emergence of sexual identity. Name-calling is a frequent strategy and power can derive from belittling and subjugating others. Rivers highlights sexuality as a potentially vulnerable element of a teenager's armoury. The high profile of sex and sexuality within western culture exacerbates these tendencies. In addition to racism and homophobia, the young people affected of course may *also* be siblings, involved in teenage intimate relationships, street-based groups and so on, with the associated peer violence and other pressures that these entail.

Although the book is primarily sociological in its orientation, it is interesting that many of our authors did not segregate sharply between social and psychological factors but acknowledged that the two were inter-linked. Family and community influences clearly have a profound effect on violent children. There is some evidence that abusive siblings are more likely to have experienced violent, neglectful parenting. Siblings who sexually abuse are themselves more likely to have had similar experiences with adults. Certain groups of children who exhibit sexually harmful behaviours have been found to have poor social skills, low self-esteem, experience of rejection by peers, and problems with intimacy. Their families typically are multi-dysfunctional with frequent changes of carers and periods of separation. Psychological studies of bullies have identified lack of empathy and high narcissism, which may stem from poor early attachments.

Whereas there may be little that governments can do in the short term to transform traditional gender roles, politicians do have choices about the sorts of economies and societies they seek to fashion, particularly relating to social inequalities. We started off this book by outlining current tendencies to perceive certain kinds of violent children as inherently 'evil'. Our authors detected little evidence of the Satanic. Instead, we argued earlier that there is often an association between negative and violent early family experiences and children who go on to harm others. None of this is automatic: influences may be indirect and causal chains and social trajectories are complex (Caprara and Rutter, 1995). There is strong international evidence of the stresses of family poverty and its adverse impact on parenting, including greater risk of child abuse (Katz *et al.*, 2007). Although making progress, UK government has missed its child poverty targets (Palmer, MacInnes and Kenway, 2006). Social mobility for the young is more complex than in previous generations and young adults lacking qualifications and skills are hardest hit in a recession – such as at the time of writing with a third of the long-term unemployed reported to be under 25 (Prince's Trust, 2009).

The influential book, *The Spirit Level* (Wilkinson and Pickett, 2009), argued that it is not poverty *per se* that leads to social problems but overall levels of *inequality*. Extreme wealth causes problems in society as well as extreme poverty. Their analysis of a range of health and social problems in rich countries – including violence, teenage births and educational failure – showed that these problems are experienced more often by poor people than rich. However, in comparing different societies, these social problems have little relationship to *average* incomes. Instead, there are close links with income differences. How individuals perceive themselves in comparison with others seems to be very important. The authors demonstrate a strong and consistent association between inequality and violence in societies. Reanalysing the UNICEF (2007) data on child wellbeing in rich countries, they also show that there is more conflict between children in unequal countries – based on those reporting fighting, bullying and finding peers unhelpful. Children in Finland, Sweden and Germany reported low levels of conflict and they were highest in the UK, France and the US.

It has been observed that New Labour governments since 1997 attempted to reduce the effects of inequality without addressing inequality itself; also that government has sought high-quality Scandinavian welfare services at US tax levels. Whatever the cause, social inequality and poverty are rife among the families of the young, and their links with children's violent behaviour are highlighted in the preceding chapters. It is important to emphasise that most poor parents manage to provide a good upbringing and most children do not become violent. Yet the challenges and temptations are considerable and the risks enhanced.

These difficulties are exemplified in our two chapters on youth crime. Young and Hallsworth (Chapter 5), writing about street-based activities, argue that youths were '… worn down by marginalisation and exclusion, struggled to survive in a society they believed did not care or cater for their needs' (p. 61). They had fought to gather the social resources necessary to maintain a sense of self-esteem. Territorial control and 'respect' were important parts of this. Similarly, Squires and Goldsmith's chapter (14) on knife crime reveals the exclusion of groups of young people from legitimate social opportunities. Youths involved are simultaneously under-protected and their coping strategies over-controlled. The criminal justice system in itself can do little to reduce violent crime among the young, the origins of which lie with wider social problems:

… in managing these groups badly, by fostering and facilitating a demonisation of young people, further ostracising and excluding them, and demonstrating a punitive lack of trust and respect, it pushes them to find their own, even more problematic and often dangerous solutions.

p. 212

While not absolving young people from their own agency and responsibility for violence, it is clear from our chapters that how adults choose to socially organise children's lives can have a profound effect on the levels of peer conflict between them.

GOVERNMENT RESPONSES

Given these social problems, to what extent have government approaches helped alleviate peer violence between children and young people? Our chapters end with a particular focus on the implications for *practitioners*, but the policy framework is clearly important too. We restrict ourselves here to government and social policy in the UK. We also omit areas that have not attracted specific responses but are part of broader policy frameworks, such as sibling abuse and children displaying sexually harmful behaviours (Chapters 4 and 9).

Overall, there are some areas in which government efforts over the past decade are felt to have made a positive contribution to children's welfare. Much more attention is now given to the problem of bullying in schools and government has funded a variety of initiatives. Of course, actually reducing the incidence of bullying is a different issue; and some other educational policies on the curriculum, the annual media denigration of pupils following the publication of exam results and restricted employment opportunities to school leavers without academic qualifications may have had a countervailing influence.

As outlined in our Introduction, the broad *Every Child Matters* policy framework (Department for Education and Skills, 2003) has been generally well received. It has identified a wider set of responsibilities and 'outcomes' for all public services dealing with children, and emphasised more of a preventive agenda. Linked to this, the *Sure Start* initiative has aimed to provide a children's centre in every community and universal early years education and family support services for families with children under four. Positive results are emerging from the evaluations (National Evaluation of Sure Start, 2008). In contrast, not all are convinced of the merits of bringing together education and social work services for children and families into a single government department, which occurred without any public debate. Britain also now has *no* senior government ministers solely responsible for education – either for school pupils, or college and university students.

One of the main policy documents outlining the framework and required responses to child protection issues of various types is *Working Together*

(Department for Children, Schools and Families, 2010b). This is also considered a useful document, which has adapted over time and been reissued following the recent child abuse tragedies of Victoria Climbié and Peter Connelly. It now covers a wider range of safeguarding situations than previously, including a longer section on peer abuse (Chapter 11). It emphasises that peer abuse should always be taken as seriously as abuse committed by an adult, and reiterates that a significant proportion of sex offences are committed by teenagers. The risks of peer violence are higher for young people living away from home but not exclusively. *Working Together* contains a strengthened section on bullying, including bullying via the internet and sexist, sexual and transphobic bullying at school. The relevance of racism is acknowledged. There is a section on teenage partner relationships (our Chapter 8) but we do not know how this is being interpreted and applied, and to what effect. The creation of the Social Work Taskforce and subsequent National College of Social Work should help address the profile and status of the social work profession (Department for Children, Schools and Families, 2010a).

To its credit, government acknowledged the link between violence against women and violence against *girls* (Home Office, 2009) and launched a £2 million publicity campaign supported by the Prime Minister and ministers across the Home Office, Education, Health and other departments. The Home Office also commissioned a review of the sexualisation of young people (Papadopoulos, 2010), which scrutinised evidence on the 'hyper-sexualisation and objectification of girls', and the 'hyper-masculinisation of boys' (p. 3). This concluded that there was a link between the increase in sexually objectifying images of women and girls, and greater acceptance of aggressive attitudes and behaviour as the norm (p. 11). Regrettably, measures to teach all pupils from the age of five that violent relationships are unacceptable were lost following the announcement of the 2010 General Election, when the Bill making personal, social, health and economic education (PSHE) a compulsory curriculum subject was shelved at the last minute lacking opposition support. Despite these steps, teenage partner violence has not been considered an urgent child welfare problem and receives nowhere near the amount of attention as domestic violence against adults.

Hence, there are a number of fields in which government responses might be expected to have some positive influence on reducing the problem of violence between children. But these must be set against areas in which our authors were more critical. For example, Brown's chapter (2) on preschool children was critical of the 'risk adverse' culture and increased adult surveillance of children's social activities, as well as the dissuasion of physically active and exuberant play.

At a more general level, government has done little to curb media excesses in demonising young people and to encourage more responsible reporting. Indeed, its criminal justice policies against youth crime and anti-social behaviour have fuelled the imbalance (Chapter 14). When under criticism, governments may find it convenient to divert attention to other vulnerable groups. General levels of youth offending have declined, although the large increases in expenditure and preventive efforts probably did not have a major influence. However, violent crime among under-16s appears to have increased and our authors argued that police-led responses are not the solution. Government policies have had little impact on the different forms of social exclusion experienced by youth in many deprived communities, which lie at its roots. In this respect, and concerning violent crime especially, Squires and Goldsmith conclude on the sombre note that we have learnt little over the past decade.

On discriminated minorities, Rivers argued that homophobic bullying has worsened in recent years following local government legislation that prohibited teaching about homosexuality 'as a pretended family relationship'. The greatest indictment in our chapter (7) concerns the 'colour-coded' way in which the British criminal justice system responded to the murder of Stephen Lawrence. His black friend at the scene of the crime was assumed by police to be responsible for the attack and the Lawrence family were treated with disrespect. Back concludes that, over the decade since the murder, the commitment to tackle racist violence has waned and, instead, been replaced by new anxieties about violent – often black – youths.

Given the range of social problems and behaviours discussed in our chapters, it is unlikely that a single model to combat violence between children and young people will suffice. Government cannot resolve all the problems but economic and social policies can influence the type of society that parents, neighbours and children inhabit. We have lived through 30 years of economic neoliberalism in the UK in which individual, acquisitive consumerism is likely to have weakened social bonds. Family life is changing and, while avoiding stereotypes, different family forms have implications for children's upbringing, socialisation and control.

Housing policy, with the reduced level and sale of public housing, has led to a diminution of social capital in disadvantaged areas. Neighbours seem less likely to become involved in other people's families: prior to her death in 2008, 7-year-old Khyra Ishaq was abused and starved by her parents in Birmingham. Neighbours stated at the trial that they had heard cries of 'let me out' from the house at night; Khyra had been observed 'whimpering' in her garden in March, wearing just her underwear; and other neighbours had caught a child from the family stealing stale bread from a bird table in their garden. Yet accounts have emerged in other cases where family and friends have reported concerns to police or social workers resulting in no further action, and there seems a lack of community confidence in public authorities, fuelled by the media, to protect children's welfare.

These are large and complex issues. Professionals can do only so much and parents, as well as the wider community, have key roles to promote children's welfare and safety, including peer violence. Government policies must address extreme inequality, gender and ethnic relations. Compared to our other European partners, the UK position is anomalous regarding age of criminal responsibility (see Introduction); and the reluctance to acknowledge that, in England, 10-year-olds should not be tried in adult criminal courts symbolises the historical legacy in this country and society's ambivalence towards children, especially youths. Much else stems from this.

We are conscious that we have had little to say about resources. As this book goes to press, the Coalition Government is proposing deep cuts to public expenditure to reduce the deficit following the provision of £850 billion to avert the collapse of the banking system (National Audit Office, 2009). Various options are being proposed, including discontinuing quangos, removing unnecessary bureaucracy and regulation, and restricting salaries. Some areas may be protected but maintaining high-quality children's services should be a major priority.

IMPLICATIONS FOR PROFESSIONALS

Faced with these serious challenges, which are often structural, practitioners can sometimes feel powerless and deskilled. However, there is evidence in our chapters that local professionals can mitigate some of the problems we have described. For example, Stanley and colleagues (Chapter 15) showed how school-based initiatives to combat teenage intimate partner violence can be delivered more effectively to boys. Some schools experience more bullying than others; and peer violence in residential children's homes varies (Chapter 6). Individuals can and do make a difference.

Where appropriate, our chapters concluded with a range of suggestions as to how to address the problems concerned. Professionals working in particular areas probably have most to learn from the specific chapters concerned. Overall, there appear to be six broad themes that can be of general relevance.

Initially, it is important to recognise that the problems of peer violence are quite likely to have been distorted. Practitioners should undertake their own detailed inquiries to investigate the exact nature of the problems concerned before responses can be planned.

Second, practitioners should not overlook gender issues. The nature of problems is likely to be different for boys and girls, and responses should take this into account. As one author put it, a 'one size fits all' approach is unlikely to be successful.

A third general conclusion from our chapters is that the problems we have discussed are likely to be compounded for children from disadvantaged minorities, including minority ethnic groups and lesbian and gay youth. (Because of the constraints of space, we did not include a chapter on disability which would have been interesting.) Problems do not exist in isolation but some children will be subject to multiple stresses. Caprara and Rutter (1995) have shown how the effects of multiple stresses are *cumulative*: more than simply the sum total of individual problems. However, importantly for practitioners, the opposite must also be true and resolving one problem area can have a disproportionately beneficial effect.

Fourth, most public attention is probably given to *physical* violence. There are many other potential forms of violence and physical violence is not necessarily seen by children as the most damaging. Sexual exploitation is related to physical violence but has an added dimension. Intimidation and emotional violence can also be very harmful, including name-calling, impugning reputations and coercive control.

A fifth point is that authors writing on youth issues have shown how young people may lack the basic skills to 'back down'. For adolescents, lacking social capital and the inability to derive traditional economic and social status, other concerns such as territory and personal 'respect' may be substitutes. Professionals should be aware of this and young people may need help to deal with these conflicts.

Furthermore, it is important that peer violence and children's related problems are perceived *holistically*. Violence is likely to be related to a wider set of problems. Without being deterministic, our chapters showed that children who are instigators of violence may also be victims as well. These behaviours should be seen in the overall context of children's lives. Peer violence often, but not always, is worsened for children living in deprived communities. Parenting is likely to be more effective if the stresses of poverty are alleviated, and so professionals should help families to deal with economic problems including debt.

FINAL THOUGHTS

So having reached the end of the book, some final thoughts persist. We remain convinced that peer violence between children is a major social problem that requires closer attention of the right sort. The evidence shows that children experience high levels of violent and otherwise harmful behaviours. Although developing coping strategies, they are less well equipped than adults to deal with these stresses due their physical, social and psychological immaturity. They are subjected to these tensions in a variety of social sites. Adult society is not always sympathetic. It is disconcerting that, in an advanced nation such as ours, young people experience so much dissatisfaction and harm. Social injustice flourishes and girls and minorities are more likely to be on the receiving end. Peer violence overall has probably not increased in recent years but there is little evidence that it has been successfully tackled. Taken together, this is a sober set of conclusions. Readers may not have found this book an enjoyable read, but it is hoped that the analysis and suggestions will be of some use in understanding and tackling the problems.

REFERENCES

Caprara, G. and Rutter, M. (1995) Individual development and social change, in *Psychosocial Disorders in Young People: Time Trends and their Causes* (eds M. Rutter and D. Smith), Wiley, Chichester.

Cohen, S. (1972) *Folk Devils and Moral Panics: The Creation of the Mods and Rockers*, Routledge, London.

Department for Children, Schools and Families (DCSF) (2010a) *Building a Safe and Confident Future: Implementing the Recommendations of the Social Work Taskforce*, DCSF, London.

Department for Children, Schools and Families (2010b) *Working Together to Safeguard Children: A Guide to Inter-Agency Working to Safeguard and Promote the Welfare of Children*, DCSF, London.

Department for Education and Skills (DfES) (2003) *Every Child Matters*, Cm 5860, DfES, London.

Home Office (2009) *Together We Can End Violence Against Women and Girls*, Home Office, London.

Katz, I., Corylon, J., La Placa V. and Hunter, S. (2007) *The Relationship Between Parenting and Poverty*, Joseph Rowntree Foundation, York.

McRobbie, A. and Thornton, S. (1995) Rethinking 'moral panic' for multi-mediated social worlds', *British Journal of Sociology*, **46** (4), 559–74.

National Audit Office (NAO) (2009) *Maintaining Financial Stability across the United Kingdom Banking System*, NAO, London.

National Evaluation of Sure Start (2008) *The Impact of Sure Start Local Programmes on Three Year Olds and their Families*, HMSO, London

Palmer, S. (2007) *Toxic Childhood: How the Modern World is Damaging our Children and What We Can Do About It*, Orion Publishing Group, London.

Palmer, G., MacInnes, T. and Kenway, P. (2006) *Monitoring Poverty and Social Exclusion in the UK 2006*, New Policy Institute, London, www.jrf.org.uk/publications/monitoring-poverty-and-social-exclusion-uk-2006 (accessed 25 July 2010).

Papadopoulos, L. (2010) *Sexualisation of Young People: Review*, Home Office, London.

Parton, N. and Berridge, D. (forthcoming) Child protection in England, in *Child Protection Systems: International Trends and Orientations* (eds. N. Gilbert, N. Parton and M. Skivenes), Oxford University Press, New York.

Prince's Trust (2009) *The Cost of Exclusion: Counting the Cost of Youth Disadvantage in the UK*, Prince's Trust, London.

Thoburn, J. (2007) *Globalisation and Child Welfare: Lessons from a Cross-national Study of Children in Out-of-home Care*, Social Work Monographs, School of Social Work and Psychosocial Sciences, University of East Anglia, Norwich.

UNICEF (2007) *Child Poverty in Perspective: An Overview of Child Well-being in Rich Countries*, Innocenti Report Card 7, UNICEF Innocenti Research Centre, Florence.

Wilkinson, R. and Pickett, K. (2009) *The Spirit Level: Why More Equal Societies Almost Always Do Better*, Allen Lane, London.

Index

Children Behaving Badly? Peer Violence Between Children and Young People
Edited by Christine Barter and David Berridge
© 2011 John Wiley & Sons Ltd.